TORTURE

This depiction of a suspect being tortured

comes from a series of engravings appended

to the official text of the Austrian Empire's

Criminal Procedure Code of 1769, called

the *Constitutio Criminalis Theresiana*. The

engravings, which illustrate various means

for inflicting torture in the courts of Prague

and Vienna, were intended as guides for

local craftsmen and court functionaries in

constructing and operating such devices.

This plate shows a flaming torch being

applied to the chest of an accused who is

being racked.

TORTURE

A Collection

EDITED BY

SANFORD

LEVINSON

XXVI

Figura IV.

Entwürff des obern Leibs des Inquisiten, wie selber nach vollzogener bren, nüng von vorne anzü, sehen.

Entwürff dieses grads der peinliche Tortur nemč: des Feuers.

Latus II.

Entwürff des nač der Seiten, und vollendeten grad des Feuers anzüse, henden Inquisitens.

Erklärung der Buchstaben.

OXFORD
UNIVERSITY PRESS

2004

OXFORD
UNIVERSITY PRESS

Oxford   New York
Auckland   Bangkok   Buenos Aires   Cape Town   Chennai
Dar es Salaam   Delhi   Hong Kong   Istanbul   Karachi   Kolkata
Kuala Lumpur   Madrid   Melbourne   Mexico City   Mumbai   Nairobi
São Paulo   Shanghai   Taipei   Tokyo   Toronto

Published by Oxford University Press, Inc.,
198 Madison Avenue, New York, New York 10016

www.oup.com

Oxford is a registered trademark of Oxford University Press.

Library of Congress Cataloging-in-Publication Data
Torture : a collection / edited by Sanford Levinson.
p.   cm.
ISBN 0-19-517289-2
1. Torture—Moral and ethical aspects. 2. Human rights. 3. Political
prisoners—Legal status, laws, etc. I. Levinson, Sanford, 1941–
HV8593.T662 2004
323.4'9—dc22   2004008860

9 8 7 6 5 4 3 2 1

Printed in the United States of America
on acid-free paper

CONTENTS

Part III
Contemporary Attempts to Abolish Torture through Law

Part IV
Reflections on the Post–September 11 Debate about Legalizing Torture

TORTURE

Ariel Dorfman

The Tyranny of Terror

Is Torture Inevitable in Our Century and Beyond?

A bit over twenty-five years ago, history forced me to write a poem that, perhaps as a way of accentuating the horror I felt, came to be called "Hope."

> My son has been
> missing
> since May 8th
> of last year.
>
>> They took him
>> just for a few hours
>> they said
>> just for some routine
>> questioning.
>
> After the car left,
> the car with no license plate,
> we couldn't
>
>> find out
>
> anything else
> about him.
>
> But now things have changed.
> We heard from a compañero
> who just got out
> that five months later
> they were torturing him

in Villa Grimaldi
at the end of September
they were questioning him
in the red house
that once belonged to the Grimaldis.

They say they recognized
his voice his screams
they say.

Somebody tell me frankly
what times are these
what kind of world
what country?
What I'm asking is
how can it be
that a father's
joy
a mother's
joy
is knowing
that they
that they are still
torturing our son?
Which means
that he was alive
five months later
and our greatest
hope
will be to find out
next year
that they're still torturing him
eight months later
and he may   might   could
still be alive.[1]

It is sad—and more than sad, it is tragic—to remark that the questions asked in that poem, written over a quarter of a century ago and dealing with the horror spilling out of the Pinochet dictatorship, continue to haunt us today. We can all unfortunately repeat those words from a distressed parent, a father, perhaps a mother, unable to recognize what the world has become; can we not echo them all over again? *Somebody tell me frankly, what times are these? What kind of world? What country?*

Here is the transitory answer. More than twenty-five years after that poem was written, we live in a world where torture is practiced on a regular basis in more countries than ever—132 at the latest count, but who knows if there are not more—and where torture is being contemplated as inevitable and even beneficial in nations that call themselves democratic and respectful of the rights of their citizens. More than twenty-five years after that poem was written, I live in a country—the United States—where a leading civil rights lawyer has suggested that the courts might issue "torture warrants" as a way of fighting terrorism. We live in times where people, in this land and in so many other supposedly "civilized" nations, are so filled with primal fear that they look on with apparent indifference at the possibility of extreme maltreatment of their presumable enemies—indifference, indeed, at the evidence and televised images of this sort of maltreatment. We live in times where it is no longer abhorrent to express the need to apply electricity to the genitals of a prisoner or tear out his fingernails or keep him for days on end in a cage and blindfolded, if that will save our skin, protect our children, foster our security. The times, the country we live in, allow torture to be applied, as it always has been, in our name, by allies and so-called friends and partners.

It is also true that we live in a world where there have been some startling advances in the last twenty-five years in the struggle to abolish torture from the face of the earth and, perhaps more essentially, from the basements of humankind. Implicit in those questions—what times are these? what kind of world? what country?—was the belief that such a situation could not, should not, be normal, would someday not be normal. The queries themselves expressed the hidden desire that we would all someday find unfamiliar and absolutely strange this degrading procedure and the suffering it created, not only for the victims but for those who surrounded and survived them. Behind the questions, within the questions, there was indeed the hope that a time would dawn when such terror and absurdity would no longer seem customary or everyday, that this sort of pain inflicted by one man on a defenseless other would not even be possible to conceive. The questions contained the perverse expectation, therefore, then as now, that a day would come when we will be unable to even pose them—

not pose them at all—a day when humanity lives up to the best image of itself reflected in the mirror of the future.

If that expectation has not been fully met, and torture is as pervasive and persistent as ever, we should nevertheless be careful not to ignore some of the very significant steps taken to free the world of this plague in the latter part of the twentieth century, starting with the extraordinary organizational progress among the forces opposed to torture and human rights abuses. Over the years, a resilient army of citizens, victims, and lawyers who research, denounce, lobby, and campaign has made its appearance, growing into a transnational network of activists and concerned men and women that has been very effective in holding governments and individuals accountable for these kinds of abuse. Paramount perhaps in the growth of this movement has been the self-organization of the torture survivors themselves— the Torture Abolition and Survivors Support Coalition (TASSC) is itself a splendid example and model—accompanied by the creation of a number of medical centers dedicated to healing the psychological and physical wounds left by torture. Because this sort of profanation of the body and the mind is precisely meant to render the victims passive, mute, depressed, and ashamed; to destroy their dignity and exclude them from society; and to make them afraid for the rest of their lives, there can be nothing more encouraging than the efforts of those very victims to work actively on behalf of others who have suffered the same fate to stop that fate from devouring others.

Equally important has been the headway we have made in the field of national and particularly international law. Torture and similar abuses have been outlawed, in principle, since the adoption of the Universal Declaration of Human Rights in 1948. But it was only in 1975—more or less at the time when the poem I read was being composed, when the words that inspired that poem were being pronounced in Geneva by Edgardo Enríquez, Senior—that the General Assembly of the United Nations passed the Declaration against Torture, and one year later, in 1976, that the two U.N. covenants against human rights violations were adopted with the initial ratification of thirty-five countries, making torture a crime against humanity and, therefore, presumably, the business of all of humanity. There can be no exaggerating the momentousness of these treaties and agreements, even if they were, for the most part, ignored by the signatories in the name of national sovereignty—the unspoken principle "You do what you want to your people as long as you let me do what I want to mine." It would be too long and laborious to detail here the ways governments cheerfully disregarded the Covenants they had themselves approved and initialed; more interesting is to note how in the last ten years the nations of the world, shocked by the repetition of genocide and ethnic cleansing fifty years after Hitler's defeat, have been adopting a series of new agreements that establish, for the first time, ways in which war criminals—including, of course, those who have engaged in torture against their subjects—can be judged outside their national jurisdictions, making the international community and the courts of other countries responsible for trying those criminals and punishing them. Of all these many developments—in which the War Crimes Tribunals and the creation of the International Criminal Court stand out—perhaps the most dramatic and heartening was the arrest of General Augusto Pinochet in London in October 1998 on charges of genocide, a detention that led to extradition hearings from which transcendental legal rulings emerged. Although it began as a trial that dealt with all manner of crimes against humanity committed in Chile during the general's seventeen-year dictatorship, it was ultimately the crime of torture that decided Pinochet's fate and allowed extradition to Spain to proceed; it was the fact that the men under his command had systematically used torture that did him in and led to his defeat.

I was there in London on March 24, 1999, when the Law Lords—the equivalent of Supreme Courts in other countries—delivered their verdict, establishing what has been called the most transcendental judgement on human rights since the Nuremberg Trials. By finding sufficient cause for General Pinochet to be extradited to Spain to face charges of torture, the English judges stripped General Pinochet of his immunity as a former head of state, as a self-appointed senator, as the beneficiary of his own amnesty laws. But more crucially, they established that rulers will be held accountable, not only to their own populations, who seldom have the means to bring such rulers to trial, but also to any court in the world that is prepared to act in the name of the victims. When the Law Lords denied Pinochet's right to excuse his crimes by claiming sovereign immunity and cloak himself in his official capacity, simultaneously rejecting the Chilean government's claim that only it can judge the former strongman of Chile, they were effectively enacting universal jurisdiction for transgressions committed by any head of state that are so vast and outrageous to qualify as a crime against the whole of humankind. Because the Law Lords limited prosecution of Pinochet to crimes committed after the Convention on Torture was ratified on December 8, 1988, by the three countries (Chile, where the crimes had been committed; Spain, which was demanding extradition in the name of humanity; and England, where the arrest had taken place), it all came down to twenty-nine incidents of murder and torture, only one of which was mentioned specifically by the judges: the death by torture of seventeen-year-old Marcos Quezada Yáñez, on June 24, 1989, in the small town of Curacautín in the south of Chile. The autopsy had revealed that he had died because of the beatings and electric shocks administered to him by the police as punishment for his protesting Pinochet's policies.

It was that young man who was on my mind when I left the House of Lords that day in March 1999 and stepped into the bright London sun to be interviewed by a crew from Chilean television. The reporter listened to me explaining why this is a victory for humanity, that we have just been blessed with a great final reward to conclude this terrible and murderous century, a decisive step forward in the quest of our species for justice and equality. The reporter then asked me whether Pinochet's chance of being extradited had not radically diminished, given that the Law Lords had left only one case of torture standing, that of Marcos Quezada Yáñez.

When I answered, I was surprised by my own vehemence. "What if it were your mother who had died under torture?" I demanded of the reporter. "If it were your own mother, wouldn't you want justice to be done?"

Then I waited for her answer. I did not add any details about Marcos Quezada and what he must have felt when the electricity went through his body and he realized he could not escape the pain. I did not overdramatize my question by wondering out loud what it must have meant to be there on that grill and know that you are going to die, know that nobody can save you now. Wouldn't you want justice to be done? That's all I asked. If it were done to you and those you love, one by one by one, wouldn't you want that practice abolished? I am still waiting. I believe many of us are still waiting for an answer to that question.

Torture is, of course, a crime committed against a body.

It is also a crime committed against the imagination. Or rather, it presupposes, it requires, it craves the abrogation of our capacity to imagine others' suffering, dehumanizing them so much that their pain is not our pain. It demands this of the torturer, placing the victim outside and beyond any form of compassion or empathy, but also demands of everyone else the same distancing, the same numbness, on the part of those who know and close their eyes, those who do not want to know and close their eyes, those who close their eyes and ears and hearts. Torture does not, therefore, only corrupt those directly involved in the terrible contact between two bodies, one having all the power and the other having all the pain, one that can do what it wants and the other that cannot do anything except wait and pray and resist. Torture also corrupts the whole social fabric because it prescribes a silencing of what has been happening between those two bodies, it forces people to make believe that nothing, in fact, has been happening, it necessitates that we lie to ourselves about what is being done not far from where we talk, while we munch a chocolate bar, smile at a lover, read a book, listen to a concerto, exercise in the morning. Torture obliges us to be deaf and blind and mute. Or we could not go on living. With that incessant awareness of the incessant horror, we could not go on living.

This process of denial does not affect only bystanders. It is also something that digs deeply and fiercely consumes those who survive torture and, particularly, the relatives of those who have been tortured.

One story that springs out of the Pinochet case should suffice to display not only how we can be numbed and paralyzed by torture but also how the punishment of the perpetrator, however symbolic it may be, can help to heal the world, overcome that paralysis, and challenge apathy and silence.

I first laid eyes on María Josefa Ruiz-Tagle[2] sometime in 1974 when I was just beginning my long exile from Chile. She was a baby girl—around one and a half years old, I guess, and if I'm not mistaken she played on the floor of our kitchen in Paris with our son Rodrigo, who was then seven years old, while my wife Angelica and I chatted with her mother, Mónica Espinoza. I can remember being charmed by the beauty of the baby but even more by the serenity of the mother.

Mónica's husband, Eugenio Ruiz-Tagle Orrego—whom I had known only vaguely while he lived—had been savagely killed in Antofogasta, in the north of Chile. On September 12, 1973, the day after the Junta had taken power, Eugenio—the general manager of the National Cement Works— had voluntarily given himself up, like so many who had trusted that the military would not defile or denigrate them. A disturbing rumor had sprung up after his death: that his right-wing father in Santiago had taken his time in pressuring the military to release his wayward offspring, apparently because he thought that nothing much could happen to the young man, given the traditional civility of Chile's armed forces, or maybe trusting that his son's blue-blooded heritage would protect him—which made it even more heartbreaking when his mother demanded that Eugenio's tightly sealed coffin be opened and discovered his body and face mutilated almost beyond recognition.

And yet, I always wondered if those reports of his father's guilty detachment and subsequent intolerable loss did not constitute a fabrication, of the sort that often circulate in uncertain and violent times, an attempt by a repressed community to forge a story of how the murder of a rebellious son awakens a conservative progenitor to the true evil of a regime he helped to bring into being.

What was no fabrication, however, was how that death had devastated the family: you could see it in the deep well of sorrow that Mónica seemed to be floating in when my wife and I met her in Paris almost a year after the execution of her husband. And yet, at the same time, there was an unexpected purity in her gaze as I recall it, as if she had decided not to give fate the satisfaction of seeing her cry, as if all the tears had dried up inside her before coming out. Or was it a quiet resilience, a decision she seemed to have taken that she was going to get on with life no matter how hard that might be, for the sake of the baby but also in the name of her dead love, who would not have wanted the murder of his body to have also murdered her future? So I was not entirely surprised when I heard, some months later, that she had settled into a stable relationship with José Joaquín Brunner, one of Chile's most prominent intellectuals, a man would bring up María Josefa as if she were his own child.

The little girl was told, from an early age, that her biological father, Eugenio, had died in front of a firing squad, but no other details were forthcoming. She conjured up, María Josefa wrote many years later, a sort of romantic scene—a death occasioned by a diffuse group of men, none of whom was identifiably responsible, perhaps a way of keeping that violence done to her father from overwhelming and poisoning her life, allowing her not to dwell on the face of the man or the men who were personally responsible for that homicide. She always sensed, nevertheless, that underneath the silence surrounding and covering that remote death there lurked something more dreadful, some secret terror that was all the more fearful because nobody dared to name it. And then, one day, when she was twelve, a strange hunch led her to probe and explore what might lie behind a photograph in her grandmother's house, a picture that showed María

Josefa herself at around two years of age taking a bath in a small tub. Was it the clean water in which she was bathing in the picture that provoked her to undo the frame that held it and go beyond the false innocence of that child she had once been? Perhaps, because what she found were three pages concealed by her grandmother and written by two of her father's friends who had witnessed the way he had been mistreated before he died, witnesses who had been tortured themselves but who had, by a miracle, survived, instead of being killed by what became known later on as the Caravan of Death, La Caravana de la Muerte. Reading those words from the past, María Josefa found out that her father Eugenio had not been shot by a firing squad. To use her own words: "He was missing an eye. They had carved out his nose. His face was deeply burnt in many places. His neck had been broken. Stabs and bullet wounds. The bones broken in a thousand parts. They had torn the nails from his hands and from his feet. And they had told him that they were going to kill me and my mother."

But she said nothing. She kept those words, those images, inside—like the country itself, that did not want to know what had happened and that could not deal with its own memories.

Many years later, in 1999, after she had Lucas, her first baby—at the same age, twenty-six, her father had reached upon his death—she held the baby in her arms one morning and realized that her father had also been able to hold her and get to know her. She burst into tears and felt the irresistible need to write to the progenitor who had given her life—the need to tell her story, to write what it meant to be the child not only of a murdered man but of a country that did not want to confront and name that death. She denounced how everything around her had been built so that she and everyone else would not have to look the past in the face. Built, she said, so that people would not have to go to sleep every night feeling afraid.

Still, however, she kept those intimate words to herself—until a year and a half later, in November 2000, when Eugenio's body was exhumed from the Antofagasta cemetery and taken for a second burial to the Wall of Memory in Santiago, the place where the victims of the dictatorship are commemorated. Then she allowed an actor to publicly read out, on that occasion, the words she had written to her father.

For the tears that had been kept hidden all these years to come out—the tears I had not been able to see when Angélica and I sat with her mother Mónica in that kitchen in Paris and watched the fatherless child playing—

for that to happen, first Pinochet had to be arrested and put on trial, and then Eugenio's name had to be cleared. It had to be affirmed that he was not a terrorist but a victim, that he was not a criminal but a hero, that his death was terrible but had not been entirely in vain, as it had come back to haunt the man who had ordered it. Only when Eugenio was able to come back from the dead could his daughter come out into the light of day.

But that is not the end of the story. When you bring something out from its hiding place, other things emerge, one thing leading to another. Eugenio Ruiz-Tagle still had one more service to perform for his family, his friends, and his country.

A few months after María Josefa had decided to make her secret thoughts public, the English home secretary, adducing what turned out to be spurious health problems, returned Pinochet to Chile, where he faced charges of murder, kidnapping, and conspiracy to torture. When Judge Juan Guzmán managed to strip the former dictator of his parliamentary immunity and placed him under house arrest at the end of January 2001, his lawyers immediately appealed, insisting that their client was innocent, that there was no proof that he had known about any of the deaths he was accused of, including that of Eugenio Ruiz-Tagle. One week later, on February 7, 2001, the online newspaper *El Mostrador* published the most damning document yet in the whole case. Back in 1973 the justice minister—probably because of Ruiz-Tagle's family connections—had informed Pinochet, then commander-in-chief of the army, of the young man's torture and extrajudicial execution by the officers from the Caravan of Death. In his own handwriting, Pinochet answered the minister that he was to deny the facts and conceal them, instructing him to say that "Mr. Ruiz-Tagle was executed due to the grave charges that existed against him. [Say that] there was no torture according to our information." Needless to say, any possible investigation into that death had been quashed at that time.

This piece of news occasioned yet another revelation the next day in the same online newspaper. Carlos Bau, an accountant at the cement works where Eugenio had served as general manager—and who had given himself up to the authorities the same September 12—told the story of Ruiz-Tagle's daily torture at the air force base of Cerro Moreno in Antofagasta during the month that preceded his execution. The soldiers had wanted the prisoners to confess that they had weapons and explosives. (Pinochet's subordinates were trying to assemble a justification for the repression their commander-in-chief had unleashed, proof that there was a war and that the enemy was armed and dangerous.) It turned out that, far from protecting him, Ruiz-Tagle's surnames had made his tormentors pick him out for special treatment—maybe to teach him a lesson, maybe because they had class resentments of their own, maybe because a Ruiz-Tagle should have known better than to associate with the Allendista riffraff. Whatever the reasons, Eugenio was always the first to be beaten. And every time, Bau reported, that there was a session, while Eugenio was being mocked and kicked and cut, he did not let a cry out, kept what he was feeling inside— just like his wife a year later in Paris, and like his daughter through most of her life. But Bau added one more detail that had not up till that moment been public knowledge in Chile: the identity of the officer who had initiated the beatings, who had begun it all by landing Eugenio a kick in the genitals as an introduction to what was to await him in the days ahead. It was Lieutenant Hernán Gabrielli Rojas—who happened to be, twenty-eight years later, in the year 2001, the present acting commander-in-chief of the Chile air force. The very same man.

Are you sure? the journalist asked Bau.

Absolutely sure.

And in the next days, Bau's identification was confirmed by several other witnesses—Hernán Vera, Juan Ruz, and another victim, an officer called Navarro, who added that he had also seen Gabrielli torturing a fourteen-year-old boy.

General Gabrielli's response on February 12 was not only to proclaim his innocence but to announce that he was suing Bau and the others for libel, invoking a clause in the Law of National Security that shields a commander-in-chief from slander. The charges were subsequently dismissed. ("We weren't slandering him," Bau adduced; "we were just telling the truth about him.") Later in the year, in spite of ferocious resistance from the air force, Gabrielli was forced to step down from his post.

What can we learn from this series of incidents and disclosures?

Terror, the aftermath of torture, once it has burrowed into us, is not conquered in one revelatory flash. It is a slow, zigzag process, just like memory itself. Let me make myself clearer; let me implicate myself in the blindness that terror creates. I had, in fact, read the name Gabrielli as the tormentor of Ruiz-Tagle back in 1976 or 1977, when Carlos Bau, having already served three years of a forty-year prison sentence, which had been commuted into twenty years of banishment, arrived in Holland (where I had just moved with my family, from Paris). Bau had no qualms in recounting his terrifying story—though what I recalled above all afterward of that conversation was an image that surged into my head and stayed with me through the years: my realization that when one has been tortured it is as if for the rest of one's life one will be wearing sunglasses behind one's eyes. A few days after Carlos arrived in Amsterdam, he journeyed to Geneva to offer his testimony to the Human Rights Commission, and that's how, some time later, I was able to read his words at my leisure. That's when I read, I must have read, the name of Gabrielli. Except that it completely slipped my mind. Not that peculiar. So many names and things and circumstances that we forget. No, what is special, what is painfully revealing, is that even though Carlos and the others had mentioned Gabrielli whenever they spoke about their experience, everybody else in Chile also forgot that name. Or simply did not pay attention. Or did not dare to pay attention. Or did not want to face the consequences of paying attention.

Until the moment was right.

Until Pinochet's arrest and arraignment, his submission to the law like any mortal, broke his aura of invulnerability, shattering the dread with which he had frozen our hearts.

If María Josefa was finally able to speak and if the rest of us were able to finally hear what Carlos Bau had been telling us over and over for years, it was because they were no longer alone; it was because so many others near and faraway slowly began to open up. I am not making this up: over and over I meet, on each visit to my country, people who used to keep their eyes on the ground or shift them around while speaking of the years of terror and now lift those eyes and meet my own gaze. I could tell, for instance, the story of Felipe Agüero, the twin brother of my former brother-in-law Nacho, who, after watching Carlos Bau and his fellow detainees bring down an air force general for torture committed twenty-eight years ago, had then been inspired to finger one of his academic colleagues at the Catholic University as an interrogator in the infamous Estadio Nacional in Santiago, a certain political science professor named Emilio Meneses. I could retell Felipe's story and many others.

Better to add just one more: when I was working against Pinochet in the plebiscite of 1988, I met an old toothless woman in a shantytown not far from our house in La Reina who told me that she dared not vote against Pinochet, "because his eye sees everything, especially in the polling booth."

I ran into her again twelve years later, a few months after the general had been placed under house arrest in Santiago. This time she told me several jokes—obscene ones, at that—about the old bastard.

She no longer cared if Pinochet was secretly listening to her.

I would have liked to end this foreword with these final images of people conquering their fear, of torture victims hounding their tormentors, of solidarity and hidden sunshine in the midst of the fog, so that we can presume and declare that these victories will accumulate until we finally have a world free of this sort of pain. But I need to temper the reader's optimism; I cannot help but trouble that reader and trouble myself by advancing a more dire question, more drastic and radical than what country is this? what times do we live in? what kind of world?—a question that wonders if it will ever be possible to completely abolish torture.

The question that needs to be examined was posed, most forcefully and bluntly, over 130 years ago, by a great Russian writer, using as his spokesperson someone who may, arguably, have been his greatest character:

> I challenge you—answer. Imagine that you are creating a fabric of human destiny with the object of making men happy in the end, giving them peace and rest at last, but that it was essential and inevitable to torture to death only one tiny creature—that little child beating its breast with its fist, for instance—and to found that edifice on its unavenged tears, would you consent to be the architect on those conditions? Tell me, and tell the truth.

These are the words of Ivan Karamazov, tempting his brother Alyosha, recently become a monk, Ivan testing Alyosha's faith in God, demanding if he is ready to build the joy and harmony and paradise of the human species on the eternal agony of one innocent youngster, and they are as relevant today as when they were first invented by the Russian novelist Feodor Dostoevski for his masterpiece *The Brothers Karamazov*. Ivan has preceded his question with stories about suffering children—a seven-year-old girl beaten over and over by her parents in sensual delirium and then enclosed in a freezing wooden outhouse and made to eat her own excrement; an eight-year-old serf boy torn to pieces by hounds in front of his mother for the edification of a landowner—true cases, plucked from newspapers and archives by Dostoevski, that horrify us and yet merely hint at the almost unimaginable cruelty that awaited humanity in the years to come. What would Ivan say if he had witnessed the way the twentieth century ended up refining pain, industrializing pain, producing pain on a massive, rational, technological scale, a century that would produce manuals on pain and how to inflict it, training courses on how to increase it and catalogues that explained where to acquire the instruments that ensured that pain would be unlimited, a century that handed out medals for those who had written the manuals and commended those who designed the courses and rewarded and enriched those who had produced the instruments in those catalogues of death?

I did not reproduce that passage from *The Brothers Karamazov*, however, in order to accumulate more episodes of horror—by now few people alive on this Earth can claim that they are not aware of the torments and afflictions that some men are capable of wreaking upon others. I evoke Ivan's words because they take us into the impossible heart of the matter regarding torture; they demand that we confront the real and inevitable dilemma that the existence and persistence of torture poses to the world, particularly after the terrorist attacks of September 11, 2001. Ivan Karamazov's words remind us that torture is justified by those who practice it: this is the price, we are told, that needs to be paid by the suffering few in order to guarantee happiness to the rest of society, the enormous majority given security and well-being by those horrors inflicted in some dark cellar, some faraway pit, some abominable police station. Make no mistake: every regime that tortures does so in the name of salvation, some superior goal, some promise of paradise. Call it communism, call it the free market, call it the free world, call it the national interest, call it fascism, call it the leader, call it civilization, call it the service of God, call it what you will, the cost of paradise, the promise of some sort of paradise, says Ivan Karamazov, will always be hell for at least one person somewhere, sometime.

So we must face this truth: torturers do not generally think of themselves as evil but rather as guardians of the common good, dedicated patriots who get their hands dirty and endure perhaps some sleepless nights in order to deliver the blind ignorant majority from violence and anxiety. Even if those who torture must be aware that, due to merely statistical reasons, there has to be a chance that one of their prisoners must inevitably be innocent of what he or she is accused of, the torturers are willing to let those who are blameless suffer the frightening fate of the supposedly guilty. It is not clear how many of the citizens of this country or any other country in the world would react if they were brazenly confronted by Ivan Kara-mazov's question, whether they would consciously be able to accept that their dreams of heaven depend on an eternal inferno of distress for one innocent child. We can only hope that, like Alyosha, they would answer no. Doestoevski makes Alyosha answer softly—notice to that word *softly*—to his brother's question. "No, I would not consent." He would not consent to have the happiness of everyone built upon the suffering of one child.

I should leave it there, this ethical conundrum, saying that the choice is stark and that, finally, the truly moral path is clear and clean, but I will allow myself to take Ivan's question a bit farther, trouble our waters of uncertainty yet a bit more.

What if the person being eternally tortured for our well-being is guilty?

What if we could erect a future of love and harmony on the everlasting pain of someone who had himself committed mass murder, who had tortured children; what if we were invited to enjoy Eden all over again while one despicable human being was receiving over and over again the horrors he imposed on others?

Would we answer no?

Would we answer that torture is always, definitely, absolutely, unacceptable?

Speaking only for myself, I can only hope that I would say no to such a temptation, such a proposal. I can only hope that we would have the compassion and the wisdom to reject the path of rage. I can only pray that we would not act as if we were gods, knowing better than our fellows what is right and what is wrong, who deserves to live and who to die. I can only pray that humanity will have the courage to say no, no to torture, no to torture under any circumstance whatsoever, no to torture, no matter who the enemy, what the accusation, what sort of fear we harbor; no to torture no matter what kind of threat is posed to our safety; no to torture anytime, anywhere; no to torturing anyone; no to torture. I can only hope and plead and pray that a day will come when the very question of torture will have been forever abolished from our midst.

Notes

This essay is a revised version of a keynote speech delivered on June 25, 2002, at a conference in Washington, D.C., organized by Sister Dianna Ortiz and the TASSC, that brought together survivors of torture from around the world with experts on this subject, in order to discuss ways to abolish this form of human rights violation. Part of it was published in the London *Guardian* on May 8, 2004.

1. Taken from my book of poems *In Case of Fire in a Foreign Land: New and Collected Poems in Two Languages* (Durham, N.C.: Duke University Press, 2002).
2. This rendering of Maria Josefa's story has been adapted from my recent book *Exorcising Terror: The Incredible, Unending Trial of General Augusto Pinochet* (Seven Stories, 2002).

ACKNOWLEDGMENTS

Several years ago, I vowed that I would never again take on the task of trying to gather a collection of freshly written essays. It has been my my experience, both as editor and sometime contributor to such collections, that they invariably take a far longer time than anticipated. I broke this resolution because of my belief that the topic of torture is especially significant and that there needs to be much greater public discussion of the topic. I was fortunate to be able to recruit an unusually fine group of contributors, and I am truly grateful to each and every one of them for producing their essays in what, for academics, is record time. In at least one case, the final version was completed within two weeks of giving birth, which is ample testimony to the dedication of the participants.

All of the contributors, I know from reading their drafts, have a number of individuals they would like to thank for assistance in the preparation of their manuscripts. I think it best, though, that each of us, including myself, thank those who read drafts and made suggestions privately.

I do, however, want to make one truly heartfelt public acknowledgment—to our editor at the Oxford University Press, Dedi Felman. This project would never have gotten off the ground if she had not encouraged it at every single stage. It is, for example, far easier to get busy people to take the time to write essays if one can say, when initially speaking to them, that the Oxford University Press has exhibited great interest in publishing the collection. But her help has gone far beyond supplying the imprimatur of one of the world's distinguished presses, and she is an essential part of every aspect of this book, from its initial organization to its final cover design.

With regard to other books I have written or edited, I have always taken great pleasure—indeed, it has served as an incentive to complete the book—in being able to honor someone, whether a family member or a friend or academic mentor, by "dedicating" the book to him or her. There is, however, no such "dedication" at the front of this book. One reason is that any given person might well have mixed feelings about being the dedicatee of a book on what is truly one of the grimmest possible topics imaginable. It is also undoubtedly true that no reader, including any possible dedicatee, will agree with (or, perhaps, even find morally tolerable) every single one of the essays, as exemplified by the fact that several of the essays take unusually sharp issue with one another. I was tempted, therefore, to dedicate the book simply to "victims of torture." That seemed, however, an ultimately sentimental gesture, especially inasmuch as several of the essays, including my own, countenance the possibility that under some very restricted circumstances, it might be the "lesser evil" to engage in torture—though all of us agree that a "lesser evil" is not therefore made into a positive "good." So this book goes into the world without a dedicatee. I am, however, pleased to say that every contributor concurred in a suggestion that all of the royalties attached to this book will go not to the authors but rather to the Torture Abolition and Survivors Support Coalition.

The essays in this book were all written before the May 2004 disclosures of abuses—including allegations of torture—in Iraq and Afghanistan (not to mention secret CIA prisons around the world). No doubt many of the authors would wish to rewrite some of their remarks. But the brutal fact is that far less rewriting would be necessary than some might wish. I take the liberty of quoting from the first paragraph of my contribution to the *Village Voice*, May 12, 2004:

> For over a decade, the United States has lived with a loose definition of "torture" that is significantly out of line with that of most of the rest of the world and invites the kind of manufactured distinctions that give lawyering a bad name. Moreover, officials in both Congress and the executive branch have winked and nodded at practices such as sending prisoners to countries that will do our dirty work for us.

Thus, to quote myself once more, "The only thing new about recent revelations is the pictures." This book was conceived in the belief that the issue of torture would not in fact go away, as much as it would be wonderful to believe the opposite. What recent events reveal is that it is more important than ever that Americans take responsibility for what has been, is being, and will be done in their name. The point of this book is that the questions raised by what has been called "highly coercive interrogation" are scarcely easy to resolve. But it is not difficult to say that any such resolution should be done in public and not, as has been the case over the past several years, behind closed doors and with almost no public discussion.

—Sanford Levinson

ACKNOWLEDGMENTS

Sanford Levinson

Contemplating Torture

An Introduction

Why should one take valuable time and expend equally valuable intellectual and emotional energy thinking about torture? Not only is the subject grim, but it is also the case, as almost all of the following essays point out, that torture is unequivocally and absolutely forbidden by the law of civilized nations (including the United States). Remarkable proof of sorts of this universal condemnation is provided by a rather unlikely source, an Argentinian torturer who said, even as he defended his participation in Argentina's "Dirty War," that "[t]he day we stop condemning torture—although we tortured—the day we become insensitive to mothers who lose their guerilla sons—although they are guerillas—is the day we stop being human beings."[1] Such abhorrence of torture is at the heart of the defense the United States and its supporters offered most strongly of Iraq and the deposing of Saddam Hussein—especially following the failure to find any weapons of mass destruction or otherwise substantiate any plausible threat posed by Iraq to American national security. Even opponents of the Iraq war (like myself) are reluctant to say that it would have been "better" had Saddam Hussein in effect been left free to continue torturing his enemies, a likely result of a failure to resort to war.

That torture should be universally condemned is not just the belief of political theorists or philosophers. The principle is written into some of the most basic documents of international law, including the United Nations Convention Against Torture and Other Cruel, Inhuman or Degrading Treatment or Punishment, which entered into force in 1987 and has since been ratified by 130 countries (excerpts of the Convention appear on pages 40–42). A key article of the Convention, accepted by the United States Senate when ratifying it in behalf of the United States, specified that "[n]o exceptional circumstances *whatsoever* [emphasis added], whether a state of war or a threat of war, internal political instability or any other public emergency, may be invoked as a justification of torture." The word "whatsoever" is powerful indeed. Every constitutional lawyer is aware that the assertion of "compelling state interests" often suffices to limit, say, the reach of the First Amendment and its proclamation that Congress "shall make *no* law" abridging freedom of speech or press. Yet the Convention makes it as clear as language can possibly do that *no* interest, however "compelling," will avail a government that tries to assert the "necessity" of torturing a hapless suspect. The state simply cannot do it, period, at least if one takes the words of the Convention seriously.

So what, a reader may well ask, is there to think about or contemplate? If truth is beauty and beauty truth, then it is equally obvious that torture is both ugly and evil, and "That is all you know and all you need to know" to realize that it is indeed absolutely beyond the pale for any nation that deems itself civilized. To be sure, some of the contributors to this book would unequivocally endorse this message, especially Ariel Dorfman, who, in his eloquent and moving foreword, and elsewhere, speaks from the depths of his own experience with the vicious regime of General Pinochet in Chile. It is no small matter to disagree with Dorfman or with Elaine Scarry, whose book *The Body in Pain*, written two decades ago, is perhaps the canonical examination of what it is that makes torture the epitome of evil. This being acknowledged, it is important to emphasize at the outset that the essays that follow, though joined together in the belief that torture is indeed evil, nonetheless are part of an increasingly important debate over the possibility that torture, at least in some carefully specified circumstances, might be a "lesser evil" than some other "greater evil" that menaces society. At that point, so the argument goes, it is indeed necessary to "contemplate" the possibility of torture in all senses of that word.

Any such argument obviously runs contrary to the sweeping condemnation seen in the United Nations Convention or the philosophical arguments carefully set out in Henry Shue's classic essay (chapter 2). Yet Michael Walzer wrote an equally classic essay (chapter 3) in which he explicitly endorses the necessity of having political leaders who are willing, in dire circumstances, to "dirty their hands" by engaging in quite horrendous actions, including torture. Their saving grace, if that is the right word, is feeling suitably guilty about violating what most people indeed wish *were* an "absolute" prohibition. The use of the subjunctive here is telling; it is simply not true, as an empirical matter, that torture is nonexistent, even, as will be shown hereafter, in presumptively "civilized" states.

Juxtaposing Shue and Walzer should make clear what is at stake in this debate, especially when complemented by the contribution of the Chicago political philosopher Jean Bethke Elshtain. Elshtain's distinctive contribution is the embedding of her own reflections on the morality of torture within theologically informed analysis.

Whatever the (alleged) contemporary consensus regarding torture, one must realize that torture has not in fact always been condemned, nor, of course, has it disappeared, even among signatories of the United Nations Convention. As to the past, the Yale legal historian John Langbein offers a brief overview of the legal history of torture, noting that it was condemned only relatively recently in our two millennia of recorded history of the subject. Aristotle, for example, defended it. And Jerome Skolnick, the dean of American sociologists of police practices, notes as well that the "third degree" was an accepted part of those practices until at least World War II.

Moreover, a number of parties to the Torture Convention have been accused of committing torture, while others, including Great Britain and Israel, have explicitly been found by courts to have engaged in the "cruel, inhuman or degrading treatment" also covered by the Convention. The European Court of Human Rights found that Great Britain had engaged in such conduct, and the Northern Ireland professor of law (and human rights scholar) Fionnuala Ni Aoláin assesses the relevance of such transnational institutions within the European context generally. More surprising, in a way, is that the Israeli Supreme Court itself condemned certain practices of Israeli security agencies, in an opinion by the president of the Court, Aharon Barak, substantial parts of which are reprinted here (chapter 9). Almost no one, of course, believes that other signatories to the Convention could conceivably survive strict scrutiny of their practices.

Indeed, one might have recourse to the basic distinction of American legal realists between "law on the books" and "law in action" when trying to determine the actual frequency of torture and, even more so, of "cruel, inhuman or degrading treatment." The contribution of the Yale law professor Oona Hathaway to this book assesses the behavior of countries that have ratified a variety of antitorture conventions and those that have not, and she comes to the rather dispiriting conclusion that there is little difference, with regard to respecting this basic human right, between the ratifiers and nonratifiers of the conventions. (What is most dispiriting is that at times there is a negative correlation, so that ratifiers behave even worse than nonratifiers.)

There can be little doubt, though, that it is September 11, 2001, and its aftermath that account for this book, insofar those events served to jump-start a public debate over the methods by which states can legitimately ferret out information about terrorism. As early as October 21, 2001, Walter Pincus wrote in the *Washington Post* about the increasing frustration felt by federal law enforcement officials at the refusal of various persons detained in the wake of the attacks to disclose information they were presumed to have. The detainees resisted such standard blandishments as plea bargaining, cash, or relocation in the federal witness program. One person described as an "experienced FBI agent" is quoted saying that it could get to the point "where we . . . go to pressure."

"Pressure" is, to put it mildly, a loaded term. As Pincus explained, it can refer to anything from the use of so-called (and almost certainly nonexistent) truth drugs to application of one or another method of torture. One suggestion, for example, was extradition of suspects to countries allied with the United States that would willingly torture or threaten the safety of family members should the suspect not cooperate. A brief glance at article 3 of the Convention—"No State Party shall expel, return [*refouler*] or extradite a person to another State where there are substantial grounds for believing that he would be in danger of being subjected to torture"—should be enough to indicate the illegality of such measures. Yet reliable journalists have reported that the United States has indeed turned over suspected terrorists to such allies as Egypt, Jordan,and Morocco, which are presumably willing to use methods the United States does not use. As one Morroccan intelligence officer told a reporter for the *New York Times,* "I am allowed to use all means in my possession" when interrogating a suspect. "You have to fight all his resistance at all levels"[2]

One consequence of such "rendering"—the technical term for sending suspects held by the United States to another country—has apparently been a significant regression in Morocco's efforts at achieving greater recognition of human rights.[3] In any event, as an American official inelegantly but candidly told reporters for the *Washington Post*," We don't kick the [expletive] out of them. We send them to other countries so that they can kick the [expletive] out of them."[4]

As a matter of political fact, not a single major American political figure has engaged in significant criticism of such policies. Most, no doubt, would agree with the comments of Senator John D. Rockefeller IV, the ranking Democratic member of the Senate Intelligence Committee, following the capture in Pakistan of a high-ranking official of al-Qaeda. Referring to the possibility of turning the official over to a more torture-accepting ally, Rockefeller said, "I wouldn't rule it out. I wouldn't take anything off the table where he is concerned, because this is the man who has killed hundreds and hundreds of Americans over the past ten years."[5]

Judge Richard Posner writes in his own contribution to this book that "only the most doctrinaire civil libertarians (not that there aren't plenty of them) deny that if the stakes are high enough, torture is permissible. No one who doubts that should be in a position of responsibility," and he criticizes Dorfman's absolute rejection of torture in his foreword as not only "overwrought in tone but irresponsible in content." No one should believe that Posner is unaware of the awfulness of torture or of the duty of judges to protect people against being tortured. Indeed, he had earlier ruled, with regard to allegations of torture made against the Chicago Police Department, that "even a murderer has a right to be free from torture."[6] And he takes Alan Dershowitz to task, with regard to his proposal for "torture warrants" that would legitimate selected instances of torture, for potentially contributing to the overuse of torture by normalizing its use. Yet Posner, in the end, would presumably agree with an American official, described as having supervisory responsibility over suspected terrorists captured in Afghanistan, who was quoted as saying: "If you don't violate someone's human rights some of the time, you probably aren't doing your job."[7]

"Torture," as a term, tends to be a "placeholder," an abstract word that is made concrete by the knowledge (and imagination) of the reader. John Langbein's essay, for example, includes an illustration of medieval forms of torture that probably conform to one's basic image of the practice (Langbein also supplied the illustration on the title page). We must, though, necessarily ask ourselves what precisely constitutes "torture," as distinguished not only from "inhuman and degrading acts," which are also forbidden by the United Nations Convention, but also, and even more significantly, from what might be termed "merely unattractive" methods of interrogation that are, nonetheless, distinguishable from those that are forbidden. Although American military officials emphasize that torture is not a permissible option, they have also been reported as saying that "under the Geneva Convention, anything *short of torture* [emphasis added] is permissible to get a hardened Qaeda operative to spill a few scraps of information that could prevent terrorist attacks."[8] And a teacher at an army "interrogation school" tells his students that the job for which he is training them "is just a hair's-breadth away from being an illegal specialty under the Geneva Convention."[9] What all lawyers (and most laypersons) know is that legal prohibitions often act as implicit permission to do, at least as a matter of law, anything short of what is prohibited. The "letter of the law" often takes precedent over any "spirit" that might be thought to inhabit it.

The opinion of the Israeli Supreme Court mentioned earlier spells out (and condemns) actual interrogation practices; these might be compared with those described in what has become a classic article, filed on December 26, 2002, in the *Washington Post,* concerning American interrogation methods in Afghanistan. According to intelligence specialists familiar with CIA methods, those who refuse to cooperate are sometimes kept standing or kneeling for hours, in black hoods or spray-painted goggles. "At times they are held in awkward, painful positions and deprived of sleep with a 24-hour bombardment of lights—subject to what are known as 'stress and duress' techniques." Another common technique is sleep deprivation, vividly described by Menachem Begin, who was subjected to it as part of his own torture as a young man in the Soviet Union. The spirit of a sleep-deprived prisoner, Begin writes, "is wearied to death, his legs are unsteady, and he has one sole desire to sleep, to sleep just a little, not to get up, to lie, to rest, to forget. . . . Anyone who has experienced this desire knows that not even hunger or thirst are comparable with it."[10] It should be clear, though, that nothing lawyers say can be a complete substitute for actual knowledge of what occurs in interrogation rooms behind closed doors. Indeed, I actively solicited a contribution from a current member of the United States armed forces who specializes in interrogation and the teaching of interrogation practices. He was quite willing to contribute but was prevented from doing so by superior authority, who, among other things, apparently did not trust the motivations behind this book, which are indeed to encourage a public debate about contemporary interrogation practices. I deeply regret his absence.

It should be clear, though, that state authorities have incentives to offer particularly horrific requirements for something to be considered "torture";

this serves in effect to legitimate actual interrogation practices, such as those just described. This is, after all, what "coming close, but not crossing the line" is all about.

Thus it is no small matter that the United States, when ratifying the United Nations Convention in 1994, adopted a definition of torture that was considerably more state-protective than the UN's definition. In particular, according to the Senate,

> (a) . . . the United States understands that, in order to constitute torture, an act must be *specifically intended* to inflict *severe* physical or mental pain or suffering and that mental pain or suffering refers to *prolonged* mental harm caused by or resulting: from (1) the intentional infliction or threatened infliction of *severe* physical pain or suffering;
>
> (2) the administration or application, or threatened administration or application, of mind altering substances or other procedures calculated to disrupt *profoundly* the senses or the personality;
>
> (3) the threat of *imminent* death; or
>
> (4) the threat that another person will *imminently* be subjected to death, *severe* physical pain or suffering, or the administration or application of mind altering substances or other procedures calculated to *disrupt profoundly* the senses or personality. . . .

It should occasion no surprise that each and every one of the italicized passages was diligently parsed in documents that were disclosed in May and June 2004 as a result of the furor over Abu Ghraib and allegations that the abuses that took place there reflected official policies regarding interrogation of suspected terrorists. Especially important were memoranda written by the Office of Legal Counsel (OLC) within the Justice Department for submission to White House Counsel Alberto Gonzales and by a "working group" within the Defense Department that submitted a report to Secretary of Defense Donald Rumsfeld in March 2003. According to the OLC, for example, only acts "of an extreme nature" could "rise to the level of torture. . . . Physical pain amounting to torture must be equivalent in intensity to the pain accompanying serious physical injury, such as organ failure, impairment of bodily function, or even death." Anything less than this, according to then-OLC head (and now federal judge) Jay Bybee, appears to be considered "merely" inhuman and degrading and therefore not "torture" at all. John Parry's article offers further illumination about some significant differences in how torture has been defined in international and domestic law.

In any event, all of us, whether lawyers or ordinary citizens, are forced to try to synthesize the two competing realities of, first, the absolute prohibition against torture and other inhuman and degrading acts and, second, the obvious fact that not only is it occurring but also, just as significantly, serious and thoughtful people appear to justify it. Richard Weisberg suggests that I am mistaken in calling for such a "synthesis," that the task of the moral and humane intellectual is to join Dorfman (and others) in unequivocal, unlimited opposition to the very idea of torture. Sober people have suggested, in effect, that nothing less than the notion of a democratic civilization may be at stake. "There is a line which democracies cross at their peril," wrote the editors of the *Economist*. It is defined as "threatening or inflicting actual bodily harm" to those from whom the state seeks information (and, obviously, those whom it wishes to punish). "On one side of that line stand societies sure of their civilized values. That is the side America and its allies must choose," they concluded. I do not wish to deny the force (or eloquence) of such arguments. But even one who accepts them in full still cannot avoid engaging in grim and unattractive discussions about what methods of interrogation, by stopping "short" of banned practices, are therefore defined as acceptable.

As already suggested, some critics have condemned any such discussions. Interestingly enough, they do not necessarily argue that, as a matter of fact, torture ought never be contemplated, only that it should never gain the degree of legitimacy that comes via a debate in which one necessarily concedes the "reasonableness" of competing positions. Thus, one can admit that even the most absolute rules are made to be broken, at least on occasion, but nonetheless maintain as well that it is important to express in public the absolutist position. Because of the value instantiated, any such breaking should take place out of public view (or the space occupied by public discussion) and ought never be admitted to.

Exemplary in this regard is the Slovenian social theorist Slavoj Zizek, who is vehemently opposed to books like this one. Indeed, "essays . . . which do not advocate torture outright, [but] simply introduce it as a legitimate topic of debate, are even more dangerous than an explicit endorsement of torture." Unlike the latter, which would be "too shocking" for most people to accept, "the mere introduction of torture as a legitimate topic allows us to entertain the idea while retaining a pure conscience." This serves, he argues, to legitimize torture and "changes the background of ideological presuppositions and options much more radically than its outright advocacy."[11] He is, not surprisingly, critical of Alan Dershowitz, a leading figure in the contemporary debate. (It is, therefore, appropriate that Dershowitz, in his contribution to this book, discusses not only his intellectual position but also the tone of some of the criticisms that have been leveled at him.) Yet Zizek seems caught in a self-contradiction, inasmuch as he himself writes: "OK, we can well imagine that in a specific situation, confronted with the proverbial 'prisoner who knows' and whose words can save thousands, we would resort to torture. . . . [F]ollowing the unavoidable brutal urgency of the moment, we should simply do it" (and, presumably, refrain from talking about it). I analogize Zizek's position to the "don't ask, don't tell" policy adopted by the Clinton Administration with regard to gays and lesbians in the military. Perhaps one can defend such an approach by quoting the old maxim about hypocrisy being the tribute that vice pays to virtue. In this case, the element of hypocrisy that is involved in the cognoscente being aware that the reality of legal practice is different from what the naive outsider might believe is amply justified by the reinforcement of the undoubted virtue of an ethic of no-torture. Even if one is normatively drawn to this version of "don't ask, don't tell," the practical difficulty is that the victims of torture, if they are left to live, will almost undoubtedly wish to invoke some kind of ex post legal process, whether by seeking the criminal punishment of their torturers or suing for civil damages for violation of their legal right not to be tortured.

Gays and lesbians in the military, however insulted they are by the "don't ask, don't tell" policy, have a certain incentive to remain silent about their activity. Those who are tortured, in contrast, have no such incentive. The only way to guarantee their silence is to adopt what is said to be the practice of professional killers and to kill *all* eyewitnesses to a crime, explaining that it's "professional, not personal." But nobody who defends the pragmatic necessity of unacknowledged torture would move to this next step. One must, therefore, wrestle with the response of the legal system to the almost inevitable *public* aspect of torture.

Zizek's seeming assent to the proposition that torture might indeed be thinkable in a least one "specific situation" is not unique even among self-professed "absolutists." The Harvard law professor Charles Fried postulates a situation "where killing an innocent person may save a whole nation." He writes that "it seems *fanatical* to maintain the absoluteness of the judgment, to do right even if the heavens will in fact fall."[12] What gives Fried's comments added force is precisely that he is generally grouped with that group of legal philosophers who indeed take rights extremely seriously and who, therefore, are generally critical of utilitarians who immediately focus on consequences when deciding what rights people have in given situations. But Fried, like many other professed antiutilitarians, recognizes what might be called a "catastrophe exception" to his general argument.

Fried's concession may be especially troublesome insofar as he seems to license doing *anything* if deemed necessary to prevent the heavens from falling. Would this legitimate, for example, threatening injury or death to the innocent child of a suspected terrorist as a means of procuring the relevant information? This is not a small point, as Miriam Gur-Ayre, in her analysis of the Israeli Supreme Court decision, demonstrates. She emphasizes the distinction between justifying torture as a means of "self-defense" against the specific perpetrator of an evil and justifying it under the general notion of its being "necessary," in Fried's terms, "to save a whole nation." "Necessity" defenses can take a far more open-ended form than is provided by responses to those who actually threaten one's life.

In any event, the plausibility of Machiavelli's and Weber's critique of absolutist moralism, evoked by Michael Walzer in his powerful essay defending the necessity, on occasion, to "dirty" one's hands, seems to be strongest when the state, as the legitimate instantiation of an otherwise decent society, is indeed fundamentally at risk. But that, obviously, requires some real discussion about *what* precisely counts as a "catastrophe" and, just as important, *who* gets to determine whether the relevant conditions have been met. It is, for example, presumed, without serious discussion, that the events of September 11 constituted just the kind of "catastrophe" that justifiably generated the kind of conversation this book represents. Catastrophic it was, obviously, for the victims, their families, and the city of New York. In no serious sense, though, was it a genuine "existential threat" to the maintenance of American society, other than to remind us, yet again, that we are vulnerable to certain kinds of terrorism, as had been amply illustrated, of course, less than a decade earlier when the World Trade Center was bombed, or with the demolition of American embassies in Africa.

The previous paragraph might well create a certain tension (or anger) on the part of readers, because, we have been told, over and over again, that September 11 was a day that, like Pearl Harbor, will not only live in infamy but also, and more important, will, indeed, *must,* fundamentally change the way we lead our lives. These changes will include, of course, the modification—some would say "suspension"—of ordinary civil liberties, beginning with habeas corpus and the right to consult an attorney and moving on, perhaps, to being subject to torture should one not be forthcoming with what the United States deems necessary information. It would be good to be able to engage in a serious discussion as to what exactly are the predicate conditions for something being declared a "catastrophe," and, of course, why in the world we would necessarily trust a highly politicized state elite, with its own potential political interests in creating a perception of danger, to be reliable in such declarations.

Oren Gross offers a troubling discussion of the idea of the "emergency power" and the degree to which it should be domesticated, as it were, by being made part of what might be termed "ordinary law." He tellingly quotes the German—many would add "Nazi"—philosopher Carl Schmitt, who wrote that "[t]here exists no norm that is applicable to chaos [or catastrophe]."

So are we doomed, as it were, to contemplate torture? Some would sidestep the need for any such discussion, not by simply emphasizing its fundamental immorality but rather by claiming that it is in fact inefficacious, that is to say counterproductive, in achieving its goals of gaining valuable information. As one expert put it, "pain alone will often make people numb and unresponsive. You have to engage people to get into their minds and learn what is there."[13]

It would obviously be wonderful if this were correct, for then the problem of torture essentially vanishes, assuming, of course, that we are referring to the potential of torture as a way of procuring information about future actions. If torture never achieves its purpose and, indeed, is harmful not only to the victims but even to the police themselves (since false statements made only to stop the pain send them astray), then the obvious question is why any rational police officer would ever engage in it. If torture is in fact inefficient, then one must be a sadist to defend it. One virtue of this response is that it appears "tough-minded," unlike what some might deem merely "moralistic" arguments that we should adhere to the prohibition even if adherence imposes serious costs on innocent people.

An unfortunate reality, though, is that we really have no idea how reliable torture is as a way of obtaining information. One cannot even imagine carrying out methodologically sophisticated tests except in a totalitarian society. With regard to the effectiveness or futility of torture, we have only anecdotes and counteranecdotes, none of them dispositive. The Israeli Supreme Court, even while invalidating a number of standard operating procedures of the Israeli security services, nonetheless agreed that the use of some of these procedures "in the past has led to the thwarting of murderous attacks." Similarly, an essayist in the *New York Review of Books*, reviewing a number of books on the Algerian struggle for independence in the 1950s, asked, "Was torture [by the French] effective?" Alas, if the books under review are reliable, the answer seems to be yes. "[T]orture enabled the French to gather information about future terrorist strikes and to destroy the infrastructure of terror in Algiers."[14] Similarly, Alan Dershowitz has offered as an example of torture "working" a 1995 episode when "Philippine authorities tortured a terrorist into disclosing information that may have foiled plots to assassinate the pope and to crash eleven commercial airliners carrying approximately four thousand passengers into the Pacific Ocean, as well as a plan to fly a private Cessna filled with explosives into CIA headquarters."[15] Such grandiose plans could easily have been dismissed prior to September 11, but not now.

Obviously, there are many instances of torture that are totally inefficacious by any measure. But even this claim concedes the legitimacy of engaging in some kind of cost-benefit analysis, which for some people is itself horrendous, inasmuch as it necessarily rejects the absolutism of the imperative "Do not torture" and accepts the possibility that torture *might* be acceptable. One might say that accepting the legitimacy of even one instance of "efficacious" torture is morally disastrous. This comes close to the position of Ivan Karamazov, who refused to respect, let alone worship, a God who would kill an innocent child even if that would save the entire world. Surely no self-respecting state would preserve itself by losing its soul. Let justice be done, though the heavens fall! Yet Charles Fried, as I have mentioned, suggests that this is the position of a fanatic, and I find it difficult to disagree with Fried.

So one might ask the classic question "What is to be done?" If one accepts the absolutism of the prohibition, then the answer is "Nothing," save redoubled efforts to assure compliance. If one accepts some version of the critique of absolutism, though, then this answer seems, at the very least, incomplete. So what *is* to be done as one approaches this particular moral Rubicon?

Alan Dershowitz, a noted civil libertarian who nonetheless rejects the absolutism of the prohibition, suggests an alternative: if one accepts the possibility of even one instance of "legitimate torture," the state must first procure a "torture warrant" explicitly authorizing the activity. Zizek condemns Dershowitz's view as "extremely dangerous" insofar as "it gives legitimacy to torture, and thus opens up the space for more torture." Zizek is not alone in this view; Posner expresses similar reservations, as does Seth Kreimer, in a powerful article addressing the specific issue of the status of torture within current American constitutional doctrine.[16] One should recognize, though, that this ultimately raises an empirical question: What approach to torture, among those just outlined, best reduces or eliminates its actual occurrence?

It turns out to be surprisingly hard to avoid granting some element of "legitimacy" to torture, unless one resolutely believes, in the face of all the evidence, that any and all known events of torture will be prosecuted with significant severity under a doctrine of what lawyers call "strict liability," that is, limiting the legal issue to whether the alleged activity occurred at all, accepting no possible arguments by the defendant that it was justifiable or even excusable. As illustrated by a number of the articles—and by Justice Barak's opinion for the Israeli Supreme Court—few theorists, and no legal systems, have endorsed such strict liability. Most telling, in a way, is that even Professor Shue, who insists that all acts of "torture ought to remain illegal," nonetheless added immediately that "anyone who sincerely believes such an act to be the least available evil" should be

> placed in the position of needing to justify his or her act morally in order to defend himself or herself legally. . . . Anyone who thinks an act of torture is justified should have no alternative but to convince a group of peers in a public trial that all necessary conditions for a morally permissible act were indeed satisfied. . . . If the situation approximates those in the imaginary examples in which torture seems possible to justify, *a judge can surely be expected to suspend the sentence.* (Emphasis added)

This argument is quite similar to that adopted by the Israeli Supreme Court, which left open the possibility that an interrogator accused of torture or inhumane acts could be exculpated upon demonstrating that the acts in question could be viewed as "immediately necessary for the purpose of saving the life, liberty, body, or property, of either himself or his fellow persons, from substantial danger of [imminent] serious harm" and that there were no "alternative means for avoiding the harm."

The principal point is that this scarcely avoids legitimizing at least some acts of torture. What else, after all, is conveyed by accepting the possibility of acquittal, suspension of sentence, or gubernatorial and presidential pardons of what would be perceived as "morally permissible" torture? State officials would then be giving their formal imprimatur to actions that the various conventions condemn without exception.

If one is truly committed to the absolutism set forth in the United Nations Convention, torture would indeed have to be a strict liability offense; any variation in punishment, based on the level of culpable evil, takes away from the element of strict liability. Once one decides to listen to the torturer's story, as well as that of the person tortured, one enters into a far more complicated moral and legal universe, spelled out by Mark Osiel in his reflections on Argentinian torturers, which have implications far beyond that benighted country. The Argentinian torturers may have been moral monsters, but, as Osiel demonstrates, they were *complex* monsters, with more to tell us than we might like to hear.

Few governments, including the United States, Great Britain, and Israel, among others that could no doubt be cited, appear eager, or even particularly willing, to prosecute as criminals agents of the state who engaged in violations of the relevant prohibitions. As John Conroy writes, "throughout the world torturers are rarely punished, and when they are, the punishment rarely corresponds to the severity of the crime."[17] Miscreants, for example, sometimes lose their jobs, but they rarely go to jail.

Conroy's explanation for the infrequency of punishment is derived from the very title of his excellent book *Unspeakable Acts, Ordinary People.* Torturers cannot be reduced to the obvious "sadists" one would, for moral clarity's sake, like them to be. They view themselves as servants of a state fighting a just war; indeed, as Osiel points out, they are often encouraged in their views by the clergy—in the case of Argentina, Catholic priests. What is just as bad, alas, is that the victims of torture will often indeed be unattractive, across one or another dimension, and the alleged torturers will often be able sincerely to argue—in front of jurors or judges far more inclined to identify with them than with the tortured—that they believed they were acting to protect society. Can anyone genuinely imagine, for example, that an alleged terrorist claiming to have been tortured by or with the knowledge of American officials could win a jury trial for damages in the United States today, even assuming that one could surmount various immunity defenses that might prevent ever getting to the jury?

If one believes in the probability of what might be termed the under-enforcement of the norm against torture—and any other view is willfully naive—then we should at least consider, and not merely dismiss, Dershowitz's suggestion that we look at torture before it occurs, so to speak, when the state pleads for a warrant, rather than from the after-the-fact perspective when the torturer, even assuming that he is charged with a criminal offense or sued by his victim, might be all too able to persuade a judge or jury of his "acceptable" motives. To be sure, we can wonder if there really are a sufficient number of detached magistrates to withstand the blandishments of the state. A noted Israeli philosopher is not alone in suggesting that any prior authorization of torture will inevitably coarsen society and lead to its "normalization."

Are there ways to guard against such a possibility, especially if one is suspicious, as I am, that after-the-fact legal controls are likely to be inefficacious? First, unlike the authorizations to engage in wiretaps of alleged foreign agents, which are granted by a secret court, all torture warrants should be public, with written opinions that can be subjected to analysis even if the opinion cannot specify all the evidence that persuaded the judge that this is one of the rare cases justifying the warrant. Second, the person the state proposes to torture should be in the courtroom, so that the judge can take no refuge in abstraction. The judge should be fully aware of his or her personal complicity in the act of torture.

Making the judge complicit in torture would have certain consequences. One might be that certain judges would simply stand down, because of their adherence to the absolute proscription of the practice. Justice Scalia has recently argued that a judge is sufficiently complicit in the act of capital punishment that no judge who believes that capital punishment is immoral should remain on the bench in such cases. Similarly, whether or not the judge actually puts the hood over the head, he should have no doubt that he is collaborating in what even Argentinian torturers recognized as presumptively evil activity. He should know that he is, therefore, potentially at risk if a later court finds the grant of the warrant to have been unreasonable.

Consider also the possibility that anyone against whom a torture warrant is issued receives a significant payment as "just compensation" for the denial of his or her right not to be tortured. Perhaps the very notion of "just compensation" is offensive in such contexts, especially if it suggests that the compensation is simply the amoral "price" the state pays for torture. But the *ex ante* assignment of such a price, especially if it is substantial and paid to *everyone* who is tortured, might itself serve to limit the incidence of torture. And, especially if one emphasizes the word "just," it might help to serve, as with the comment of the Argentinian torturer, to reinforce the paradoxical notion that one must condemn the act even if one comes to the conclusion that it is indeed justified in a particular situation. This is, after all, what Walzer means by the duty to acknowledge that one's hands are "dirty" even if one, as a political leader, did in fact serve the legitimate interests of the society.

Conclusion: In Our Name

It is vitally important that we discuss what is being done in our name. As the *Economist* has written, discussion in the United States has been all too "desultory."[18] It is, perhaps, a dreadful play on words to describe torture as too painful to think about. Yet it is of extraordinary importance to defining who we are as a people and how seriously we take our most solemn commitments. Perhaps law cannot speak fully during time of war; with regard to torture, though, all that law needs to do is whisper, given the remarkably categorical ban on torture that it contains.

There is a special reason for the United States, among all countries, to choose adherence to the no-torture "taboo" (and to behave as if it really means it, which would mean, among other things, the end of "rendering" suspects to torture-friendly countries). One might well believe in a "contagion affect." If the United States is widely believed to accept torture as a proper means of fighting the war against terrorism, then why should any other country refrain? The United States is, for better and, most definitely, for worse, the "new Rome," the giant colossus bestriding the world and claiming, as well, to speak in behalf of good against evil. Part of the responsibility attached to being such a colossus may be the need to accept certain harms that lesser countries need not accept. Our very size and power may require that we limit our responses in a way that might not be true of smaller countries more "existentially" threatened by their enemies than the United States has yet been.

This is a very powerful case, and much in me wishes simply to endorse it without further ado. At the very least, I strongly agree that the United States must be willing to bear significant costs—greater than many other countries—before it accepts the possibility of torture. "Catastrophe" must be taken seriously as a limiting condition, rather than as a rhetorical term to be evoked whenever something appalling happens.

Still, we must be aware that condemning torture is only the beginning of the necessary conversation, at least so long as most of us end up endorsing "vigorous questioning short of torture." We must be as attentive, intellectually and emotionally, to "inhuman and degrading" acts as to "torture," lest we fall victim to accepting anything "short of torture" as in fact fully acceptable, morally even if not legally. In any event, anyone who accepts the necessity of line-drawing—and that must mean anyone who thinks seriously about this topic—must be willing to defend quite awful conduct that comes right up to the line. There is no way to avoid the moral difficulties generated by the possibility of torture. We are staring into an abyss, and no one can escape the necessity of a response.

Notes

1. Admiral Mayorga, quoted in Tina Rosenberg, *Children of Cain: Violence and the Violent in Latin America* (1991), 126.

2. Eric Lichtblau and Adam Liptak, "Threats and Responses: The Suspect; Questioning to Be Legal, Humane and Aggressive, The White House Says," *New York Times,* March 4, 2003, A13.

3. "Bad Memories Reawakened," *Economist,* January 11, 2003, 36.

4. See Dana Priest and Barton Gellman, "U.S. Decries Abuse but Defends Interrogations," *Washington Post,* December 26, 2002, A1.

5. Lichtblau and Liptak, "Threats and Reponses."

6. *Wilson v. City of Chicago,* 6 F.3d 1233, 1236 (7th Cir. 1993). Judge Posner said, moreover, that this right entailed "the correlative right to present his claim of torture to a jury that has not been whipped into a frenzy of hatred."

7. Priest and Gellman, "U.S. Devries Abuse."

8. Eric Schmitt, "There Are Ways to Make Them Talk," *New York Times,* June 16, 2002, sec. 4, 1.

9. Jess Bravin, "Interrogation School Tells Army Recruits How Grilling Works; Thirty Techniques in Sixteen Weeks, Just Short of Torture; Do They Yield Much?", *Wall Street Journal,* April 26, 2002, A1.

10. Quoted in John Conroy, *Unspeakable Acts, Ordinary People: The Dynamics of Torture* (New York: Knopf, 2000), 34.

11. Slavoj Žižek, *Welcome to the Desert of the Real* (London: Verso, 2002), 103–104.

12. Charles Fried, *Right and Wrong* (Cambridge, Mass.: Harvard University Press, 1978), 10. Emphasis added.

13. Don Van Natta, Jr., "Questioning Terror Suspects in a Dark and Surreal World," *New York Times,* Mrach 9, 2003, A1.

14. Adam Shatz, "The Torture of Algiers," *New York Review of Books,* November 21, 2002, 53, 57.

15. Alan M. Dershowitz, *Why Terrorism Works: Understanding the Threat, Responding to the Challenge* (New Haven, Conn.: Yale University Press, 2002), 137.

16. Seth F. Kreimer, "Too Close to the Rack and the Screw: Constitutional Constraints on Torture in the War on Terror," *University of Pennsylvania Journal of Constitutional Law* 6 (2003); 278.

17. Conroy, *Unspeakable Acts,* 25–26.

18. Editorial, "Is Torture Ever Justified?" *Economist,* January 11, 2003, 11.

Appendix: Selected Articles of the United Nations Convention against Torture and Other Inhuman and Degrading Acts

Article 1

1. For the purposes of this Convention, the term "torture" means any act by which severe pain or suffering, whether physical or mental, is intentionally inflicted on a person for such purposes as obtaining from him or a third person information or a confession, punishing him for an act he or a third person has committed or is suspected of having committed, or intimidating or coercing him or a third person, or for any reason based on discrimination of any kind, when such pain or suffering is inflicted by or at the instigation of or with the consent or acquiescence of a public official or other person acting in an official capacity. It does not include pain or suffering arising only from, inherent in or incidental to lawful sanctions. . . .

Article 2

1. Each State Party shall take effective legislative, administrative, judicial or other measures to prevent acts of torture in any territory under its jurisdiction.

2. No exceptional circumstances whatsoever, whether a state of war or a threat of war, internal political instability or any other public emergency, may be invoked as a justification of torture.

3. An order from a superior officer or a public authority may not be invoked as a justification of torture.

Article 3

1. No State Party shall expel, return [*refouler*] or extradite a person to another State where there are substantial grounds for believing that he would be in danger of being subjected to torture.

2. For the purpose of determining whether there are such grounds, the competent authorities shall take into account all relevant considerations including, where applicable, the existence in the State concerned of a consistent pattern of gross, flagrant or mass violations of human rights.

Article 4

1. Each State Party shall ensure that all acts of torture are offences under its criminal law. The same shall apply to an attempt to commit torture and to an act by any person which constitutes complicity or participation in torture.

2. Each State Party shall make these offences punishable by appropriate penalties which take into account their grave nature. . . .

Article 11

Each State Party shall keep under systematic review interrogation rules, instructions, methods and practices as well as arrangements for the custody and treatment of persons subjected to any form of arrest, detention or imprisonment in any territory under its jurisdiction, with a view to preventing any cases of torture.

Article 12

Each State Party shall ensure that its competent authorities proceed to a prompt and impartial investigation, wherever there is reasonable ground to believe that an act of torture has been committed in any territory under its jurisdiction.

Article 13

Each State Party shall ensure that any individual who alleges he has been subjected to torture in any territory under its jurisdiction has the right to complain to, and to have his case promptly and impartially examined by, its competent authorities. . . .

Article 15

Each State Party shall ensure that any statement which is established to have been made as a result of torture shall not be invoked as evidence in any proceedings, except against a person accused of torture as evidence that the statement was made.

Article 16

1. Each State Party shall undertake to prevent in any territory under its jurisdiction other acts of cruel, inhuman or degrading treatment or punishment which do not amount to torture as defined in article I, when such acts are committed by or at the instigation of or with the consent or acquiescence of a public official or other person acting in an official capacity. . . .

Following are URLs for various internal documents of the Executive Branch, leaked to the public in May and June 2004, relating to Executive Branch authority to order coercive interrogation, including torture.

January 25, 2002, Memorandum from Alberto Gonzales to The President, "Decision re Application of the Geneva Convention on Prisoners of War to the Conflict with al Qaeda and the Taliban." http://msnbc.msn.com/id/4999148/site/newsweek/

The Gonzales draft generated two responses from the State Department:

1. Memo from Colin Powell to White House Counsel on "Draft Decision Memorandum for the President on the Applicability of the Geneva Convention to the Conflict in Afganistan." 26 January 2002. http://msnbc.msn.com/id/4999363/site/newsweek/

2. Legal Advisor to the State Department, William H. Taft IV, "Comments on Your Paper on the Geneva Convention." http://www.nytimes.com/packages/html/politics/20040608 DOC.pdf

August 1, 2002, Memorandum from Jay Bybee, Office of Legal Counsel of Department of Justice, to Alberto Gonzales, Counsel to the President, on "Standards for Interrogation." http://www.washingtonpost.com/wp-srv/nation/documents/dojinterrogationmemo20020801.pdf

Working Group Report [to Secretary of Defense Donald Rumsfeld] on Detainee Interrogations in the Global War on Terrorism: Assessment of Legal, Historical, Policy, and Operational Considerations. http://online.wsj.com/public/resources/documents/military_0604.pdf

Philosophical Considerations

Henry Shue

Torture

But no one dies in the right place
Or in the right hour
And everyone dies sooner than his time
And before he reaches home.
—Reza Baraheni

Whatever one might have to say about torture, there appear to be moral reasons for not saying it. Obviously I am not persuaded by these reasons, but they deserve some mention. Mostly, they add up to a sort of Pandora's box objection: if practically everyone is opposed to all torture, why bring it up, start people thinking about it, and risk weakening the inhibitions against what is clearly a terrible business?

Torture is indeed contrary to every relevant international law, including the laws of war. No other practice except slavery is so universally and unanimously condemned in law and human convention. Yet, unlike slavery, which is still most definitely practiced but affects relatively few people, torture is widespread and growing. According to Amnesty International, scores of governments are now using some torture—including governments which are widely viewed as fairly civilized—and a number of governments are heavily dependent upon torture for their very survival.[1]

So, to cut discussion of this objection short, Pandora's box is open. Although virtually everyone continues ritualistically to condemn all torture publicly, the deep conviction, as reflected in actual policy, is in many cases not behind the strong language. In addition, partial justifications for some of the torture continue to circulate.[2]

One of the general contentions that keeps coming to the surface is: since killing is worse than torture, and killing is sometimes permitted, especially in war, we ought sometimes to permit torture, especially when the situation consists of a protracted, if undeclared, war between a government and its enemies. I shall try first to show the weakness of this argument. To establish that one argument for permitting some torture is unsuccessful is, of course, not to establish that no torture is to be permitted. But in the remainder of the essay I shall also try to show, far more interestingly, that a comparison between some types of killing in combat and some types of torture actually provides an insight into an important respect in which much torture is morally worse. This respect is the degree of satisfaction of the primitive moral prohibition against assault upon the defenseless. Comprehending how torture violates this prohibition helps to explain—and justify—the peculiar disgust which torture normally arouses.

The general idea of the defense of at least some torture can be explained more fully, using "just-combat killing" to refer to killing done in accord with all relevant requirements for the conduct of warfare.[3] The defense has two stages.

A Since (1) just-combat killing is total destruction of a person,
      (2) torture is—usually—only partial destruction or temporary incapacitation of a person, and
      (3) the total destruction of a person is a greater harm than the partial destruction of a person is,
then (4) just-combat killing is a greater harm than torture usually is;

B since (4) just-combat killing is a greater harm than torture usually is, and
      (5) just-combat killing is sometimes morally permissible,
then (6) torture is sometimes morally permissible.

To state the argument one step at a time is to reveal its main weakness. Stage B tacitly assumes that if a greater harm is sometimes permissible, then a lesser harm is too, at least sometimes. The mistake is to assume that the only consideration relevant to moral permissibility is the amount of harm done. Even if one grants that killing someone in combat is doing him or her a greater harm than torturing him or her (Stage A), it by no means follows that there could not be a justification for the greater harm that was not applicable to the lesser harm. Specifically, it would matter if some killing could satisfy other moral constraints (besides the constraint of minimizing harm) which no torture could satisfy.[4]

A defender of at least some torture could, however, readily modify the last step of the argument to deal with the point that one cannot simply weigh amounts of "harm" against each other but must consider other relevant standards as well by adding a final qualification:

(6') torture is sometimes morally permissible, provided that it meets whichever standards are satisfied by just-combat killing.

If we do not challenge the judgment that just-combat killing is a greater harm than torture usually is, the question to raise is: Can torture meet the standards satisfied by just-combat killing? If so, that might be one reason in favor of allowing such torture. If not, torture will have been reaffirmed to be an activity of an extremely low moral order.

Assault upon the Defenseless

The laws of war include an elaborate, and for the most part long-established, code for what might be described as the proper conduct of the killing of other people. Like most codes, the laws of war have been constructed piecemeal and different bits of the code serve different functions.[5] It would almost certainly be impossible to specify any one unifying purpose served by the laws of warfare as a whole. Surely major portions of the law serve to keep warfare within one sort of principle of efficiency by requiring that the minimum destruction necessary to the attainment of legitimate objectives be used.

However, not all the basic principles incorporated in the laws of war could be justified as serving the purpose of minimizing destruction. One of the most basic principles for the conduct of war (*jus in bello*) rests on the distinction between combatants and noncombatants and requires that insofar as possible, violence not be directed at noncombatants.[6] Now, obviously, there are some conceptual difficulties in trying to separate combatants and noncombatants in some guerrilla warfare and even sometimes in modern conventional warfare among industrial societies. This difficulty is a two-edged sword; it can be used to argue that it is increasingly impossible for war to be fought justly as readily as it can be used to argue that the distinction between combatants and noncombatants is obsolete. In any case, I do not now want to defend or criticize the principle of avoiding attack upon noncombatants but to isolate one of the more general moral principles this specific principle of warfare serves.

It might be thought to serve, for example, a sort of efficiency principle in that it helps to minimize human casualties and suffering. Normally, the armed forces of the opposing nations constitute only a fraction of the respective total populations. If the casualties can be restricted to these official fighters, perhaps total casualties and suffering will be smaller than they would be if human targets were unrestricted.

But this justification for the principle of not attacking noncombatants does not ring true. Unless one is determined a priori to explain everything in terms of minimizing numbers of casualties, there is little reason to believe that this principle actually functions primarily to restrict the number of casualties rather than, as its own terms suggest, the *types* of casualties.[7] A more convincing suggestion about the best justification which could be given is that the principle goes some way toward keeping combat humane, by protecting those who are assumed to be incapable of defending themselves. The principle of warfare is an instance of a more general moral principle which prohibits assaults upon the defenseless.[8]

Nonpacifists who have refined the international code for the conduct of warfare have not necessarily viewed the killing involved in war as in itself any less terrible than pacifists view it. One fundamental function of the distinction between combatants and noncombatants is to try to make a terrible combat fair, and the killing involved can seem morally tolerable to nonpacifists in large part because it is the outcome of what is conceived as a fair procedure. To the extent that the distinction between combatants and noncombatants is observed, those who are killed will be those who were directly engaged in trying to kill their killers. The fairness may be perceived to lie in this fact: that those who are killed had a reasonable chance to survive by killing instead. It was kill or be killed for both parties, and each had his or her opportunity to survive. No doubt the opportunities may not have been anywhere near equal—it would be impossible to restrict wars to equally matched opponents. But at least none of the parties to the combat were defenseless.

Now this obviously invokes a simplified, if not romanticized, portrait of warfare. And at least some aspects of the laws of warfare can legitimately be criticized for relying too heavily for their justification on a core notion that modern warfare retains aspects of a knightly joust, or a duel, which have long since vanished, if ever they were present. But the point now is not to attack or defend the efficacy of the principle of warfare that combat is more acceptable morally if restricted to official combatants, but to notice one of its moral bases, which, I am suggesting, is that it allows for a "fair fight" by means of protecting the utterly defenseless from assault. The resulting picture of war—accurate or not—is not of victim and perpetrator (or, of mutual victims) but of a winner and a loser, each of whom might have enjoyed, or suffered, the fate of the other. Of course, the satisfaction of the requirement of providing for a "fair fight" would not by itself make a conflict morally acceptable overall. An unprovoked and otherwise unjustified invasion does not become morally acceptable just because attacks upon noncombatants, use of prohibited weapons, and so on are avoided.

At least part of the peculiar disgust which torture evokes may be derived from its apparent failure to satisfy even this weak constraint of being a "fair fight." The supreme reason, of course, is that torture begins only after the fight is—for the victim—finished. Only losers are tortured. A "fair fight" may even in fact already have occurred and led to the capture of the person who is to be tortured. But now that the torture victim has exhausted all means of defense and is powerless before the victors, a fresh assault begins. The surrender is followed by new attacks upon the defeated by the now unrestrained conquerors. In this respect torture is indeed not analogous to the killing in battle of a healthy and well-armed foe; it is a cruel assault upon the defenseless. In combat the other person one kills is still a threat when killed and is killed in part for the sake of one's own survival. The torturer inflicts pain and damage upon another person who, by virtue of now being within his or her power, is no longer a threat and is entirely at the torturer's mercy.

It is in this respect of violating the prohibition against assault upon the defenseless, then, that the manner in which torture is conducted is morally more reprehensible than the manner in which killing would occur if the laws of war were honored. In this respect torture sinks below even the well-regulated mutual slaughter of a justly fought war.

Torture within Constraints?

But is all torture indeed an assault upon the defenseless? For, it could be argued in support of some torture that in many cases there is something beyond the initial surrender which the torturer wants from the victim and that in such cases the victim could comply and provide the torturer with whatever is wanted. To refuse to comply with the further demand would then be to maintain a second line of defense. The victim would, in a sense, not have surrendered—at least not fully surrendered—but instead only retreated. The victim is not, on this view, utterly helpless in the face of unrestrainable assault as long as he or she holds in reserve an act of compliance which would satisfy the torturer and bring the torture to an end.

It might be proposed, then, that there could be at least one type of morally less unacceptable torture. Obviously the torture victim must remain defenseless in the literal sense, because it cannot be expected that his or her captors would provide means of defense against themselves. But an alternative to a capability for a literal defense is an effective capability for surrender, that is, a form of surrender which will in fact bring an end to attacks. In the case of torture the relevant from of surrender might seem to be a compliance with the wishes of the torturer that provides an escape from further torture.

Accordingly, the constraint on the torture that would, on this view, make it less objectionable would be this: the victim of torture must have available an act of compliance which, if performed, will end the torture. In other words, the purpose of the torture must be known to the victim, the purpose must be the performance of some action within the victim's power to perform, and the victim's performance of the desired action must produce the permanent cessation of the torture. I shall refer to torture that provides for such an act of compliance as torture that satisfies the constraint of possible compliance. As soon becomes clear, it makes a great difference what kind of act is presented as the act of compliance. And a person with an iron will, a great sense of honor, or an overwhelming commitment to a cause may choose not to accept voluntarily cessation of the torture on the terms offered. But the basic point would be merely that there should be some terms understood so that the victim retains one last portion of control over his or her fate. Escape is not defense, but it is a manner of protecting oneself. A practice of torture that allows for escape through compliance might seem immune to the charge of engaging in assault upon the defenseless. Such is the proposal.

One type of contemporary torture, however, is clearly incapable of satisfying the constraint of possible compliance. The extraction of information from the victim, which perhaps—whatever the deepest motivations of torturers may have been—has historically been a dominant explicit purpose of torture is now, in world practice, overshadowed by the goal of the intimidation of people other than the victim.[9]. . . The function of general intimidation of others, or deterrence of dissent, is radically different from the function of extracting specific information under the control of the victim of torture, in respects which are central to the assessment of such torture. This is naturally not to deny that any given instance of torture may serve, to varying degrees, both purposes—and, indeed, other purposes still.

Terroristic torture, as we may call this dominant type, cannot satisfy the constraint of possible compliance, because its purpose (intimidation of persons other than the victim of the torture) cannot be accomplished and may not even be capable of being influenced by the victim of the torture. The victim's suffering—indeed, the victim—is being used entirely as a means to an end over which the victim has no control. Terroristic torture is a pure case—the purest possible case—of the violation of the Kantian principle that no person may be used *only* as a means. . . .

The degree of need for assaults upon the defenseless initially appears to be quite different in the case of torture for the purpose of extracting information, which we may call *interrogational torture.*[10] This type of torture needs separate examination because, however condemnable we ought in the end to consider it overall, its purpose of gaining information appears to be consistent with the observation of some constraint on the part of any torturer genuinely pursuing that purpose alone. Interrogational torture does have a built-in end-point: when the information has been obtained, the torture has accomplished its purpose and need not be continued. Thus, satisfaction of the constraint of possible compliance seems to be quite compatible with the explicit end of interrogational torture, which could be terminated upon the victim's compliance in providing the information sought. In a fairly obvious fashion the torturer could consider himself or herself to have completed the assigned task—or probably more hopefully, any superiors who were supervising the process at some emotional distance could consider the task to be finished and put a stop to it. A pure case of interrogational torture, then, appears able to satisfy the constraint of possible compliance, since it offers an escape, in the form of providing the information wanted by the torturers, which affords some protection against further assault.

Two kinds of difficulties arise for the suggestion that even largely interrogational torture could escape the charge that it includes assaults upon the defenseless. It is hardly necessary to point out that very few actual instances of torture are likely to fall entirely within the category of interrogational torture. Torture intended primarily to obtain information is by no means always in practice held to some minimum necessary amount. To the extent that the torturer's motivation is sadistic or otherwise brutal, he or she will be strongly inclined to exceed any rational calculations about what is sufficient for the stated purpose. In view of the strength and nature of a torturer's likely passions—of, for example, hate and self-hate, disgust and self-disgust, horror and fascination, subservience toward superiors and aggression toward victims—no constraint is to be counted upon in practice.

Still, it is of at least theoretical interest to ask whether torturers with a genuine will to do so could conduct interrogational torture in a manner which would satisfy the constraint of possible compliance. In order to tell, it is essential to grasp specifically what compliance would normally involve. Almost all torture is "political" in the sense that it is inflicted by the government in power upon people who are, seem to be, or might be opposed to the government. Some torture is also inflicted by opponents of a government upon people who are, seem to be, or might be supporting the government. Possible victims of torture fall into three broad categories: the ready collaborator, the innocent bystander, and the dedicated enemy.

First, the torturers may happen upon someone who is involved with the other side but is not dedicated to such a degree that cooperation with the torturers would, from the victim's perspective, constitute a betrayal of anything highly valued. For such a person a betrayal of cause and allies might indeed serve as a form of genuine escape.

The second possibility is the capture of someone who is passive toward both sides and essentially uninvolved. If such a bystander should happen to know the relevant information—which is very unlikely—and to be willing to provide it, no torture would be called for. But what if the victim would be perfectly willing to provide the information sought in order to escape the torture but does not have the information? . . . The victim has no convincing way of demonstrating that he or she cannot comply, even when compliance is impossible. (Compare the reputed dunking test for witches: if the woman sank, she was an ordinary mortal.)

Even a torturer who would be willing to stop after learning all that could be learned, which is nothing at all if the "wrong" person is being tortured, would have difficulty discriminating among pleas. Any keeping of the tacit bargain to stop when compliance has been as complete as possible would likely be undercut by uncertainty about when the fullest possible compliance had occurred. . . .

Finally, when the torturers succeed in torturing someone genuinely committed to the other side, compliance means, in a word, betrayal; betrayal of one's ideals and one's comrades. The possibility of betrayal cannot be counted as an escape. Undoubtedly some ideals are vicious and some friends are partners in crime—this can be true of either the government, the opposition, or both. Nevertheless, a betrayal is no escape for a dedicated member of either a government or its opposition, who cannot collaborate without denying his or her highest values.[11]

For any genuine escape must be something better than settling for the lesser of two evils. One can always try to minimize one's losses—even in dilemmas from which there is no real escape. But if accepting the lesser of two evils always counted as an escape, there would be no situations from which there was no escape, except perhaps those in which all alternatives happened to be equally evil. On such a loose notion of escape, all conscripts would become volunteers, since they could always desert. And all assaults containing any alternatives would then be acceptable. An alternative which is legitimately to count as an escape must not only be preferable but also itself satisfy some minimum standard of moral acceptability. A denial of one's self does not count.

Therefore, on the whole, the apparent possibility of escape through compliance tends to melt away upon examination. The ready collaborator and the innocent bystander have some hope of an acceptable escape, but only provided that the torturers both (1) are persuaded that the victim has kept his or her part of the bargain by telling all there is to tell and (2) choose to keep their side of the bargain in a situation in which agreements cannot be enforced upon them and they have nothing to lose by continuing the torture if they please. If one is treated as if one is a dedicated enemy, as seems likely to be the standard procedure, the fact that one actually belongs in another category has no effect. On the other hand, the dedicated enemies of the torturers, who presumably tend to know more and consequently are the primary intended targets of the torture, are provided with nothing which can be considered an escape and can only protect themselves, as torture victims always have, by pretending to be collaborators or innocents, and thereby imperiling the members of these two categories.

Morally Permissible Torture?

Still, it must reluctantly be admitted that the avoidance of assaults upon the defenseless is not the only, or even in all cases an overriding, moral consideration. And, therefore, even if terroristic and interrogational torture, each in its own way, is bound to involve attacks upon people unable to defend themselves or to escape, it is still not utterly inconceivable that instances of one or the other type of torture might sometimes, all things considered, be justified. Consequently, we must sketch the elements of an overall assessment of these two types of torture, beginning again with the dominant contemporary form: terroristic. . . .

Much of what can be said about terroristic torture can also be said about instances involving interrogational torture. This is the case primarily because in practice there are evidently few pure cases of interrogational torture.[12] An instance of torture which is to any significant degree terroristic in purpose ought to be treated as terroristic. But if we keep in mind how far we are departing from most actual practice, we may, as before, consider instances in which the *sole* purpose of torture is to extract certain information and therefore the torturer is willing to stop as soon as he or she is sure that the victim has provided all the information the victim has.

Interrogational torture would in practice be difficult to make into less of an assault upon the defenseless. The supposed possibility of escape through compliance turns out to depend upon the keeping of a bargain which is entirely unenforceable within the torture situation and upon the making of discriminations among victims that would usually be difficult to make until after they no longer mattered. In fact, since any sensible willing collaborator will cooperate in a hurry, only the committed and the innocent are likely to be severely tortured. More important, in the case of someone being tortured because of profoundly held convictions, the "escape" would normally be a violation of integrity.

As with terroristic torture, any complete argument for permitting instances of interrogational torture would have to include a full specification of all necessary conditions of a permissible instance, such as its serving a supremely important purpose (with criteria of importance), its being the least harmful means to that goal, its having a clearly defined and reachable endpoint, and so on. This would not be a simple matter. Also as in the case of terroristic torture, a considerable danger exists that whatever necessary conditions were specified, any practice of torture once set in motion would gain enough momentum to burst any bonds and become a standard operating procedure. Torture is the ultimate shortcut. If it were ever permitted under any conditions, the temptation to use it increasingly would be very strong.

Nevertheless, it cannot be denied that there are imaginable cases in which the harm that could be prevented by a rare instance of pure interrogational torture would be so enormous as to outweigh the cruelty of the torture itself and, possibly, the enormous potential harm which would result if what was intended to be a rare instance was actually the breaching of the dam which would lead to a torrent of torture. There is a standard philosopher's example which someone always invokes: suppose a fanatic, perfectly willing to die rather than collaborate in the thwarting of his own scheme, has set a hidden nuclear device to explode in the heart of Paris. There is no time to evacuate the innocent people or even the movable art treasures—the only hope of preventing tragedy is to torture the perpetrator, find the device, and deactivate it.

I can see no way to deny the permissibility of torture in a case *just like this*. To allow the destruction of much of a great city and many of its people would be almost as wicked as purposely to destroy it, as the Nazis did to London and Warsaw, and the Allies did to Dresden and Tokyo, during World War II. But there is a saying in jurisprudence that hard cases make bad law, and there might well be one in philosophy that artificial cases make bad ethics. If the example is made sufficiently extraordinary, the conclusion that the torture is permissible is secure. But one cannot easily draw conclusions for ordinary cases from extraordinary ones, and as the situations described become more likely, the conclusion that the torture is permissible becomes more debatable.

Notice how unlike the circumstances of an actual choice about torture the philosopher's example is. The proposed victim of our torture is not someone we suspect of planting the device: he *is* the perpetrator. He is not some pitiful psychotic making one last play for attention: he *did* plant the device. The wiring is not backwards, the mechanism is not jammed: the device *will* destroy the city if not deactivated.

Much more important from the perspective of whether general conclusions applicable to ordinary cases can be drawn are the background conditions that tend to be assumed. The torture will not be conducted in the basement of a small-town jail in the provinces by local thugs popping pills; the prime minister and chief justice are being kept informed; and a priest and a doctor are present. The victim will not be raped or forced to eat excrement and will not collapse with a heart attack or become deranged before talking; while avoiding irreparable damage, the antiseptic pain will carefully be increased only up to the point at which the necessary information is divulged, and the doctor will then immediately administer an antibiotic and a tranquilizer. The torture is purely interrogational.[13]

Most important, such incidents do not continue to happen. There are not so many people with grievances against this government that the torture is becoming necessary more often, and in the smaller cities, and for slightly lesser threats, and with a little less care, and so on. Any judgment that torture could be sanctioned in an isolated case without seriously weakening existing inhibitions against the more general use of torture rests on empirical hypotheses about the psychology and politics of torture. There *is* considerable evidence of all torture's metastatic tendency. If there is also evidence that interrogational torture can sometimes be used with the surgical precision which imagined justifiable cases always assume, such rare uses would have to be considered.

Does the possibility that torture might be justifiable in some of the rarefied situations which can be imagined provide any reason to consider relaxing the legal prohibitions against it? Absolutely not. The distance between the situations which must be concocted in order to have a plausible case of morally permissible torture and the situations which actually occur is, if anything, further reason why the existing prohibitions against torture should remain and should be strengthened by making torture an international crime. An act of torture ought to remain illegal so that anyone who sincerely believes such an act to be the least available evil is placed in the position of needing to justify his or her act morally in order to defend himself or herself legally. The torturer should be in roughly the same position as someone who commits civil disobedience. Anyone who thinks an act of torture is justified should have no alternative but to convince a group of peers in a public trial that all necessary conditions for a morally permissible act were indeed satisfied. If it is reasonable to put someone through torture, it is reasonable to put someone else through a careful explanation of why. If the situation approximates those in the imaginary examples in which torture seems possible to justify, a judge can surely be expected to suspend the sentence. Meanwhile, there is little need to be concerned about possible injustice to justified torturers and great need to find means to restrain totally unjustified torture.

Notes

The time and facilities for this study were provided by the Center for Philosophy and Public Policy of the University of Maryland. For careful critiques of earlier versions I am also grateful to Michael Gardner, Robert Goodin, Ernest Schlaretzki, and especially Peter G. Brown and the editors of *Philosophy & Public Affairs*.

1. See Amnesty International, *Report on Torture* (New York: Farrar, Straus and Giroux, 1975), 21–33.

2. I primarily have in mind conversations which cannot be cited, but for a written source see Roger Trinquier, *La Guerre Moderne* (Paris: La Table Ronde, 1961), 39, 42, 187–191. Consider the following: "Et c'est tricher que d'admettre sereinement que l'artillerie ou l'aviation peuvent bombarder des villages où se trouvent des femmes et des enfants qui seront inutilement massacrés, alors que le plus souvent les ennemis visés auront pu s'enfuir, et refuser que des spécialistes en interrogeant un terroriste permettent de se saisir des vrais coupables et d'épargner les innocents" (42).

3. By "just combat" I mean warfare which satisfies what has traditionally been called *jus in bello*, the law governing how war may be fought once underway, rather than *jus ad bellum*, the law governing when war may be undertaken.

4. Obviously one could also challenge other elements of the argument—most notably, perhaps, premise (3). Torture is usually humiliating and degrading—the pain is normally experienced naked and amidst filth. But while killing destroys life, it need not destroy dignity. Which is worse, an honorable death or a degraded existence? While I am not unsympathetic with this line of attack, I do not want to try to use it. It suffers from being an attempt somehow just to intuit the relative degrees of evil attached respectively to death and degradation. Such judgments should probably be the outcome, rather than the starting point, of an argument. The rest of the essay bears directly on them.

5. See James T. Johnson, *Ideology, Reason, and the Limitation of War: Religious and Secular Concepts 1200–1740* (Princeton: Princeton University Press, 1975). Johnson stresses the largely religious origins of *jus ad bellum* and the largely secular origins of *jus in bello*.

6. For the current law, see Geneva Convention Relative to the Protection of Civilian Persons in Time of War, 12 August 1949 [1955], 6 U.S.T. 3516; T.I.A.S. No. 3365; 75

U.N.T.S. 287. Also see United States, Department of the Army, *The Law of Land Warfare*, Field Manual 27-10 (Washington, DC: Government Printing Office, 1956), chap. 5, "Civilian Persons"; and United States, Department of the Air Force, *International Law—The Conduct of Armed Conflict and Air Operations*, Air Force Pamphlet 110-31 (Washington, DC: Government Printing Office, 1976), chap. 3, "Combatants, Noncombatants and Civilians."

7. This judgment is supported by Stockholm International Peace Research Institute, *The Law of War and Dubious Weapons* (Stockholm: Almqvist and Wiksell, 1976), 9: "The prohibition on deliberately attacking the civilian population as such is not based exclusively on the principle of avoiding unnecessary suffering."

8. To defend the bombing of cities in World War II on the ground that *total* casualties (combatant and noncombatant) were thereby reduced is to miss, or ignore, the point.

9. See Amnesty International, *Report on Torture*, 69.

10. These two categories of torture are not intended to be, and are not, exhaustive.

11. Defenders of privilege customarily portray themselves as defenders of civilization against the vilest barbarians. Self-deception sometimes further smooths the way to treating whoever are the current enemies as beneath contempt and certainly unworthy of equal respect as human beings. Consequently, I am reluctant to concede, even as a limiting case, that there are probably rare individuals so wicked as to lack integrity, or anyway to lack any integrity worthy of respect. But what sort of integrity could one have violated by torturing Hitler?

Any very slight qualification here must not, however, be taken as a flinging wide open of the doors. To be beyond the pale in the relevant respect must involve far more than simply serving values which the torturers find abhorrent. Otherwise, license has been granted simply to torture whoever are one's greatest enemies—the only victims very many torturers would want in any case. Unfortunately, I cannot see a way to delimit those who are genuinely beyond the pale which does not beg for abuse.

12. Amnesty International, *Report on Torture*, 24–25, 114–242.

13. For a realistic account of the effects of torture, see *Evidence of Torture: Studies by the Amnesty International Danish Medical Group* (London: Amnesty International, 1977). Note in particular: "Undoubtedly the worst sequelae of torture were psychological and neurological" (12). For suggestions about medical ethics for physicians attending persons being tortured, see "Declaration of Tokyo: Guidelines for Medical Doctors Concerning Torture," in United Nations, General Assembly, Note by the Secretary-General, *Torture and other Cruel, Inhuman or Degrading Treatment or Punishment in relation to Detention and Imprisonment* (UN Document A/31/234, 6 October 1976, 31st Session), annex 2.

Michael Walzer

Political Action
The Problem of Dirty Hands

In a 1971 issue of *Philosophy & Public Affairs* there appeared a symposium on the rules of war which was actually (or at least more importantly) a symposium on another topic.[1] The actual topic was whether or not a man can ever face, or ever has to face, a moral dilemma, a situation where he must choose between two courses of action both of which it would be wrong for him to undertake. Thomas Nagel worriedly suggested that this could happen and that it did happen whenever someone was forced to choose between upholding an important moral principle and avoiding some looming disaster. R. B. Brandt argued that it could not possibly happen, for there were guidelines we might follow and calculations we might go through which would necessarily yield the conclusion that one or the other course of action was the right one to undertake in the circumstances (or that it did not matter which we undertook). R. M. Hare explained how it was that someone might wrongly suppose that he was faced with a moral dilemma: sometimes, he suggested, the precepts and principles of an ordinary man, the products of his moral education, come into conflict with injunctions developed at a higher level of moral discourse. But this conflict is, or ought to be, resolved at the higher level; there is no real dilemma. . . .

In modern times the dilemma appears most often as the problem of "dirty hands," and it is typically stated by the Communist leader Hoerderer in Sartre's play of that name: "I have dirty hands right up to the elbows. I've plunged them in filth and blood. Do you think you can govern innocently?"[2] My own answer is no, I don't think I could govern innocently; nor do most of us believe that those who govern us are innocent—as I shall argue later—even the best of them. But this does not mean that it isn't possible to do the right thing while governing. It means that a particular act of government (in a political party or in the state) may be exactly the right thing to do in utilitarian terms and yet leave the man who does it guilty of a moral wrong. The innocent man, afterwards, is no longer innocent. If on the other hand he remains innocent, chooses, that is, the "absolutist" side of Nagel's dilemma, he not only fails to do the right thing (in utilitarian terms), he may also fail to measure up to the duties of his office (which imposes on him a considerable responsibility for consequences and outcomes). Most often, of course, political leaders accept the utilitarian calculation; they try to measure up. One might offer a number of sardonic comments on this fact, the most obvious being that by the calculations they usually make they demonstrate the great virtues of the "absolutist" position. Nevertheless, we would not want to be governed by men who consistently adopted that position.

The notion of dirty hands derives from an effort to refuse "absolutism" without denying the reality of the moral dilemma. Though this may appear to utilitarian philosophers to pile confusion upon confusion, I propose to take it very seriously. . . .

I

Let me begin, then, with a piece of conventional wisdom to the effect that politicians are a good deal worse, morally worse, than the rest of us (it is the wisdom of the rest of us). Without either endorsing it or pretending to disbelieve it, I am going to expound this convention. For it suggests that the dilemma of dirty hands is a central feature of political life, that it arises not merely as an occasional crisis in the career of this or that unlucky politician but systematically and frequently. . . .

. . . The politician has, or pretends to have, a kind of confidence in his own judgment that the rest of us know to be presumptuous in any man.

The presumption is especially great because the victorious politician uses violence and the threat of violence—not only against foreign nations in our defense but also against us, and again ostensibly for our greater good. This is a point emphasized and perhaps overemphasized by Max Weber in his essay "Politics as a Vocation."[3] It has not, so far as I can tell, played an overt or obvious part in the development of the convention I am examining. The stock figure is the lying, not the murderous, politician—though the murderer lurks in the background, appearing most often in the form of the revolutionary or terrorist, very rarely as an ordinary magistrate or official. Nevertheless, the sheer weight of official violence in human history does suggest the kind of power to which politicians aspire, the kind of power they want to wield, and it may point to the roots of our half-conscious dislike and unease. The men who act for us and in our name are often killers, or seem to become killers too quickly and too easily.

Knowing all this or most of it, good and decent people still enter political life, aiming at some specific reform or seeking a general reformation. They are then required to learn the lesson Machiavelli first set out to teach: "how not to be good."[4] Some of them are incapable of learning; many more profess to be incapable. But they will not succeed unless they learn, for they have joined the terrible competition for power and glory; they have chosen to work and struggle as Machiavelli says, among "so many who are not good." They can do no good themselves unless they win the struggle, which they are unlikely to do unless they are willing and able to use the necessary means. So we are suspicious even of the best of winners. It is not a sign of our perversity if we think them only more clever than the rest. They have not won, after all, because they were good, or not only because of that, but also because they were not good. No one succeeds in politics without getting his hands dirty. This is conventional wisdom again, and again I don't mean to insist that it is true without qualification. I repeat it only to disclose the moral dilemma inherent in the convention. For sometimes it is right to try to succeed, and then it must also be right to get one's hands dirty. But one's hands get dirty from doing what it is wrong to do. And how can it be wrong to do what is right? Or, how can we get our hands dirty by doing what we ought to do?

II

It will be best to turn quickly to some examples. I have chosen two, one relating to the struggle for power and one to its exercise. . . . Let us imagine a politician who wants to do good only by doing good, or at least he is certain that he can stop short of the most corrupting and brutal uses of political power. Very quickly that certainty is tested. What do we think of him then?

He wants to win the election, someone says, but he doesn't want to get his hands dirty. This is meant as a disparagement, even though it also means that the man being criticized is the sort of man who will not lie, cheat, bargain behind the backs of his supporters, shout absurdities at public meetings, or manipulate other men and women. Assuming that this particular election ought to be won, it is clear, I think, that the disparagement is justified. If the candidate didn't want to get his hands dirty, he should have stayed at home; if he can't stand the heat, he should get out of the kitchen, and so on. His decision to run was a commitment (to all of us who think the election important) to try to win, that is, to do within rational limits whatever is necessary to win. But the candidate is a moral man. He has principles and a history of adherence to those principles. That is why we are supporting him. Perhaps when he refuses to dirty his hands, he is simply insisting on being the sort of man he is. And isn't that the sort of man we want?

Let us look more closely at this case. In order to win the election the candidate must make a deal with a dishonest ward boss, involving the granting of contracts for school construction over the next four years. Should he make the deal? . . .

Because he has scruples . . . we know him to be a good man. But we view the campaign in a certain light, estimate its importance in a certain way, and hope that he will overcome his scruples and make the deal. It is important to stress that we don't want just *anyone* to make the deal; we want *him* to make it, precisely because he has scruples about it. We know he is doing right when he makes the deal because he knows he is doing wrong. I don't mean merely that he will feel badly or even very badly after he makes the deal. If he is the good man I am imagining him to be, he will feel guilty, that is, he will believe himself to be guilty. That is what it means to have dirty hands.

All this may become clearer if we look at a more dramatic example, for we are, perhaps, a little blasé about political deals and disinclined to worry much about the man who makes one. So consider a politician who has seized upon a national crisis—a prolonged colonial war—to reach for power. He and his friends win office pledged to decolonization and peace; they are honestly committed to both, though not without some sense of the advantages of the commitment. In any case, they have no responsibility for the war; they have steadfastly opposed it. Immediately, the politician goes off to the colonial capital to open negotiations with the rebels. But the capital is in the grip of a terrorist campaign, and the first decision the new leader faces is this: he is asked to authorize the torture of a captured rebel leader who knows or probably knows the location of a number of bombs hidden in apartment buildings around the city, set to go off within the next twenty-four hours. He orders the man tortured, convinced that he must do so for the sake of the people who might otherwise die in the explosions—even though he believes that torture is wrong, indeed abominable, not just sometimes, but always.[5] He had expressed this belief often and angrily during his own campaign; the rest of us took it as a sign of his goodness. How should we regard him now? (How should he regard himself?)

Once again, it does not seem enough to say that he should feel very badly. But why not? Why shouldn't he have feelings like those of St. Augustine's melancholy soldier, who understood both that his war was just and that killing, even in a just war, is a terrible thing to do?[6] The difference is that Augustine did not believe that it was wrong to kill in a just war; it was just sad, or the sort of thing a good man would be saddened by. But he might have thought it wrong to torture in a just war, and later Catholic theorists have certainly thought it wrong. Moreover, the politician I am imagining thinks it wrong, as do many of us who supported him. Surely we have a right to expect more than melancholy from him now. When he ordered the prisoner tortured, he committed a moral crime and he accepted a moral burden. Now he is a guilty man. His willingness to acknowledge and bear (and perhaps to repent and do penance for) his guilt is evidence, and it is the only evidence he can offer us, both that he is not too good for politics and that he is good enough. Here is the moral politician: it is by his dirty hands that we know him. If he were a moral man and nothing else, his hands would not be dirty; if he were a politician and nothing else, he would pretend that they were clean.

III

Machiavelli's argument about the need to learn how not to be good clearly implies that there are acts known to be bad quite apart from the immediate circumstances in which they are performed or not performed. He points to a distinct set of political methods and strategems which good men must study (by reading his books), not only because their use does not come naturally, but also because they are explicitly condemned by the moral teachings good men accept—and whose acceptance serves in turn to mark men as good. These methods may be condemned because they are thought contrary to divine law or to the order of nature or to our moral sense, or because in prescribing the law to ourselves we have individually or collectively prohibited them. Machiavelli does not commit himself on such issues, and I shall not do so either if I can avoid it. The effects of these different views are, at least in one crucial sense, the same. They take out of our hands the constant business of attaching moral labels to such Machiavellian methods as deceit and betrayal. Such methods are simply bad. They are the sort of thing that good men avoid, at least until they have learned how not to be good.

Now, if there is no such class of actions, there is no dilemma of dirty hands, and the Machiavellian teaching loses what Machiavelli surely intended it to have, its disturbing and paradoxical character. He can then be understood to be saying that political actors must sometimes overcome their moral inhibitions, but not that they must sometimes commit crimes. I take it that utilitarian philosophers also want to make the first of these statements and to deny the second. From their point of view, the candidate who makes a corrupt deal and the official who authorizes the torture of a prisoner must be described as good men (given the cases as I have specified them), who ought, perhaps, to be honored for making the right decision when it was a hard decision to make. There are three ways of developing this argument. First, it might be said that every political choice ought to be made solely in terms of its particular and immediate circumstances—in terms, that is, of the reasonable alternatives, available knowledge, likely consequences, and so on. Then the good man will face difficult choices (when his knowledge of options and outcomes is radically uncertain), but it cannot happen that he will face a moral dilemma. Indeed, if he always makes decisions in this way, and has been taught from childhood to do so, he will never have to overcome his inhibitions, whatever he does, for how could he have acquired inhibitions? Assuming further that he weighs the alternatives and calculates the consequences seriously and in good faith, he cannot commit a crime, though he can certainly make a mistake, even a very serious mistake. Even when he lies and tortures, his hands will be clean, for he has done what he should do as best he can, standing alone in a moment of time, forced to choose.

This is in some ways an attractive description of moral decision-making, but it is also a very improbable one. For while any one of us may stand alone, and so on, when we make this or that decision, we are not isolated or solitary in our moral lives. Moral life is a social phenomenon, and it is constituted at least in part by rules, the knowing of which (and perhaps the making of which) we share with our fellows. The experience of coming up against these rules, challenging their prohibitions, and explaining ourselves to other men and women is so common and so obviously important that no account of moral decision-making can possibly fail to come to grips with it. Hence the second utilitarian argument: such rules do indeed exist, but they are not really prohibitions of wrongful actions (though they do, perhaps for pedagogic reasons, have that form). They are moral guidelines, summaries of previous calculations. They ease our choices in ordinary cases, for we can simply follow their injunctions and do what has been found useful in the past; in exceptional cases they serve as signals warning us against doing too quickly or without the most careful calculations what has not been found useful in the past. But they do no more than that; they have no other purpose, and so it cannot be the case that it is or even might be a crime to override them. Nor is it necessary to feel guilty when one does so. Once again, if it is right to break the rule in some hard case, after conscientiously worrying about it, the man who acts (especially if he knows that many of his fellows would simply worry rather than act) may properly feel pride in his achievement.

But this view, it seems to me, captures the reality of our moral life no better than the last. It may well be right to say that moral rules ought to have the character of guidelines, but it seems that in fact they do not. Or at least, we defend ourselves when we break the rules as if they had some status entirely independent of their previous utility (and we rarely feel proud of ourselves). The defenses we normally offer are not simply justifications; they are also excuses. Now, as Austin says, these two can *seem* to come very close together—indeed, I shall suggest that they can appear side by side in the same sentence—but they are conceptually distinct, differentiated in this crucial respect: an excuse is typically an admission of fault; a justification is typically a denial of fault and an assertion of innocence.[7] Consider a well-known defense from Shakespeare's *Hamlet* that has often reappeared in political literature: "I must be cruel only to be kind."[8] The words are spoken on an occasion when Hamlet is actually being cruel to his mother. I will leave aside the possibility that she deserves to hear (to be forced to listen to) every harsh word he utters, for Hamlet himself makes no such claim—and if she did indeed deserve that, his words might not be cruel or he might not be cruel for speaking them. "I must be cruel" contains the excuse, since it both admits a fault and suggests that Hamlet has no choice but to commit it. He is doing what he has to do; he can't help himself (given the ghost's command, the rotten state of Denmark, and so on). The rest of the sentence is a justification, for it suggests that Hamlet intends and expects kindness to be the outcome of his actions—we must assume that he means greater kindness, kindness to the right persons, or some such. It is not, however, so complete a justification that Hamlet is able to say that he is not *really* being cruel. "Cruel" and "kind" have exactly the same status; they both follow the verb "to be," and so they perfectly reveal the moral dilemma.[9]

When rules are overridden, we do not talk or act as if they had been set aside, canceled, or annulled. They still stand and have this much effect at least: that we know we have done something wrong even if what we have done was also the best thing to do on the whole in the circumstances. Or at least we feel that way, and this feeling is itself a crucial feature of our moral life. Hence the third utilitarian argument, which recognizes the usefulness of guilt and seeks to explain it. There are, it appears, good reasons for "over-valuing" as well as for overriding the rules. For the consequences might be very bad indeed if the rules were overridden every time the moral calculation seemed to go against them. It is probably best if most men do not calculate too nicely, but simply follow the rules; they are less likely to make mistakes that way, all in all. And so a good man (or at least an ordinary good man) will respect the rules rather more than he would if he thought them merely guidelines, and he will feel guilty when he overrides them. Indeed, if he did not feel guilty, "he would not be such a good man." It is by his feelings that we know him. Because of those feelings he will never be in a hurry to override the rules, but will wait until there is no choice, acting only to avoid consequences that are both imminent and almost certainly disastrous.

The obvious difficulty with this argument is that the feeling whose usefulness is being explained is most unlikely to be felt by someone who is convinced only of its usefulness. He breaks a utilitarian rule (guideline), let us say, for good utilitarian reasons: but can he then feel guilty, also for good utilitarian reasons, when he has no reason for believing that he *is* guilty? Imagine a moral philosopher expounding the third argument to a man who actually does feel guilty or to the sort of man who is likely to feel guilty. Either the man won't accept the utilitarian explanation as an account of his feeling about the rules (probably the best outcome from a utilitarian point of view) or he will accept it and then cease to feel that (useful) feeling. But I do not want to exclude the possibility of a kind of superstitious anxiety, the possibility, that is, that some men will continue to feel guilty even after they have been taught, and have agreed, that they cannot possibly *be* guilty. It is best to say only that the more fully they accept the utilitarian account, the less likely they are to feel that (useful) feeling. . . .

V

. . . No doubt we can get our hands dirty in private life also, and sometimes, no doubt, we should. But the issue is posed most dramatically in politics for the three reasons that make political life the kind of life it is, because we claim to act for others but also serve ourselves, rule over others, and use violence against them. It is easy to get one's hands dirty in politics and it is often right to do so. But it is not easy to teach a good man how not to be good, nor is it easy to explain such a man to himself once he has committed whatever crimes are required of him. At least, it is not easy once we have agreed to use the word "crimes" and to live with (because we have no choice) the dilemma of dirty hands. Still, the agreement is common enough, and on its basis there have developed three broad traditions of explanation, three ways of thinking about dirty hands, which derive in some very general fashion from neoclassical, Protestant, and Catholic perspectives on politics and morality. I want to try to say something very briefly about each of them, or rather about a representative example of each of them, for each seems to me partly right. But I don't think I can put together the compound view that might be wholly right.

The first tradition is best represented by Machiavelli, the first man, so far as I know, to state the paradox that I am examining. The good man who aims to found or reform a republic must, Machiavelli tells us, do terrible things to reach his goal. Like Romulus, he must murder his brother; like Numa, he must lie to the people. Sometimes, however, "when the act accuses, the result excuses."[10] This sentence from *The Discourses* is often taken to mean that the politician's deceit and cruelty are justified by the good results he brings about. But if they were justified, it wouldn't be necessary to learn what Machiavelli claims to teach: how not to be good. It would only be necessary to learn how to be good in a new, more difficult, perhaps roundabout way. That is not Machiavelli's argument. His political judgments are indeed consequentialist in character, but not his moral judgments. We know whether cruelty is used well or badly by its effects over time. But that it is bad to use cruelty we know in some other way. The deceitful and cruel politician is excused (if he succeeds) only in the sense that the rest of us come to agree that the results were "worth it" or, more likely, that we simply forget his crimes when we praise his success.

It is important to stress Machiavelli's own commitment to the existence of moral standards. His paradox depends upon that commitment as it depends upon the general stability of the standards—which he upholds in his consistent use of words like good and bad. If he wants the standards to be disregarded by good men more often than they are, he has nothing with which to replace them and no other way of recognizing the good men except by their allegiance to those same standards. It is exceedingly rare, he writes, that a good man is willing to employ bad means to become prince.[11] Machiavelli's purpose is to persuade such a person to make the attempt, and he holds out the supreme political rewards, power and glory, to the man who does so and succeeds. The good man is not rewarded (or excused), however, merely for his willingness to get his hands dirty. He must do bad things well. There is no reward for doing bad things badly, though they are done with the best of intentions. And so political action necessarily involves taking a risk. But it should be clear that what is risked is not personal goodness— *that is thrown away*—but power and glory. If the politician succeeds, he is a hero; eternal praise is the supreme reward for not being good.

What the penalties are for not being good, Machiavelli doesn't say, and it is probably for this reason above all that his moral sensitivity has so often been questioned. He is suspect not because he tells political actors they must get their hands dirty, but because he does not specify the state of mind appropriate to a man with dirty hands. A Machiavellian hero has no inwardness. What he thinks of himself we don't know. I would guess, along with most other readers of Machiavelli, that he basks in his glory. But then it is difficult to account for the strength of his original reluctance to learn how not to be good. In any case, he is the sort of man who is unlikely to keep a diary and so we cannot find out what he thinks. Yet we do want to know; above all, we want a record of his anguish. That is a sign of our own conscientiousness and of the impact on us of the second tradition of thought that I want to examine, in which personal anguish sometimes seems the only acceptable excuse for political crimes.

The second tradition is best represented, I think by Max Weber, who outlines its essential features with great power at the very end of his essay "Politics as a Vocation." For Weber, the good man with dirty hands is a hero still, but he is a tragic hero. In part, his tragedy is that though politics is his vocation, he has not been called by God and so cannot be justified by Him. Weber's hero is alone in a world that seems to belong to Satan, and his vocation is entirely his own choice. He still wants what Christian magistrates have always wanted, both to do good in the world and to save his soul, but now these two ends have come into sharp contradiction. They are contradictory because of the necessity for violence in a world where God has not instituted the sword. The politician takes the sword himself, and only by doing so does he measure up to his vocation. With full consciousness of what he is doing, he does bad in order to do good, and surrenders his soul. He "lets himself in," Weber says, "for the diabolic forces lurking in all violence." Perhaps Machiavelli also meant to suggest that his hero surrenders salvation in exchange for glory, but he does not explicitly say so. Weber is absolutely clear: "the genius or demon of politics lives in an inner tension with the god of love . . . [which] can at any time lead to an irreconcilable conflict."[12] His politician views this conflict when it comes with a tough realism, never pretends that it might be solved by compromise, chooses politics once again, and turns decisively away from love. Weber writes about this choice with a passionate high-mindedness that makes a concern for one's soul seem no more elevated than a concern for one's flesh. Yet the reader never doubts that his mature, superbly trained, relentless, objective, responsible, and disciplined political leader is also a suffering servant. His choices are hard and painful, and he pays the price not only while making them but forever after. A man doesn't lose his soul one day and find it the next.

The difficulties with this view will be clear to anyone who has ever met a suffering servant. Here is a man who lies, intrigues, sends other men to their death—and suffers. He does what he must do with a heavy heart. None of us can know, he tells us, how much it costs him to do his duty. Indeed, we cannot, for he himself fixes the price he pays. And that is the trouble with this view of political crime. We suspect the suffering servant of either masochism or hypocrisy or both, and while we are often wrong, we are not always wrong. Weber attempts to resolve the problem of dirty hands entirely within the confines of the individual conscience, but I am inclined to think that this is neither possible nor desirable. The self-awareness of the tragic hero is obviously of great value. We want the politician to have an inner life at least something like that which Weber describes. But sometimes the hero's suffering needs to be socially expressed (for like punishment, it confirms and reinforces our sense that certain acts are wrong). And equally important, it sometimes needs to be socially limited. We don't want to be ruled by men who have lost their souls. A politician with dirty hands needs a soul, and it is best for us all if he has some hope of personal salvation, however that is conceived. It is not the case that when he does bad in order to do good he surrenders himself forever to the demon of politics. He commits a determinate crime, and he must pay a determinate penalty. When he has done so, his hands will be clean again, or as clean as human hands can ever be. So the Catholic Church has always taught, and this teaching is central to the third tradition that I want to examine.

Once again I will take a latter-day and a lapsed representative of the tradition and consider Albert Camus' *The Just Assassins*. The heroes of this play are terrorists at work in nineteenth-century Russia. The dirt on their hands is human blood. And yet Camus' admiration for them, he tells us, is complete. We consent to being criminals, one of them says, but there is nothing with which anyone can reproach us. Here is the dilemma of dirty hands in a new form. The heroes are innocent criminals, just assassins, because, having killed, they are prepared to die—*and will die.* Only their execution, by the same despotic authorities they are attacking, will complete the action in which they are engaged: dying, they need make no excuses. That is the end of their guilt and pain. The execution is not so much punishment as self-punishment and expiation. On the scaffold they wash their hands clean and, unlike the suffering servant, they die happy.

Now the argument of the play when presented in so radically simplified a form may seem a little bizarre, and perhaps it is marred by the moral extremism of Camus' politics. "Political action has limits," he says in a preface to the volume containing *The Just Assassins,* "and there is no good and just action but what recognizes those limits and if it must go beyond them, at least accepts death."[13] I am less interested here in the violence of that "at least"—what else does he have in mind?—than in the sensible doctrine that it exaggerates. That doctrine might best be described by an analogy: just assassination, I want to suggest, is like civil disobedience. In both men violate a set of rules, go beyond a moral or legal limit, in order to do what they believe they should do. At the same time, they acknowledge their responsibility for the violation by accepting punishment or doing penance. But there is also a difference between the two, which has to do with the difference between law and morality. In most cases of civil disobedience the laws of the state are broken for moral reasons, and the state provides the punishment. In most cases of dirty hands moral rules are broken for reasons of state, and no one provides the punishment. There is rarely a Czarist executioner waiting in the wings for politicians with dirty hands, even the most deserving among them. Moral rules are not usually enforced against the sort of actor I am considering, largely because he acts in an official capacity. If they were enforced, dirty hands would be no problem. We would simply honor the man who did bad in order to do good, and at the same time we would punish him. We would honor him for the good he has done, and we would punish him for the bad he has done. We would punish him, that is, for the same reasons we punish anyone else; it is not my purpose here to defend any particular view of punishment. In any case, there seems no way to establish or enforce the punishment. Short of the priest and the confessional, there are no authorities to whom we might entrust the task.

I am nevertheless inclined to think Camus' view the most attractive of the three, if only because it requires us at least to imagine a punishment or a penance that fits the crime. The others do not require that. Once he has launched his career, the crimes of Machiavelli's prince seem subject only to prudential control. And the crimes of Weber's tragic hero are limited only by *his* capacity for suffering and not, as they should be, by *our* capacity for suffering. In neither case is there any explicit reference back to the moral code, once it has, at great personal cost to be sure, been set aside. The question posed by Sartre's Hoerderer (whom I suspect of being a suffering servant) is rhetorical, and the answer is obvious (I have already given it), but the characteristic sweep of both is disturbing. Since it is concerned only with those crimes that ought to be committed, the dilemma of dirty hands seems to exclude questions of degree. Wanton or excessive cruelty is not at issue, any more than is cruelty directed at bad ends. But political action is so uncertain that politicians necessarily take moral as well as political risks, committing crimes that they only think ought to be committed. They override the rules without ever being certain that they have found the best way to the results they hope to achieve, and we don't want them to do that too quickly or too often. So it is important that the moral stakes be very high— which is to say, that the rules be rightly valued. That, I suppose, is the reason for Camus' extremism. Without the executioner, however, there is no one to set the stakes or maintain the values except ourselves, and probably no way to do either except through philosophic reiteration and political activity.

"We shall not abolish lying by refusing to tell lies," says Hoerderer, "but by using every means at hand to abolish social classes."[14] I suspect we shall not abolish lying at all, but we might see to it that fewer lies were told if we contrived to deny power and glory to the greatest liars—except, of course, in the case of those lucky few whose extraordinary achievements make us forget the lies they told. If Hoerderer succeeds in abolishing social classes, perhaps he will join the lucky few. Meanwhile, he lies, manipulates, and kills, and we must make sure he pays the price. We won't be able to do that, however, without getting our own hands dirty, and then we must find some way of paying the price ourselves.

Notes

1. *Philosophy and Public Affairs* 1, no. 2 (winter 1971–72): Thomas Nagel, "War and Massacre," 123–144; R. B. Brandt, "Utilitarianism and the Rules of War," 145–165; and R. M. Hare, "Rules of War and Moral Reasoning," 166–181.

2. Jean-Paul Sartre, *Dirty Hands,* in *No Exit and Three Other Plays,* trans. Lionel Abel (New York, n.d.), 224.

3. In *From Max Weber: Essays in Sociology,* trans. and ed. Hans H. Gerth and C. Wright Mills (New York, 1946), 77–128.

4. See *The Prince,* chap. 15; and see *The Discourses,* bk. 1, chaps. 9 and 18. I quote from the Modern Library edition of the two works (New York: Random House, 1950), 57.

5. I leave aside the question of whether the prisoner is himself responsible for the terrorist campaign. Perhaps he opposed it in meetings of the rebel organization. In any case, whether he deserves to be punished or not, he does not deserve to be tortured.

6. Other writers argued that Christians must never kill, even in a just war; and there was also an intermediate position which suggests the origins of the idea of dirty hands. Thus Basil the Great (bishop of Caesarea in the fourth century A.D.): "Killing in war was differentiated by our fathers from murder . . . nevertheless, perhaps it would be well that those whose hands are unclean abstain from communion for three years." Here dirty hands are a kind of impurity or unworthiness, which is not the same as guilt, though closely related to it. For a general survey of these and other Christian views, see Roland H. Bainton, *Christian Attitudes toward War and Peace* (New York, 1960), esp. chaps. 5–7.

7. J. L. Austin, "A Plea for Excuses," in *Philosophical Papers,* ed. J. O. Urmson and G. J. Warnock (Oxford: Oxford University Press, 1961), 123–152.

8. *Hamlet* 3.4.178.

9. Compare the following lines from Bertold Brecht's poem "To Posterity": "Alas, we / Who wished to lay the foundations of kindness / Could not ourselves be kind . . ." in *Selected Poems,* trans. H. R. Hays (New York, 1969), 177. This is more of an excuse, less of a justification (the poem is an *apologia*).

10. *The Discourses,* bk. 1, chap. 9, 139.

11. *The Discourses,* bk. 1, chap. 9, 171.

12. "Politics as a Vocation," 125–126. But sometimes a political leader does choose the "absolutist" side of the conflict, and Weber writes (127) that it is "immensely moving when a *mature* man . . . aware of a responsibility for the consequences of his conduct . . . reaches a point where he says: 'Here I stand; I can do no other.'" Unfortunately, he does not suggest just where that point is or even where it might be.

13. *Caligula and Three Other Plays* (New York, 1958), x. (The preface is translated by Justin O'Brian, the plays by Stuart Gilbert.)

14. *Dirty Hands,* 223.

Jean Bethke Elshtain

Reflection on the Problem of "Dirty Hands"

Torture invariably appears on the "never" list of the "forbiddens" of human politics. Genocide tops that list but torture follows close behind. There are good reasons for this. Brutal regimes historically, like Stalin's Soviet Union and Hitler's Nazi Germany, used torture as a routine dimension of the state apparatus. Enemies or alleged enemies of those two evil regimes were often tortured for the sadistic pleasure of it—not to get useful information. For torture was used primarily against internal foes of the regime. Torture was also widespread in Argentina at the time of its so-called dirty war in the late 1970s—before the restoration of constitutionalism in 1982. In my discussions with the "Mothers of the Disappeared" who had lost children to the military juntas, torture was listed as the most horrible thing imaginable that their children had suffered prior to their outright killing. One mother of three "disappeared" told me that she couldn't bear the thought that her children's last memories on earth were of being tortured. That final image of another human being torturing you, and doing so with sadistic pleasure, prior to taking your last breath, was too much for her to bear. Her health broke, and she never recovered either her health or her faith in humanity.

Before the watershed event of September 11, 2001, I had not reflected critically on the theme of torture. I was one of those who listed it in the category of "never." It did not seem to me possible that the United States would face some of the dilemmas favored by moral theorists in their hypothetical musings on whether torture could ever be morally permitted. Too, reprehensible regimes tortured. End of question. Not so, as it turns out.

The Dilemma Presented

The usual dilemma proffered in order to debate torture went something like the following (and there are many variations on the theme). A bomb has been planted in an elementary school building. There are several hundred such buildings in the city in question. A known member of a terrorist criminal gang has been apprehended. The authorities are as close to 100 percent certain as human beings can be in such circumstances that the man apprehended has specific knowledge of which school contains the deadly bomb, due to go off within the hour. He refuses to divulge the information as to which school, and officials know they cannot evacuate all of the schools, thereby guaranteeing the safety of thousands of school children. It follows that some four hundred children will soon die unless the bomb is disarmed. Are you permitted to torture a suspect in order to gain the information that might spare the lives of so many innocents? The circumstances are desperate. The villain is thoroughly villainous. The probability that he knows where the bomb is planted is as close to a certainty as human beings can be in such situations. It is also undeniably the case that, were police to see this man attempting to run into the school, bomb in hand, he would be shot outright. Is it not, therefore, acceptable in this rare instance to torture him to gain the information?

What usually followed the presentation of this, or some other, vivid example was a discussion of options within the framework of the two dominant and competing moral philosophies of modernity: deontology and utilitarianism. The deontologist says "never"—one is never permitted to use another human being as a means rather than an end in himself. The utilitarian says that the greatest good for the greatest number will be served by torturing the creep and saving the school children.[1] So—where do you stand? With Kant or with Bentham?

Most often I found myself standing with neither. I didn't realize it at the time but this "neither . . . nor" surely reflected my ethical formation within the Christian theological tradition, which is not primarily a deontological ethic (despite attempts by some Christian philosophers to assimilate Christianity to deontology). Instead, what is called up and called upon within Christianity is the concrete responsibility of neighbor-love and neighbor-regard. Where would one's responsibility lie in this circumstance? With the innocent or with the guilty? With school-children who cannot defend themselves or with a prisoner who cannot defend himself either? These are the sorts of considerations that are the stock-in-trade of the moral casuist. It is the tradition of casuistry—a discredited tradition in many quarters—that I will bring to bear in this discussion.[2]

Let me leave this particular dilemma for a moment in order to explore my "neither . . . nor" in greater detail. The burden of my argument is that, while deontology makes something called "torture" impossible, utilitarianism makes it too easy and too tempting. There is another problem, and that lies in the word itself. Is a shouted insult a form of torture? A slap in the face? Sleep deprivation? A beating to within an inch of one's life? Electric prods on the male genitals, inside a woman's vagina, or in a person's anus? Pulling out fingernails? Cutting off an ear or a breast? All of us, surely, would place every violation on this list beginning with the beating and ending with severing a body part as forms of torture and thus forbidden. No argument there. But let's turn to sleep deprivation and a slap in the face. Do these belong in the same torture category as bodily amputations and sexual assaults? There are even those who would add the shouted insult to the category of torture. But, surely, this makes mincemeat of the category. If everything from a shout to the severing of a body part is "torture," the category is so indiscriminate as to not permit of those distinctions on which the law and moral philosophy rest. If we include all forms of coercion or manipulation within "torture," we move in the direction of indiscriminate moralism and legalism—a kind of deontology run amok. At the same time, we deprive law enforcement, domestic and international, of some of its necessary tools in an often violent and dangerous world.

In the context of domestic life, we tend to place a *verbal insult*—at least we used to—in the realm of manners and basic human decency. A person who insults another is to be chastised, rebuked, even shunned. So we teach children not to insult others: "Don't be rude," we say. Nowadays, of course, because we tend to moralize and to criminalize nearly everything, shouted insults can become the occasion for lawsuits or charges of hate speech and harassment. That said, a verbal insult is rather far down on the scale of awful things that can happen to people. We think worse of a *slap in the face.* Slapping a child can lead to charges of child abuse and, whether the child is physically harmed or not, slapping demeans. If one spouse consistently slaps another, spousal abuse charges may result. A slap is meant to frighten and to demean, to remind someone of who is in the driver's seat. If a slap enters the realm of criminality and turns into a beating, we distinguish it from a *verbal insult,* for it has crossed that barrier that separates the symbolic—speech—from the corporeal—an affront to the body. A third case, *a beating with the butt of a gun,* is the most serious of all in this list of three. Such beatings are the occasion for charges of felonious assault and battery. If a policeman has beaten a person he has arrested, who is hand-cuffed and subdued, he, too, may be charged: his badge is no protection. Just as we discriminate between accidental death, manslaughter, and capital murder—for a dead body isn't just a dead body; we want to know how it got there—so we make distinctions when it comes to various 'assaults' on persons.

Just War Rules and Restraints

Now let's move to the realm of interrogation of prisoners in the context of a deadly and dangerous war against enemies who know no limits. We have seen these persons in action. We know that they torture, demean, and as-sault those they have apprehended and then exult when they have beheaded an unarmed man. (Here the murder of Daniel Pearl, a civilian, hence a noncombatant.) In warfare, the rules of *jus ad bellum* and *jus in bello* have no meaning to them. The whole point of terror is the purposeful, random killing of innocents, defined as those in no position to defend themselves. In actual war-fighting, it is often the case nowadays that some, like the United States military, take seriously those ethical restraints on war-fighting derived from the just or justified war tradition and encoded in various international conventions and agreements. Others may ignore these restraints. Never-theless, those restraints—most importantly *noncombatant immunity*—are central to the way the United States makes war. Soldiers abide by rules of engagement that limit what they can do, and to whom. Terrorists simply unleash violence. Indeed, their favorite targets are "soft targets"—persons working or dining or going to school and who are not prepared, and have no means to, defend themselves.

There are hard-bitten *Realpolitikers* who claim that restraint in war-fighting amounts to "fighting with one hand tied behind your back" and gives the enemy unfair advantage. But the rules of war-making are clear and accepted as normative by the United States. Victory alone is not the singular goal. How one achieves victory is also important. There is, of course, no pristine way to make war. You cannot make war, any more than you can govern, without getting your hands dirty. Thirty years ago, Michael Walzer plumbed the question of "dirty hands" in what has become a standard essay on the subject. Those who take responsibility for the polity and for the wars fought by a polity will, at some point, incur moral guilt—not because they have intentionally committed crimes but, rather, because the courses of action to which they have committed the polity often result in unintended harm to innocents.

Michael Walzer's "Dirty Hands"

In his important essay, Walzer references St. Augustine's "melancholy soldier, who understood both that his war was just and that killing, even in a just war, is a terrible thing to do."[3] If the war is just, and if the person killed is, like the soldier who does the killing, a combatant, we do not burden the soldier with the burden of having murdered. That would be an act of injustice. But it is appropriate that he feel the burden of it all the same. Walzer pursues the issue further by noting that Augustine "might have thought it wrong to torture in a just war, and later Catholic theorists have certainly thought it wrong. Moreover, the politician I am imagining thinks it wrong, as do many of us who supported him. Surely we have a right to expect more than melancholy from him now." (Walzer is here hypothesizing that the political leader has ordered a man tortured in order to protect civilians who might otherwise die in apartment buildings that have been booby-trapped.) "When he ordered the prisoner tortured, he committed a moral crime and he accepted a moral burden. Now he is a guilty man. His willingness to acknowledge and bear . . . his guilt is evidence, and it is the only evidence he can offer us, both that he is not too good for politics and that he is good enough."[4] He is good enough to do what is wrong but necessary in order to provide for the common defense—to protect the citizens he has a particular responsibility to protect—and he is guilty, as he should be, and as any decent person would be, at what he felt compelled to do, given his vocation of statecraft.

This imagined response of the political leader eschews the exculpatory stratagems of utilitarianism that would enable the leader to torture but to keep his hands clean at the same time. Nor is Walzer's leader a strict deontologist who must do the right thing even if thousands of innocents die, rather like the person Kant imagines who is forbidden, under Kantian de-ontology, to tell a lie even if it means turning a friend hidden about his house over to a murderer who comes inquiring as to his whereabouts.[5] As I noted earlier, there is an alternative. Although Walzer himself doesn't "name" it, he describes it. One begins with a rule-governed activity. Such rules are moral guidelines. The just war tradition is such a rule-governed activity. There may be situations that were not anticipated and that are so serious, so dire in their potential consequences, they may require over-riding the rule. The rule in question is not thereby "set aside, canceled, or annulled."[6] One is obliged to acknowledge violation of the rule and to offer reasons for why, in this circumstance, the rule was temporarily overridden. This overriding of a rule should not be easy: it should, in fact, be *in extremis*, or close to it. And one overrides the rule in recognition that a moral wrong does not make a "right" but it might bring about a "less bad" or "more just" outcome.

In his essay, Walzer associates this form of prudential reasoning with the Catholic tradition. Interestingly, his example of such Catholic reasoning is that of Albert Camus, a lapsed Catholic who was, nonetheless, in dialogue with believers throughout his life. Camus reiterated over and over again the limits that must pertain in political action. If a situation requires the break-ing of a moral rule, the person who violates the rule or goes beyond it must "acknowledge their responsibility" and, in many situations, accept punish-ment or do penance. This way of thinking differs from what Walzer char-acterizes as the "Protestant tradition" in which the rule-breaker is construed as a kind of tragic hero who has violated his own conscience. For Walzer, the latter sanctions a personal melodrama and directs our attention away from where it rightly belongs: with a system of moral rules and restraints and whether, and under what circumstances, overriding a rule may be the least bad thing to do.

The Dilemma Revisited: Statescraft and a Theologian

Now let's recall the hypothetical scenario I sketched earlier. Ask yourself who you would want in a position of judgment at that point. A person of such stringent moral and legal rectitude that he or she would not consider torture because violating his or her own conscience is the most morally serious thing a person can do? Or a person, aware of the stakes and the possible deaths of hundreds of children, who acts in the light of harsh necessity and orders the prisoner tortured? This second leader does not rank his or her "purity" above human lives. The irony, of course, is that the leader who demurs in the name of living up to a moral code we probably share with him, or her, becomes directly complicit in the deaths of hundreds of innocents. Parents, grandparents, and siblings of those children will probably curse his or her name, and they are right to do so.

Within Christian moral thinking, and the tradition of casuistry that arose from it, the statesman or stateswoman has another chance. He and she can stand before God as a guilty person and seek forgiveness. There are no second chances for school-children blown to smithereens. They will never have the opportunity to grow up in order that they, too, might one day face moral dilemmas. Albert Camus would say of the person who incurs guilt that she is certainly no saint but neither has she given in to the plague of terror. Rule-mania and the moralism that flows from it aims to insulate the statesperson from any tragic dimension: if one just follows the rules, one's conscience is clear. But the route of concrete responsibility, or neighbor-regard in Christian moral teaching, suggests another and more difficult path. Remember: the political leader who has approved torture as a way to elicit information that may save the lives of hundreds of children does *not* thereby sanction or normalize torture.

Torture remains a horror and, in general, a tactic that is forbidden. But there are moments when this rule may be overridden. The refusal to legalize and to sanction something as extreme as torture is vitally important. It follows that Alan Dershowitz's suggestion that there may be instances of "legitimate torture" and those about to undertake it should be obliged to gain a "torture warrant" to sanction the activity is a stunningly bad idea. Sanctioning torture through torture warrants partakes of the same moralistic-legalism as the statesperson who values his pure conscience above all else and who will not violate a moral norm under any circumstances. We cannot—and should not—insulate political and military leaders from the often harsh demands of necessity by up-ending the moral universe: that which is rightly taboo now becomes just another piece in the armamentarium of the state.

A certain asceticism is required of those who may be required, in a dangerous and extreme situation, to temporarily override a general prohibition. They should not seek to legalize it. They should not aim to normalize it. And they should not write elaborate justifications of it, as if there were a tick-list one can do down and, if a sufficient number of ticks appears, one is given leave to torture. The tabooed and forbidden, the extreme, nature of this mode of physical coercion must be preserved so that it never becomes routinized as just the way we do things around here. The case of the anti-Nazi theologian Dietrich Bonhoeffer offers an interesting example that points to this general truth. Bonhoeffer joined a conspiracy to assassinate Hitler. The view of Bonhoeffer and his coconspirators was that the Nazi system was so dependent on this one man that, if the "head of the snake" were cut off," the Nazi system might begin to unravel. Whether that was so or not we will never know, as the conspiracy was uncovered and its participants were shot or hanged, including Bonhoeffer.

Subsequently, some Bonhoefferians have expressed frustration that Bonhoeffer never left behind, or smuggled out, a document detailing his decision to override the command not to murder (the correct way to translate the commandment against killing). They wish there was something in the nature of a justification, by Bonhoeffer, of his deeds. But Bonhoeffer, appropriately, offered nothing of the kind. Instead, he notes Machiavelli and *necessita.* He acknowledges guilt and complicity in the name of being a Christian in an autonomous, secular world.[7] "Civil courage," he wrote, "can grow only out of the free responsibility of free men." The "ultimate question for a responsible man is not how he is to extricate himself . . . but how the coming generation is to live."[8] The key question, for Bonhoeffer, is *not* "What is the right thing for me to do?" but rather "What is to come?" In his circumstance that meant what would the future hold, unless action was taken to stop it? It would hold a world in which Nazism maintained its power and extended its sway and its genocidal policies. In our context, it is whether terrorists who know no limits and who would kill as many innocents as they can, simply because they are Americans or Jews or infidels, are to be stopped lest they murder again with the ultimate aim of establishing repressive Taliban-type regimes that institute cruelty and a perverse form of "virtue." I don't mean to suggest that these are precisely analogous situations. Nothing in history ever is. But I do agree with Bonhoeffer that the question that should animate us is: What is to come?

Redefining Torture: Torture and Severe Coercion

The observant reader will have noted that I have not, as yet, defined what torture is. I have suggested, or hinted, that it is not any and all forms of physical restraint or coercion. Let's turn to another hypothetical. Suppose you had Terry Nichols in custody before the Oklahoma City bombing. You know enough to know that (1) a public building is going to be bombed, and (2) Terry Nichols knows *who, where, and when.* How do you think about torture in such a circumstance? The position I have developed pushes in the following direction: there is no absolute prohibition to what some call torture. Once again, torture is not sufficiently disaggregated. Recall the possibilities: pulling out fingernails; grinding the teeth down or pulling teeth as does a sadistic Laurence Olivier to Dustin Hoffman in the film *Marathon Man;* raping men or women; burning breasts, genitalia; hanging for hours from the arms; crucifying; torturing the spouse or children. There should be—and are—prohibitions against such practices. In an exceptional and truly extreme circumstance, would it be defendable to do any of these things? Everything in me says no and tells me that when we think of torture it is these sorts of extreme forms of physical torment we are thinking of. If torture is the inflicting of severe and devastating pain, as the dictionary defines it, the horrors I have listed are certainly torture.

But there are other options that also come under condemnation as torture. In a striking piece, "The Dark Art of Interrogation," Mark Bowden details some of these.[9] They are called "torture lite," and, Bowden tells us, some argue that such methods are not properly torture at all. This list includes

> sleep deprivation, exposure to heat or cold, the use of drugs to cause confusion, rough treatment (slapping, shoving or shaking), forcing a prisoner to stand for days at a time or sit in uncomfortable positions, and playing on his fears for himself and his family. Although excruciating for the victim, these tactics generally leave no permanent marks and do no lasting physical harm.[10]

The Geneva Convention, however, makes no distinctions of any kind between these tactics and the horrific possibilities I noted earlier. Torture is torture, it says in effect.

But is this not like saying a dead body is a dead body, as if we could not distinguish between accidental death, involuntary manslaughter, and outright murder? The interrogators Bowden interviewed weigh a situation in which the well-being of a captive sits on one side and "lives that might be saved by forcing him to talk" on the other.[11] To bring clarity to the situation, Bowden distinguishes between torture as the horrific practices about which no decent person has any doubts as to whether they constitute torture or not and, by contrast, forms of coercion that involve "moderate physical pressure" and that do no lasting physical damage.[12] It seems to be the case, as Bowden documents it, that techniques like solitary confinement and sensory deprivation often suffice to induce a prisoner to give up sensitive information about terrorist operations. The skilled interrogator often finds that the fear that something may happen is "more effective than any drug, tactic, or torture device. . . . The threat of coercion usually weakens or destroys resistance more effectively than coercion itself."[13] Forms of psychological pressure and the arts of deception and trickery—for example, telling a captive that others have capitulated so he might as well talk—are standard tools of the interrogator's trade, though some absolutists would forbid them, too. What interrogators learn quickly is that most people want to tell their stories. It is enough, then, to get them talking, for if you succeed, the prisoner keeps talking.

Bowden concludes that few "moral imperatives make such sense on a large scale"—referring to the prohibition against torture—"but break down so dramatically in the particular."[14] When you put a microscope above the word "torture" and peer through it, you see a teeming mess of possibilities, prohibitions, complexities, legalities, and ethical perils. It follows that when human rights groups label "unpleasant or disadvantageous treatment of any kind" torture, they do a disservice to the complexity of the matter; they fail to discriminate between cases; they embrace a moralistic "code fetishism" that flies in the face of the harsh and dangerous realities of the world in which we find ourselves; and, ironically, by failing to distinguish between sleep deprivation and amputation or burning or some other horror, they elevate the former and diminish the latter.

Bowden shares with me an aversion to making torture commonplace. The ban on torture must remain. But "moderate physical pressure" to save innocent lives, "coercion" by contrast to "torture," is not only demanded in certain extreme circumstances, it is arguably the "least bad" thing to do.[15] Bowden quotes Jessica Montell, the executive director of a human rights advocacy group in Jerusalem, who recognizes—as many human rights groups do not—that the issue is a complex one. She tells him:

> If I as an interrogator feel that the person in front of me has information that can prevent a catastrophe from happening . . . I imagine that I would do what I would have to do in order to prevent that catastrophe from happening. The state's obligation is then to put me on trial for breaking the law. . . . I can evoke the defense of necessity, and then the court decides whether or not it's reasonable that I broke the law in order to avert this catastrophe. . . . It can't be that there's some prior license for me to abuse people."[16]

This is an excellent, if somewhat legalistic, description of casuistry at work: the norm remains; it may have to be broken; the one who broke it for a strong reason must nevertheless make amends in some way. In other words, the interrogator must, if called on, be prepared to defend what he or she has done and, depending on context, to pay a penalty.

An Unhappy Subject Summed Up

Let's sum up this unhappy subject. Far greater moral guilt falls on a person in authority who permits the deaths of hundreds of innocents rather than choosing to "torture" one guilty or complicit person. One hopes and prays such occasions emerge only rarely. Were I the parent or grandparent of a child whose life might be spared, I confess, with regret, that I would want officials to rank their moral purity as far less important in the overall scheme of things than eliciting information that might spare my child or grandchild and all those other children and grandchildren. But I do not want a law to "cover" such cases, for, truly, hard cases do make bad laws. Instead, we work with a rough rule of thumb in circumstances in which we believe an informant might have information that would probably spare the lives of innocents. In a world of such probabilities, we should demur from Torture 1—the extreme forms of physical torment. But Torture 2, for which we surely need a different name, like coercive interrogation, may, with regret, be used. ("Torture lite," Bowden calls it.) This is a distinction with a difference.

One puts together in a single frame, then, normative condemnation of torture with appropriate consequentionalist considerations—What is to come? To condemn outright Torture 2, or coercive interrogation, is to lapse into a legalistic version of pietistic rigorism in which one's own moral purity is ranked above other goods. This is also a form of moral laziness. One repairs to a code rather than grappling with a terrible moral dilemma. The neighbor-regard in Christian moral thinking ranks concrete responsibility ahead of rigid rule-following. This neighbor-regard involves concern for forms of life and how best to make life at least slightly more just or, to cast it negatively, slightly less unjust. One is willing to pay a price and, if necessary, to incur moral guilt, when the lives of others are at stake.[17]

Notes

The title of this chapter reflects my indebtedness to Michael Walzer's classic essay "Political Action: The Problem of Dirty Hands," most of which is reprinted in chapter 3.

1. Clearly, I am simplifying each of these perspectives, especially utilitarianism, which comes in several varieties, e.g., rule utilitarianism, act utilitarianism, and so on. But this broad characterization of the direction these respective moral philosophies tend is correct.

2. The Protestant brief against casuistry was that it was "Jesuitical" and a way wily Jesuits used to wiggle out of various circumstances or to wheedle and maneuver people toward conclusions that were opposite what they began with. Casuistry took a major hit in the condemnations of Blaise Pascal and lost much credibility. Despite this, legal reasoning is primarily of a casuistical nature.

3. Walzer, "Political Action," p. 65 herein.

4. Ibid.

5. Kant's stringency infuriated the anti-Nazi theologian and martyr Dietrich Bonhoeffer, who declares that Kant carries the principle of not telling a lie to cruel absurdities. Bonhoeffer denounces the "fanatical devotee of truth" who "can make no allowance for human weakness" and who "betrays the community in which he lives." This version of 'truth' demands "its victims" even as the truth-teller remains "proud" and "pure." See Dietrich Bonhoeffer, *Ethics* (New York: Simon and Schuster, 1995), 361, 363.

6. Walzer, "Political Action," p. 68 herein.

7. Readers can turn both to his *Ethics* and his *Letters and Papers from Prison* (New York: MacMillan, 1972).

8. Bonhoeffer, *Letters and Papers from Prison*, 6–7.

9. Mark Bowden, "The Dark Art of Interrogation," *Atlantic Monthly,* October 2003, 51–76.

10. Ibid., 53.

11. Ibid., 54.

12. Ibid., 54.

13. Ibid., 60.

14. Ibid., 70.

15. Ibid., 74.

16. Ibid., 76.

17. These concluding considerations emerged in correspondence with Randall Newman concerning Reinhold Niebuhr and the incompleteness of his spelling out of neighbor-love as a form of justice.

Torture as Practiced

Part II

CAPVT   XXXVIII.

De repetitione quæstionis, siue tor-
turæ.

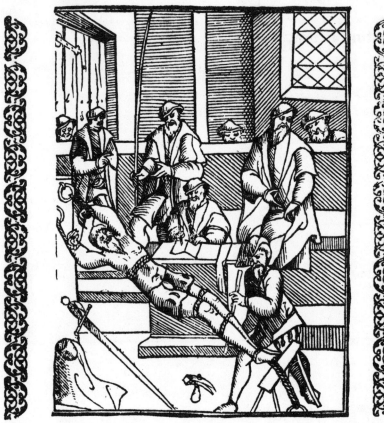

This woodcut from a leading sixteenth-century European criminal procedure manual shows the accused being examined under torture in the presence of the court, clerk, and court functionaries. The illustration is from Joost Damhoulder's *Praxis Rerum Criminalium* (Antwerp edition, 1562) and appears here courtesy of the D'Angelo Law Library at the University of Chicago Law School.

John H. Langbein

The Legal History of Torture

Efforts to accommodate the use of torture within the Western legal tradition have a long history. For half a millennium the law courts of continental Europe tortured suspected persons to obtain evidence. They acted openly and according to law. Investigation under torture was a routine part of criminal procedure in late medieval and early modern times. The jurists and judges who elaborated and administered this system were aware of the dangers of coerced evidence, and accordingly, they framed rules of safeguard meant to make tortured confessions reliable. Across the centuries it became clear that the safeguards were far from safe. In the end, the European states conceded that the long experiment with torture was a failure, and across the eighteenth century they banned the use of torture from their legal systems.

At the dawn of the twenty-first century we are hearing fresh suggestions that the authorities should be allowed to resort to torture, now for the purpose of dealing with suspected terrorists. The future may bring circumstances in which the need for information is so great that governments will again experiment with torture. The deep lesson of the past, however, is that the error rate will be high—probably too high.

This essay explains how European criminal procedure became dependent on the use of torture, and why that torture-centered law of proof failed. The experience on the Continent is contrasted with that in England, where, despite some temptations in early modern times, the use of torture did not become a part of ordinary criminal procedure.

The European Law of Torture

The law of torture developed as an adjunct to the law of proof, that is, to the rules that governed the quality and quantity of evidence needed to convict someone accused of a serious crime.[1] Because it was the judges who administered the rules about whom, how, and when to torture, the system has come to be known as "judicial torture."[2] The European law of proof emerged in the city-states of northern Italy in the thirteenth century. It spread across the Continent together with the rest of Roman-canon criminal and civil procedure as part of the broader movement known as the reception of Roman law.[3] Investigation under torture was reserved for cases of serious crime, for which the sanction was death or maiming.

The European law of proof displaced an earlier system of proof, the ordeals, conducted under the auspices of the church. The ordeals purported to achieve absolute certainty in criminal adjudication through the happy expedient of having the judgments rendered by God, who could not err.[4] The church effectively destroyed the ordeals by a decision of the Fourth Lateran Council in 1215.[5] The new criminal procedure aspired to an equivalent level of safeguard—absolute certainty—for adjudication by mortals. Although mere humans, judges, were to replace God in the judgment seat, they would be constrained by a law of proof so objectively sound that the awesome substitution of mortal for divine adjudication would be unobjectionable. The new law of proof would eliminate human discretion, hence the possibility of human error, from the determination of guilt or innocence.

The Two-Eyewitness Rule

The Italian glossators who developed the European law of proof based it on the rule that conviction would require the testimony of two unimpeachable eyewitnesses to the gravamen of the crime. Such evidence would be, in the famous phrase, "clear as the noonday sun." Without such evidence, a criminal court could not convict an accused who contested the charges against him. Only if the accused voluntarily confessed the offense could the court convict him without eyewitness testimony. A corollary of the rule that conviction required two eyewitnesses or voluntary confession was that conviction could not be based on circumstantial evidence. Circumstantial evidence depends for its efficacy on the subjective persuasion of the court, which must decide whether to draw the inference of guilt from the evidence of circumstance. Thus, for example, it would not have mattered in this system that a murder suspect had been seen departing the scene of the crime, and that the bloody dagger and the stolen loot were found in his possession. Since no eyewitness saw him actually slay the victim, the court could not convict him of the crime.

By insisting on certainty as the standard of proof, the European jurists solved one problem by creating another. They made the judgment of mortals acceptable in place of the judgment of God, but they bound themselves to a law of proof that as a practical matter could be effective only in cases involving overt crime or repentant criminals. Something had to be done to extend the system to unrepentant persons who committed clandestine crimes. The two-eyewitness rule was hard to compromise or evade, but the confession rule seemed to invite "the cruel and stupid subterfuge."[6] To go from accepting a voluntary confession to coercing a confession from someone against whom there was already strong suspicion was a step increasingly taken in the thirteenth century. The law of torture grew up to regulate this process of generating confessions.

Safeguards for Torture

The spirit of safeguard that inspired the unworkable formal law of proof also permeated the subterfuge. The largest chapter of the European law of torture concerned the prerequisites for examination under torture. European jurists devised what modern American lawyers would call a standard of probable cause, designed to ensure that only persons highly likely to be guilty would be examined under torture. Torture was permitted only when a so-called half proof had been established against the suspect. That meant either one eyewitness, or circumstantial evidence that satisfied elaborate requirements of gravity. In the example in which a suspect was caught with the dagger and the loot, each of those indicia would have been reckoned as a quarter proof, which, cumulated to a half proof, would have been sufficient to permit the authorities to examine the suspect under torture.

In this way the law of torture overcame the prohibition against using circumstantial evidence. Circumstantial evidence was not consulted directly on the ultimate question of guilt or innocence but on a question of preliminary procedure: whether or not to examine the accused under torture. Even there the law attempted to limit judicial discretion by promulgating ostensibly objective criteria for evaluating the indicia and assigning numerical values to them (eighth proofs, quarter proofs, half proofs). Vast legal treatises were compiled to guide investigating magistrates in computing whether there was sufficient cause to examine the suspect under torture.

In addition to the probable cause rules, further safeguards were devised to govern the application of torture. These rules were meant to enhance the reliability of a tortured confession. Torture was not supposed to be used to wring out an abject, unsubstantiated confession of guilt. Rather, the examining magistrate was supposed to use torture to elicit from the accused the factual detail of the crime—information that, in the words of a celebrated German statute of 1532, "no innocent person can know."[7] The examiner was forbidden to engage in so-called suggestive questioning, that is, supplying the accused with the detail that the examiner wanted to hear from him. Moreover, the information that the suspect admitted under torture was supposed to be verified to the extent feasible. Thus, for example, if the accused confessed to the crime, he was supposed to be asked what he had done with the loot and the weapon or whatever, in order that these objects, when fetched, could corroborate the confession.

Defects of Safeguard

Alas, because torture tests endurance rather than veracity, innocent persons might (as one sixteenth-century handbook on criminal procedure warned) yield to "the pain and torment and confess things that they never did."[8] For a variety of reasons, the safeguards never proved adequate. If the examining magistrate engaged in suggestive questioning, even accidentally, his lapse could not always be detected or prevented. If the accused knew something about the crime but was still innocent, what he did know might be enough to give his confession verisimilitude. In some jurisdictions the requirement of verification was not enforced or was enforced indifferently.

In order to achieve a verbal or technical reconciliation with the requirement of the formal law of proof that the confession be voluntary, the law treated a confession extracted under torture as involuntary, hence ineffective, unless the accused repeated it free from torture at a hearing held a day or so later. Sometimes the accused who had confessed under torture did recant when asked to confirm his confession. But seldom to avail: The examination under torture could thereupon be repeated. When an accused confessed under torture, recanted, and was then tortured anew, he learned quickly enough that only a "voluntary" confession at the ratification hearing would save him from further agony in the torture chamber. Thus, Johannes Julius, the seventeenth-century burgomaster of Bamburg, Germany, writing from his dungeon cell where he was awaiting execution, told his daughter why he had confessed to witchcraft "for which I must die. It is all falsehood and invention, so help me God. . . . They never cease to torture until one says something."[9] Against the coercive force of the engines of torture, no safeguards were ever found that could protect the innocent and guarantee the truth. The agony of torture created an incentive to speak, but not necessarily to speak the truth.

These shortcomings in the law of torture were identified even in the Middle Ages and were the subject of emphatic complaint in Renaissance and early modern times. Cases arose recurrently in which the real culprit was detected after an innocent accused had confessed under torture and been convicted and executed. In the eighteenth century, as the law of torture was finally about to be abolished, along with the system of proof that had required it, Beccaria[10] and Voltaire[11] became famous as critics of judicial torture by pointing to such cases, but they were latecomers to a critical legal literature nearly as old as the law of torture itself. Judicial torture survived the centuries not because its defects had been concealed but in spite of their having been long revealed. The two-eyewitness rule, the cornerstone of the European law of proof, had left the criminal procedure inextricably dependent on the tortured confession.

Abolition

The European states abolished the system of judicial torture within about two generations. Frederick the Great all but abolished torture within a month of his accession to the Prussian throne in 1740; torture was used for the last time in Prussia in 1752 and was definitely abolished in 1754. In 1770, Saxony and Denmark abolished torture; in 1776, Poland and Austria-Bohemia; in 1780, France; in 1786, Tuscany; in 1787, the Austrian Netherlands (Belgium); and in 1789, Sicily. Early in the nineteenth century, abolition reached the last corners of the Continent.[12]

The conventional historical account of this abolition movement placed great weight on the influence of the publicists of the Enlightenment. By denouncing the dangers of torture, Beccaria and Voltaire and the other writers were thought to have inspired the absolutist monarchs (in particular, Frederick the Great in Prussia, Maria Theresa and Joseph II in Austria and other Habsburg possessions, and Louis XVI in France) to issue their respective abolition decrees. Thereafter, it was said, the European states revised their laws of criminal procedure in the nineteenth century to permit the criminal courts to condemn accused criminals on the basis of what is now the modern standard of proof, known as free (in the sense of unrestricted) judicial evaluation of the evidence (*conviction intime, freie Beweiswürdigung*).

This account of the abolition movement is improbable for two reasons. First, it treats the moral outrage awakened by the Enlightenment writers as decisive, even though they were not advancing any arguments against torture that had not been known for centuries. Second, the conventional account presupposes that the abolition of torture in the eighteenth century preceded the abolition of the European law of proof, which occurred in the nineteenth century—an unlikely sequence when we recall that the old law of proof made criminal procedure unworkable without torture.

Modern scholarship[13] has put forth a different account of the history of the abolition of judicial torture. It has come to be understood that the European law of proof underwent changes in the sixteenth and seventeenth centuries, which were linked to a great change in penology, namely, the development of the sanction of penal servitude (the forerunner of imprisonment) as an alternative to the blood sanctions of medieval law.[14] The medieval law of proof formed at a time when serious crime was punished by death or maiming. These blood sanctions and the law of proof had been defined in terms of each other. When, however, the systems of incarceral punishment developed in the sixteenth and seventeenth centuries, the courts were able to treat that relationship as a restriction. The old law of proof, requiring two eyewitnesses or voluntary confession, was said to pertain only to the old blood sanctions. The courts deemed themselves able to impose the new and less severe punishments according to a less strict standard of proof, one of persuasion (*conviction intime*) rather than certainty. This development, by making it possible to convict an accused without confession or the testimony of two eyewitnesses, is what finally allowed European criminal procedure to escape its dependence on torture.

The courts did not have to invent the lesser standard of proof but only to extend it from the sphere of petty crime. When the new modes of punishment appeared, there were already two distinct systems of proof in simultaneous operation. For serious crimes punishable with the blood sanctions, the two-eyewitness rule and its subsidiary system of judicial torture governed. For petty crimes, however, where the sanctions were fines, minor corporal punishments, or short-term imprisonment, the standard of proof had not been certainty, but merely subjective persuasion of the court. Torture had been unnecessary, indeed forbidden, in such cases.

In the sixteenth and seventeenth centuries the courts analogized the application of the new sanction of penal servitude, even in cases of serious crime, to the ancient procedure for petty crime, which had also employed noncapital sanctions. In a case in which a noncapital punishment was being imposed, for whatever offense, courts began to treat the old law of proof as inapplicable, because it never had applied to noncapital cases. Thereafter, the old law of proof survived, but it had lost its grip. The standards of the old law continued to be obeyed in easy cases, where the prosecution entailed a voluntary confession or two eyewitnesses. But in the cases in which there was neither, compliance with the old law of proof was no longer essential. In precisely those cases in which it had previously been necessary to use torture, it now became possible to punish the culprit without meeting the standard of proof that had required torture. With the two-eyewitness rule effectively bypassed in this way, the European courts could base convictions wholly or partially on circumstantial evidence.[15] Torture thereupon fell into such steep disuse that the eighteenth-century abolition movement was largely symbolic.

England's Escape

The system of judicial torture was never known in England. English courts did not investigate under torture. The English were not possessed of "any unusual degree of humanity or enlightenment."[16] Rather, they were the beneficiaries of a criminal procedure so crude that torture was unnecessary. Whereas the Europeans had turned to the Roman-canon law of proof in order to legitimate a system of adjudication by professional judges, in England the replacement for the ordeals was the trial jury. The medieval English jury was assembled from men living near the scene of the crime, a body of neighbors who gave their verdict based on what they already knew or had heard rather than what they learned at trial.[17] "Our criminal procedure," wrote the historian Frederic William Maitland, "had hardly any place for a law of evidence." The English accepted "the rough verdict of the countryside, without caring to investigate the logical processes, if logical they were, of which that verdict was the outcome."[18]

On the Continent, as Maitland observed, torture "came to the relief of a law of evidence which made conviction well-nigh impossible." In England, by contrast, "neither the stringent rules of legal proof nor the cruel and stupid subterfuge [of torture] became endemic."[19] Even after the rise of the common law of evidence in the eighteenth and nineteenth centuries, an Anglo-American jury was and remains able to convict an accused on circumstantial evidence alone, less evidence than the European law of proof stipulated as a mere precondition for further investigation under torture.

In Renaissance times the English produced a celebratory literature denouncing the use of torture in Continental legal systems and extolling its absence in England.[20] In truth, however, the English did experiment with using torture to investigate crime, primarily treason, in the Tudor-Stuart period. In at least eighty-one cases during the century 1540 from 1640, the Privy Council issued warrants authorizing investigation under torture. (The archives are imperfect, and there may have been some further cases that are no longer traceable.) Most of the known cases of occurred under Elizabeth I (1558–1603), when the English Reformation and the growth of Spanish power induced a sense of extreme national peril about domestic plots and foreign intrigue. The use of torture subsided early in the seventeenth century and appears to have lapsed after 1640.[21]

Torture was used in England only when authorized by the Privy Council (or, exceptionally, by the monarch). Because the English never lodged the power to investigate under torture with ordinary law enforcement officers[22] or courts, this century of experiment with torture left hardly a trace in Anglo-American criminal procedure. Blackstone, who knew of some of the cases, dismissed the use of torture as having been extralegal. He said of the rack, the principal device used to torture suspects in England, that it was "an engine of state, not of law."[23] Sir Edward Coke, who served as an examiner under several Elizabethan torture warrants, wrote in his *Third Institute* (composed around 1630) that "there is no law to warrant tortures in this land, nor can they be justified by any prescription, being so lately brought in."[24] The legal basis, such as it was, for the use of torture in the eighty-one known cases appears to have been the notion of sovereign immunity,[25] a defensive doctrine that spared the authorities from having to supply affirmative justification for what they were doing.

History's Lessons

The European law of torture was suffused with the spirit of safeguard, yet it was never able to correct for the fundamental unreliability of coerced evidence. The attempted safeguards regulated both who could be tortured and how. The rules of probable cause meant to restrict investigation under torture to persons highly likely to be guilty. It is, however, in the nature of a difficult criminal investigation that a person may be near to the events yet nonetheless be innocent of the crime. Thus, despite the rules of probable cause, many an innocent suspect went to the torture chamber. Once there, he commonly found that the rules that were meant to protect him did not. The prohibition on suggestive questioning was hard to enforce, and the verification requirement was intrinsically equivocal.

I see little reason to think that modern circumstances would make investigation under torture more reliable. Modern technology would probably allow us to do a better job of winnowing suspects and of monitoring and hence deterring suggestive questioning. There is, however, no escape from the reality that not every suspect is guilty, and that, for many reasons, information extracted under torture comes with no guarantee of reliability. Terrorists willing to die for their cause would also be willing to plant false tales under torture.

Another insight from history is the danger that, once legitimated, torture could develop a constituency with a vested interest in perpetuating it. We have seen in recent years how the enterprise of enforcing the drug laws in the United States has made law enforcement agencies as dependent on the resulting forfeitures as the junkies are on the dope.[26] In a similar vein, Sir James Fitzjames Stephen recorded an observation made to him in India in 1872 about the proclivity of the native police for torturing suspects. "It is far pleasanter to sit comfortably in the shade rubbing red pepper into some poor devil's eyes than to go about in the sun hunting up evidence."[27]

History's most important lesson is that it has not been possible to make coercion compatible with truth.

Notes

1. This section follows John H. Langbein, *Torture and the Law of Proof: Europe and England in the Ancien Régime* (1977), 3–17, which contains citations to the historical sources and scholarly literature.

2. For example, in the leading study of the juristic literature, Piero Fiorelli, *La tortura giudiziaria nel diritto comune,* 2 vols. (1953–54).

3. For an English-language account of the reception in the German states, see John P. Dawson, *A History of Lay Judges* (1960), 102–112, and *The Oracles of the Law* (1968), 176–242.

4. For a succinct account, see T.F.T. Plucknett, *A Concise History of the Common Law,* 5th ed. (1956), 113–115; see also Paul R. Hyams, "Trial by Ordeal: The Key to Proof in the Early Common Law," in *On the Laws and Customs of England: Essays in Honor of Samuel E. Thorne* (1981), 90. Regarding the worldview of the ordeal, see Peter Brown, "Society and the Supernatural: A Medieval Change," *Daedalus* 104 (1975): 133, reprinted in Peter Brown, *Society and the Holy in Late Antiquity* (1982), 302.

5. See *Disciplinary Decrees of the General Councils,* ed. H. J. Schroeder (1937) (reprinting and translating canon 18 of the Fourth Lateran Council), 258. Regarding the background to abolition, see Robert Bartlett, *Trial by Fire and Water: The Medieval Judicial Ordeal* (1986), 70–90; R. C. van Caenegem, "The Law of Evidence in the Twelfth Century," in *Proceedings of the Second International Congress of Medieval Canon Law,* ed. S. Kuttner and Joseph Ryan (1965); J. W. Baldwin, "The Intellectual Preparation for the Canon of 1215 against Ordeals," *Speculum* 36 (1961): 613.

6. Maitland's term. Frederick Pollock and Frederic W. Maitland, *The History of English Law before the Time of Edward I,* 2nd ed. (Cambridge: 1898) (hereafter Maitland, *HEL*), 660.

7. *Constitutio Criminalis Carolina,* sec. 54 (1532), translated in John H. Langbein, *Prosecuting Crime in the Renaissance: England, Germany, France* (1974), 282.

8. Joost Damhouder, *Practique iudiciaire es causes criminelles [Praxis Rerum Criminalium]* (Antwerp, 1564), 44.

9. Quoted in Hugh R. Trevor-Roper, *The European Witch-Craze of the Sixteenth and Seventeenth Centuries* (1969), 84.

10. Cesare Beccaria, *Of Crimes and Punishments,* trans J. Grigson (1964), chap. 12, pp. 31–37 (1st ed. 1764).

11. *Oeuvres complètes de Voltaire* (Paris: 1835), 411, 441–442. See generally Peter Gay, *Voltaire's Politics* (1959), 273–308; Marcello Maestro, *Voltaire and Beccaria as Reformers of Criminal Law* (1942).

12. For the details on the legislation, see Langbein, *Torture,* 61–64, 177–179.

13. Bernard Schnapper, "Les Peines arbitraires du XIIIe au XVIIIe siècle: Doctrines savantes et usages français," *Tijdschrift voor Rechtsgeschiedenis* 41 (1973): 237; 42 (1974): 81; Langbein, *Torture,* 45–69.

14. See John H. Langbein, "The Historical Origins of the Sanction of Imprisonment for Serious Crime," *Journal of Legal Studies* 5 (1976: 5); Thorsten Sellin, *Pioneering in Penology: The Amsterdam Houses of Correction in the Sixteenth and Seventeenth Centuries* (1944).

15. Regarding the development in the German states, see Langbein, *Torture*, 47–50, and sources cited there; for France, see 50–60.

16. Maitland, *HEL*, 660.

17. See Daniel Klerman, "Was the Jury Ever Self-Informing?" in *The Trial in History: Judicial Tribunals in England and Europe, 1200–1700*, ed. Maureen Mulholland and Brian Pullan (2003), 58.

18. Maitland, *HEL*, 660–661.

19. Ibid., 659–660.

20. E.g., John Fortescue, *De Laudibus Legem Anglie*, ed. S. B. Chrimes (1942) (written c. 1470), 46–47. Thomas Smith, *De Republica Anglorum*, ed. Mary Dewar (1982) (written c. 1585), 117–118.

21. I have catalogued and analyzed eighty-one torture warrants in Langbein, *Torture*, 81–128; see also James Heath, *Torture and English Law: An Administrative History from the Plantagenets to the Stuarts* (1982), identifying these eighty-one cases. The first scholarly account was David Jardine, *A Reading on the Use of Torture in the Criminal Law of England Previously to the Commonwealth* (London, 1837).

22. English criminal procedure functioned without a professional police and prosecutorial corps until the nineteenth century. Local justices of the peace (JPs) conducted investigatorial and charging functions, supported by local constables. Both the JPs and the constables were unpaid amateurs engaged in civic service. I have emphasized in Langbein, *Torture*, 137–138, that "it would have been unthinkable to allow them to operate torture chambers of their own. . . . They were prone to faction and notoriously difficult for the central authorities to control."

23. William Blackstone, *Commentaries on the Law of England*, 4 vols. (Oxford: Oxford University Press, 1765–69), 4: 321.

24. Edward Coke, *The Third Part of the Institutes of the Laws of England: Concerning High Treason, and Other Pleas of the Crown, and Criminal Causes* (London, 1644) (posthumous publication, written c. 1620s–1630s), 35.

25. I have explained why the historical evidence points in this direction; see Langbein, *Torture*, 129–31.

26. Our plea bargaining system supplies another example of the way vested interests coalesce around coercive criminal procedures. On the coercive nature of plea bargaining, see John H. Langbein, "Torture and Plea Bargaining," *University of Chicago Law Review* 46 (1978): 1. The theme of the vested interests of judges, defense counsel, and especially prosecutors in plea bargaining was developed in Alschuler's trilogy of articles: Albert W. Alschuler, "The Trial Judge's Role in Plea Bargaining," *Columbia Law Review* 76 (1976): 1059; "The Defense Attorney's Role in Plea Bargaining," *Yale Law Journal* (1975) 84: 1179. "The Prosecutor's Role in Plea Bargaining," *University of Chicago Law Review* 36 (1968): 50.

27. James Fitzjames Stephen, *A History of the Criminal Law of England*, 3 vols. (London, 1883), 1: 442 n. 1.

Jerome H. Skolnick

American Interrogation
From Torture to Trickery

Citizens of the United States do not usually consider torture to be a feature of the nation's heritage. But it is there, hidden by other labels. Slaves were whipped as punishment for offenses, real or imaginary. After the Civil War and into the 1930s, the public torments of Southern "lynchings" were inflicted on black men in the interests of upholding a racist social order.[1] And when "Negroes" were arrested they were "frequently beaten in the wagon on the way to jail or later when they are already safely locked up."[2]

Whether the rhetorically powerful word "torture" should be applied to instances of painful abuse permitted on the basis of a caste status is open to question. The horror of the institution of slavery is that slaves no have lawful claim against the brutal punishments or sexual crimes of their owners. And, as I will discuss later, in the case of *Brown v. Mississippi* (and other famous southern cases of that era, such as *Screws v. U.S.*),[3] neither did Southern blacks in the first half of the twentieth century have legal redress for the crimes committed against them by police.

Less widely known to contemporary Americans are the painful and hidden practices of interrogation, known as the "third degree," as they were practiced throughout the United States. Police considered these measures necessary to draw confessions from recalcitrant criminals thought to be deserving of harsh inquiry and punishment. In what follows, I try to develop a narrative of the connection between lynching, the third degree, and the evolving jurisprudence of domestic American interrogation.

Lynchings and Police Whippings

The line between vigilante and official justice was scarcely discernible in the segregated South. It did not disappear easily, and not completely until the beginnings of the civil rights movements of the 1960s and the demise of legal segregation. The post–Civil War white South faced the enormous dilemma of absorbing a population of former slaves, while maintaining social and political dominance. A solution was to further develop and affirm theories of racial inferiority that justified slavery, and to use tactics of terror and torture—within and outside law—to maintain caste superiority. Punishment for transgressions of unwritten inequality norms, which arose during slavery and carried over to the twentieth century, came to be a responsibility for all whites. Local police and courts were expected to assist in upholding caste etiquette, as were lesser functionaries such as bus drivers and railroad conductors.

Lynching was accepted by the post–Civil War white power structure against those who violated—or were thought to violate—the customs and institutions that had arisen to keep blacks in a subordinated caste position. The lynching itself was a dreadful ritual of beating, burning, and humiliation. The dead, mutilated body was hanged for all to see and to remember—the "strange fruit" of Lillian Smith's celebrated novel.[4] The tortured body served the double purpose of affirming the God-given racial superiority of all whites against any black and of intimidating black men who might think of challenging the reigning social order.

Mississippi blacks passed around stories, which became legends, about sex, bloodshed, and the meaninglessness of the official legal order. In one of these, a boy is called inside a house by a partially undressed white woman. He comprehends his dilemma. If he refuses her advances, she will cry out and say that he tried to rape her, and he will be lynched. But if he accepts, and is discovered, he will also be lynched. In the story, he is arrested and acquitted because the woman's husband, who understands what really happened, testifies on his behalf. Following his acquittal he is assaulted by a gang of white boys who tie his feet to the back of a car and speed off "with the black boy's crushed, bloody head bouncing from the roadbed."[5]

Although the term "lynching" rightly summons visions of mob violence, law enforcement officials were often implicated, sometimes as participants, more often as sympathetic observers. Arthur Raper, who studied lynchings in the 1930s, estimated that at least half were carried out with police officers participating and that in nine-tenths of the others, police either condoned or winked at the mob action.[6]

Southern lynchings were carried out during the Depression decade, when the United States Supreme Court was beginning to impose more rigorous Constitutional standards on Southern courts. *Powell v. Alabama*,[7] decided in 1932, was the most famous case of the era. Popularly known as the Scottsboro case, it involved charges against nine indigent black youths who were accused of having raped two white girls in a freight car traveling through Alabama. The trial became internationally known and discussed, as Northern white liberals and the Communist Party came to the defense of the youths. Since there had been no adequate representation for the black youths at their trial, the Court reversed their convictions, mandating the appointment of counsel for indigent defendants in capital cases.

Stung by charges of a "lawless" South brought about by the publicity of the Scottsboro case, by the mid-1930s Southern law enforcement officials tried to offset mob violence by directing into the criminal justice system incidents that might earlier have provoked a public lynching. A charge of murdering a white man was more likely to find its way into court than a charge of raping a white woman, which was more likely to elicit a lynching.[8]

What a trial could mean in practice, however, is exposed in the sociologically revealing—and legally groundbreaking—United States Supreme Court case *Brown v. Mississippi*,[9] decided in 1936. No evidence, except for their confessions, was produced against three black tenant farmers accused of murdering a white planter. It took only ten days from the time of their arrest to convict them of capital murder. "A speedy trial for the suspected blacks would go a long way," a local newspaper editorialized, "toward removing any apprehension of attempted violence on the part of allegedly enraged citizens of Kemper." In other words, a speedy capital trial with its outcome ordained would prevent a public lynching.[10]

Instead, the suspects were arrested and privately tortured by the police. How the confessions were induced is described in the opinion of the chief justice of the United States Supreme Court, Charles Evans Hughes:

> Dial, a deputy sheriff, accompanied by others, came to the home of Ellington, one of the defendants, and requested him to accompany them to the house of the deceased, and there a number of white men were gathered, who began to accuse the defendant of the crime. Upon his denial, they seized him, and with the participation of the deputy

they hanged him by a rope to the limb of a tree, and having let him down, they hung him again, and when he was let down the second time, and he still protested his innocence, he was tied to a tree and whipped, and still declining to accede to the demands that he confess, he was finally released and he returned with some difficulty to his home, suffering intense pain and agony. The record of the testimony shows that the signs of the rope on his neck were plainly visible during the so-called trial. A day or two thereafter the said deputy, accompanied by another, returned to the home of the said defendant and arrested him, and departed with the prisoner towards the jail in an adjoining county, but went by a route which led into the State of Alabama; and while on the way, in that State, the deputy stopped and again severely whipped the defendant, declaring that he would continue the whipping until he confessed, and the defendant then agreed to confess to such a statement as the deputy would dictate, and he did so, after which he was delivered to jail.[11]

The two other men were similarly brutalized until they confessed. The sheriff's deputy who had presided over the whippings did not deny in sworn testimony that one of the defendants had been whipped. The whipping, he said, was "not too much for a Negro, not as much as I would have done if it were left to me."[12]

Despite this acknowledgment, the tortured "confessions" were admitted as evidence by the Mississippi trial court. On appeal, the Supreme Court of Mississippi upheld the trial court's ruling. Nevertheless, a powerful and influential dissent by Judge Virgil A. Griffith, joined by Judge William D. Anderson, was to influence the United States Supreme Court to overturn the conviction.

It should also be noted that heroic white lawyers defended the accused black men. John Clark lost law business, friends, and health defending the men and bringing their appeal to the Mississippi Supreme Court. Despite powerful odds, and lack of money (which was raised in New York City by white liberals for the N.A.A.C.P.), the former governor Earl Brewer brought the case to the Supreme Court.[13]

The justices were shocked not only by the conduct of the Mississippi police but that the highest court of Mississippi could accept confessions that had been elicited by such brutality. Justice Hughes's opinion virtually adopts Judge Griffith's dissent and concludes: "It would be difficult to conceive of methods more revolting to the sense of justice than those taken to procure the confessions of these petitioners, and the use of the confessions thus obtained as the bases for conviction and sentence was a clear denial of due process."[14]

The case was remanded to the Mississippi the District Court and retried by the district attorney, John Stennis (later an influential United States Senator). Stennis negotiated a plea bargain with the attorney, Earl Brewer, which was accepted by the defendants, who had already served years in jail. They believed that no matter how tainted the evidence against them, a retrial would result in a conviction and another death sentence.[15]

Torture, Interrogation, and Terror

I have freely used the word "torture" because under contemporary human rights standards the interrogation of the suspects in *Brown v. Mississippi* would surely qualify. Nevertheless, what the court termed "revolting methods" to force the confessions is not generally referred to by that incendiary label. Nor is it in a recent decision upholding *Miranda v. Arizona*[16] by Chief Justice William Rehnquist, who references the Mississippi beatings in *Brown* as "physical coercion."[17] Yet, as I will discuss later, the word surfaces in the 2003 case of *Chavez v. Martinez.*[18]

Why the reluctance to use the word? It may be that the rhetorical force of the word "torture" connotes a room or chamber designated for that purpose by constituted authorities, or the violent methods used by authoritarian regimes and military powers. Roman law justified torture in the belief that, under torture, a guilty person would reveal detailed knowledge of the crime that an innocent person would not know. But torture was not permitted to be employed routinely against criminal suspects. "Half proof" (the testimony of one eyewitness, or strong circumstantial evidence) was required to protect the innocent from pain infliction and false confession.[19]

Foucault argues that this "penal arithmetic" was not nearly so precise at the margins. French criminal procedures were carried out in secret by magistrates who needed to weigh the persuasiveness of circumstantial evidence and the credibility of witnesses. Consequently, the confession took on added significance. It relieved the prosecutor of the obligation of providing further evidence. Moreover, it vindicated the "unequivocal authority" of the criminal law enforcement procedures, including torture, that were being applied. To achieve a "real victory" over the accused demanded confession and contrition. Those accused must if possible "judge and condemn themselves."[20] Nevertheless, torture was permitted, and its results were persuasive, Foucault argues, precisely because it was regulated. "It was certainly cruel, but it was not savage."[21]

Torture's link with interrogation may make it appear that it is legally sanctioned, that the information being sought will be introduced in a trial, as it was in *Brown v. Mississippi*. But since evidence gained by torture is currently inadmissible in civil and common law systems, contemporary torture will ordinarily be used to gain *information* rather than *evidence*.

In other contexts, torture may be used to punish or intimidate. Although torture may mimic interrogation, it doesn't follow that the interrogators care about the truth of the answer. "That something is asked *as if* the content of the answer matters," writes Elaine Scarry "does not mean that it matters."[22]

Since torture is forbidden by law, it has been interpreted as "conduct that seeks to trump law."[23] Scarry's vivid portrait of "the structure of torture" mentions a number of regimes where specially equipped torture sites have been made use of to terrorize political enemies.[24] Such torture, Scarry writes, is usually employed when power is "highly contestable" and the regime "unstable."[25]

Yet its near equivalent, if not torture itself, has been used in recent history by stable democracies. British authorities in Northern Ireland beat Irish Republican Army prisoners with batons and fists and employed practices of detention and interrogation that included forcing detainees or prisoners to stand for long hours, placing black hoods over their heads, detention in rooms with hissing sounds prior to interrogation, and deprivation of sleep and food and drink.[26] In a decision that has been criticized by human rights advocates, the European Court of Human Rights ruled that these practices were "cruel, inhuman and degrading" but refused to characterize them as "torture"—suggesting how incendiary "torture" is as a word of reproach.[27]

Similarly, Israel's General Security Services (GSS) have used "physical means," such as shaking suspects violently, sleep deprivation, and forcing suspects to wait in painful positions, when interrogating Palestinians who are thought to be terrorists or potential terrorists. When the GSS practices were challenged by a number of Israeli civil rights groups, the GSS argued that these tactics were a "necessary" defense against terrorism.

That defense was rejected by the Israeli Supreme Court in a widely her-
alded case in 1999. The court recognized the "the difficult reality in which
Israel finds herself" and that "this decision does not ease dealing with that
reality." But it concluded that "this is the destiny of democracy, as not all
means are acceptable to it, and not all practices employed by its enemies are
open before it."[28]

The Algerian French authorities used "extraordinary measures" to obtain information, justifying these with utilitarian, cost-benefit arguments
that the next victims of terrorist attacks deserve more protection than the
attackers.[29]

A similar justification probably explains how an al-Qaeda terrorist,
Jamal Beghal, was treated after he was arrested in the Dubai airport, an arrest that thwarted a planned bombing of the U.S. Embassy in Paris and
nearly prevented the 2001 bombing of the World Trade Center in New York.
After some weeks in captivity, he talked to his interrogators and "out
poured a wealth of information." His lawyer charged that he had been
"tossed into a darkened cell, handcuffed to a chair, blindfolded and beaten
and that his family was threatened."[30]

And what are we to make of the photographs, in the evening news, of
"enemy combatants" in Guantanomo Bay who are blindfolded and shackled, with slight hope of release? That they are being interrogated under
harsh conditions is not denied. Yet the word "torture" is rarely, if ever, used
in connection with these interrogations. Are these enemy combatants also
being shown in captivity strategically, as a spectacle of deterrence, to those
who might be considering terrorist acts? The prospect of death as a "martyr" might be more acceptable to a future terrorist than a life sentence at
Guantanamo Bay, where dozens of inmates have already attempted suicide.[31]

Why has the word "torture" been so rarely employed in U.S. interrogation jurisprudence? The explanation might that torture had never been
sanctioned under the common law as it was in the civil law system—or
simply because the word is so provocative. Common law courts had no
official torturers trained to administer carefully measured doses of pain to
test pleas of innocence. Torture was condoned in England in the secret eccle-
siastical courts, which had jurisdiction over religious crimes; and in "prerogative" courts, such as the King's Star Chamber, with jurisdiction over
treason and breaches of the "King's Peace." The Star Chamber and the
Court of High Commission were abolished in 1641, and in the next decades
what came to be known as "the privilege against self-incrimination" took

hold in several high-profile trials. Under the privilege, coerced confessions were regarded as inherently untrustworthy.[32]

English judges, the Supreme Court chief justice William Rehnquist pointed out in his recent majority opinion upholding *Miranda*, excluded confessions obtained by promises, threats, and force. "A free and voluntary confession is deserving of the highest credit, because it is presumed to flow from the strongest sense of guilt . . . but a confession forced from the mind by the flattery of hope or the torture of fear, comes in so questionable a shape . . . that no credit ought to be given to it, and therefore it is rejected."[33]

The Third Degree

That may have been the goal of the common law, but the aspiration was breached well into the 1960s. Although coerced confessions were already inadmissible as evidence in many Northern states, police detectives had developed interrogation practices some of which would surely qualify as "torture" under contemporary international law. They called these "the third degree" and used them against suspects irrespective of race.[34]

The origin of the term is one of those obscure legal mysteries (like why criminal trial juries in the United States are composed of twelve persons). Richard Sylvester, president of the International Association of Chiefs of Police in 1910–15, located it in the criminal justice system. The "first degree" is presumably the arrest; the "second degree" the transport to a place of confinement; and the "third degree" the interrogation. Whatever its origin, the "third degree" was a euphemism for organized, deliberate police brutality.

Sylvester describes the "sweat box," introduced after the Civil War to combat the "marauder, the bank robber and the highwayman, thieves and criminals of every kind, [who] took advantage of the exciting times to engage in their nefarious undertakings." He describes the "sweat box" as a cell with a

> monster stove adjoining, into which vegetable matter, old bones, pieces
> of rubber shoes and kindred trophies would be thrown, all to make a
> terrible heat, offensive as it was hot, to at last become so tortuous and
> terrible as to cause the sickened and perspiring object of punishment
> to reveal the innermost secrets he possessed as the compensation for
> release from the "sweat box.[35]

Captain Cornelius Willemse of the New York City police department, in a book titled *Behind the Green Lights* (of the stationhouse), contrasts the public and the police idea of the third degree in language resonant of the carefully calibrated, "cruel but not savage" practice of torture in medieval Europe . "To the public," wrote Captain Willemse, "the 'third degree' suggests only one thing—a terrifying picture of secret merciless beating of helpless men in dark cells of the stations." Detectives, said Willemse, saw it as strategic, *purposeful* pressure, not the imposition of punishment for the sake of retribution.[36]

Although Willemse acknowledged a repertoire of coercive police tactics, he took care to point out that these were not invariably violent, and were calibrated. Detectives might roll up their sleeves and carry a rubber hose but would not actually beat the suspect. Nevertheless, Willemse (like the supervising sheriff in *Brown*) acknowledges no limits on how far police might go to break down a suspect: "I never hesitated," he boasts. "I've forced confessions—with fist, blackjack and hose—from those who would have continued to rob and kill if I had not made them talk."[37]

But unlike the Mississippi sheriff who admitted that the suspect had been whipped, police in cities like New York and Chicago routinely compounded their offenses by offering false testimony about how prisoners came to have broken bones and visible bruises—falling down steps was a favored explanation. Prosecutors and judges must certainly have understood that the police were lying about how a confession had been elicited, but winked at these "third degree" interrogations.

From *Brown* to *Miranda*

Although "coerced" confessions had been inadmissible in U.S. Federal Courts since the nineteenth century, *Brown v. Mississippi* set a new judicial standard for state courts. Henceforth, to be admitted as evidence, all confessions in the United States needed to conform to "due process" and be "voluntary," concepts that (as I will show in my discussion of the latest interrogation case to be decided by the U.S. Supreme Court) have proved elusive to this day.

Following the decision in *Brown*, the Supreme Court struggled with a succession of cases to ascertain the meaning and contours of the "due process-voluntariness" standard, in cases that revealed some of what was actually occurring in police interrogation rooms. For how many hours could police grill a suspect? Thirty-six was found to be impermissible.[38] Neither could police strip off the defendant's clothes and keep him naked for some hours.[39] Nor could they threaten to bring in his ailing wife if he failed to cooperate.[40]

The police were not allowed to introduce other ruses, ploys, or pressures, such as threatening to cut off financial aid to the defendant's children, and have them taken away from her if she failed to answer questions;[41] nor could they isolate the defendant in a distant place so his friends and family couldn't effect his release, or even contact him;[42] nor could they introduce a state-employed psychiatrist as a "general practitioner" who would offer some medical relief but would obtain a confession through artful questioning.[43]

Several years later in a case where the accused's stomach was pumped to reveal the drugs he had swallowed, the Court, speaking through Justice Frankfurter, ruled that evidence obtained by means that "shock the conscience" was "constitutionally obnoxious," not only because it might be false but because "it offends the community's sense of fair play and decency."[44] In cases like these and others, the Court seemed to be applying what Yale Kamisar, Wayne LaFave, and Jerold Israel call a "police methods" as well as a "trustworthiness" test for the acceptability of evidence.[45]

Miranda v. Arizona

Of all the U.S. Supreme Court decisions addressing police interrogation, *Miranda v. Arizona*, narrowly decided by the Warren Court only thirty years after *Brown*, is the lynchpin. It is the case most widely discussed among legal scholars, and surely the best known among television and movie viewers around the world for the famous warnings known as "Miranda rights." A suspect who is in police custody must be told that he "has the right to remain silent, that anything he says can be used against him in a court of law, that he has the right to the presence of an attorney, and that if he cannot afford an attorney one will be appointed prior to any questioning if he so desires."[46] To the surprise of many legal scholars, the legal authority of the decision was reaffirmed on June 26, 2000, by the U.S. Supreme Court, in a seven-to-two decision written by Chief Justice William Rehnquist, who wrote that "Miranda, being a constitutional decision of this Court, may not be in effect overruled by an Act of Congress" (which had tried to do precisely that), "and we decline to overrule Miranda ourselves."[47]

Nevertheless, *Miranda* remains controversial for three principal reasons. First, critics from the right, notably Paul G. Casell, have charged that *Miranda* has permitted small but significant numbers of guilty persons to go free.[48] This allegation has been effectively challenged, particularly by Stephen Schulhofer.[49]

Second, critics from the left invoke what might be called the "waiver paradox." *Miranda* requires that if a suspect waives her right to remain silent, the waiver must have been given "voluntarily, knowingly and intelligently." But, left critics assert, it is not possible for most suspects to make a truly knowing and intelligent waiver without the advice of counsel, in what may be the most important legal decision of their lives. Furthermore, well-educated arrestees, or career criminals, rarely waive their right to silence or legal representation, introducing a social class bias into the rights provided by *Miranda*. Moreover, once the waiver is given, many of the coercive pressure tactics the *Miranda* court decried are now available under the "due process-voluntariness" standard.[50]

Third, a middling position is evident in Justice Rehnquist's unexpected decision in *Dickerson*. He notes that the *Miranda* warnings have become embedded in our national culture and are required as a matter of legal precedent. Moreover, subsequent decisions have reduced the impact of *Miranda* on law enforcement. It is rare that a defendant can make a "colorable argument" that a self-incriminating statement was unconstitutionally compelled. Critics of *Miranda*, like Justice Rehnquist, understand that the police have adapted to the requirement that *Miranda* warnings be offered.

Critics from the left, who advocate that an attorney should be available to counsel before a suspect waives her rights, have difficulty resolving the waiver paradox. If a suspect had the right to an attorney on the question of whether to remain silent she would routinely keep silent, virtually eliminating custodial police interrogation—something no court has ever advocated.[51]

The waiver paradox has been partly resolved by the police and by the courts in two ways. The police have learned to substitute "interviewing" for custodial interrogation. Suppose, for example, a divorced woman has been murdered and her slain body has been found in a public park. The police may want to "interview" her former husband, a current friend or recent lover, a business partner, or a neighbor. Detectives can meet each "interviewee" at his or her home or office. Since the interviewee is not yet a suspect in custody and is presumptively free to leave, the detectives may question without giving *Miranda* warnings. On the basis of the answers, each interviewee may appear to be innocent. But if any interviewee's answers seem to be incriminating, and the police make an arrest, they must (so far) give *Miranda* warnings before further questioning the suspect in a police interrogation room. And sometimes, as Richard Ofshe and Richard Leo report, suspects are told that they are free to leave, that this is simply a conversation, and given no *Miranda* warnings.[52]

Suspects who are placed under arrest, handcuffed, given *Miranda* warnings and taken into custody know that they are in trouble, that the police believe they are guilty of a serious crime. Lacking an attorney with whom to consult about whether to waive their right to silence, they often "cooperate" with the police and try to tell a story of innocence or exculpation.

The police are trained to manipulate such suspects. Typically, they will suggest incriminating justifications for the suspect's role in the crime. There are many such ploys, usually involving leading questions. In a case of rape, the police may point to the complicity of the victim. "She has a real sexy walk, so you knew she was asking for it, right?" Or "You were just driving the car, you didn't know Joe was going to shoot the liquor store manager? If you had, you never would have driven the getaway car, right?" Many police departments train their interrogators to avoid giving Miranda warnings. Such confessions are not admissible on direct testimony when the prosecutor is making her case, but she can use them to cross-examine the defendant and "impeach" his testimony should he become a witness on his own behalf—a rule that usually keeps the defendant from testifying on his own behalf.[53]

When a suspect waives his right to remain silent and to an attorney, and agrees to talk, police are permitted to lie, even about the evidence they have in their possession. "We found your DNA at the crime scene"; or "Your partner has confessed, so why not tell the truth—things will go better for you that way."[54] In some cases, police have made up stories so convincing that suspects begin to mistrust their own memories, believe the stories, and falsely confess even to capital crimes.[55]

Restitution

The whippings of the Jim Crow era, and the fists and blackjacks of the early twentieth-century period of the third degree, have largely disappeared in U.S. interrogation rooms. However much we may think we deplore deception and trickery by American police, the post-*Miranda* era of deceptive questioning has ushered in an era of psychological pressure as an alternative to physical brutality, which in some instances could surely have been characterized as "torture." This is not to presume that police brutality has disappeared on the streets and in the stationhouses. But physical force is rarely, if ever, used when the police are seeking evidence that can be introduced in a trial.[56]

Contemporary cases of known American police brutality are usually retributive or self-aggrandizing, not motivated by the enforcement of criminal law. The most famous brutality cases of the past decade are the street beating of Rodney King in Los Angeles and the beating and sodomizing of Abner Louima in a stationhouse bathroom in New York City. Had the brutality practiced on Mr. Louima been carried out in connection with an interrogation, rather than as retribution for a false belief that Mr. Louima had punched Officer Volpe, it would surely qualify as torture.

In other famous disclosures, police have used the power and cover of their uniforms to commit major crimes. They steal from drug dealers, assault them, even shoot them and plant guns, and sell drugs.[57]

Victims of police misconduct have only relatively recently begun to experience an effective legal process for restitution against serious police misconduct. It took ninety years. Not until 1961 did the Supreme Court recognize the authority of the Civil Rights Act of 1871, the post–Civil War "Ku Klux" Act. The Act provided both civil and criminal remedies for people whose constitutional rights had been violated by "persons acting under color of state law." Its civil side—42 U.S.C.S Section 1983, generally referred to as Section 1983—lay dormant for nearly a century.

Courts generally found that police and other officials who broke state laws were not working "under color of state law." But if officers—like the Mississippi sheriffs who tortured the suspects in the *Brown* case—violated the U.S. Constitution, civil suits brought under Section 1983 were defended and won by officers who would argue that they had done nothing more than what was permitted by the state.

Two cases changed the legal terrain. In 1961 the Supreme Court decided *Monroe v. Pape,*[58] a case that began when a group of thirteen Chicago cops conducted an early morning raid—without a warrant—into the home of a black Chicagoan whom they suspected of having committed a murder. The suspect's six children were rousted out of bed, marched into the living room and made to stand naked while the cops ransacked the house, opened drawers, and ripped mattresses. Finding nothing, they took the father into custody and kept him isolated for ten hours until they finally released him without charges.

By 1961 the civil rights social and legal movement was affecting the thinking of the Supreme Court, most famously in the context of school segregation. In *Monroe*, we see the Court changing, holding in essence that Section 1983's "color of state law" provision applied when officials commit constitutional violations, regardless of whether they also violate state law. As a result of putting the federal judiciary in the business of enforcing the ninety-year-old Civil Rights Act, the legal environment of police accountability began to shift radically. "Between 1961 and 1977," Justice Lewis Powell was to write later, "the number of cases filed in federal court under civil rights statutes increased from 296 to 13,113."[59]

But the *Monroe* decision also immunized local governments from liability for constitutional violations by their police.[60] Hence a victory against a local police officer might bring satisfaction but scarce compensation. The deep pocket of municipal liability was not opened until 1978, when the Court decided a case about as far removed from police misconduct as one could imagine. The plaintiff, a pregnant New York City social worker, was required to take an unpaid leave of absence. It was her department's official policy, she was told, to compel pregnant employees to take unpaid leaves of absence before such leaves were required for medical reasons. Jane Monell sued, arguing that she and other women who were parties to the lawsuit had been denied equal protection of the law by a policy that unfairly affected women and their careers.

The Supreme Court agreed with Monell's claim and established a principle that was to effect the liability of cities for a pattern of constitutional violations by their police, including but not restricted to harsh interrogation practices; when a public agency's official "custom and practice" (like the policy denying maternity leave) violates an individual's constitutional rights, the agency, as well as the employee who carried out the policy, are liable for damages. Moreover, the Court defined *custom* or *usage* broadly, to include whatever officials do routinely, whether or not legal, or in line with written agency policy. Custom or usage, the *Monell* Court wrote, may be found in "persistent and widespread . . . practices of officials which although not authorized by written law, [are] so permanent and well settled as to have the force of law."[61] Any pattern or practice of interrogation that violated civil rights would certainly quality.

Yet there was one more hurdle barring substantial compensation for a pattern of police misconduct of any kind. Plaintiffs who sue the police and the cities they work for under Section 1983 are rarely respected professionals like Jane Monell, who had access to a civil lawyer (her husband, Oscar Chase). Civil juries are not likely to award substantial damages to plaintiffs who might have a history of robbery or drug dealing. In 1976, the U.S. Congress passed a law permitting judges in civil rights cases to award *successful* plaintiff's lawyers "reasonable attorneys fees as part of the cost," independent of the amount of the award. This has led to the development of a civil rights "brutality bar" in Los Angeles and other cities—and sometimes leads to remarkable results, as when Los Angeles attorney Stephan Yagman was awarded $29,137 in attorney's fees in a case where his clients won a two-dollar verdict against the Los Angeles police department.[62]

Where Are We Now?

The most recent restitution case decided by the Supreme Court began on November 28, 1997, and involved an allegation of torture. Two Oxnard, California, police officers, Maria Pena and Andrew Salinas, were questioning a suspected drug dealer in a vacant lot. During the questioning, Oliverio Martinez rode his bicycle into the lot. He was stopped, patted down, and discovered to have a knife in his waistband. How the search escalated into a struggle and a shooting is contested. "Both sides agree, however, that Salinas yelled, 'He's got my gun!' Pena then drew her gun and shot Martinez several times, causing severe injuries that left Martinez permanently blinded and paralyzed from the waist down."[63] The officers arrested Martinez and called for an ambulance.

Sergeant Chavez, a patrol supervisor, arrived at the scene and accompanied Martinez to the hospital. He then questioned him for about ten minutes, over a forty-five-minute period, while Martinez was being treated by doctors. The following is a partial transcription of the interview.

> CHAVEZ: What happened? Olivero, tell me what happened.
> O[LIVERIO] M[ARTINEZ]: I don't know.
> CHAVEZ: I don't know what happened [*sic*]?
> O. M.: Ay! I am dying. Ay! What are you doing to me? No, . . . ! (unintelligible scream).

CHAVEZ: What happened, sir?

O. M.: My foot hurts . . .

CHAVEZ: Olivera. Sir, what happened?

O. M.: I am choking.

CHAVEZ: Tell me what happened.

O. M.: I don't know.

CHAVEZ: 'I don't know.'

O. M.: My leg hurts.

CHAVEZ: I don't know what happened [*sic*]?

O. M.: It hurts . . .

CHAVEZ: Hey, hey look.

O. M.: I am choking.

CHAVEZ: Can you hear? look listen, I am Benjamin Chavez with the police here in Oxnard, look.

O. M.: I am dying, please.

O. M.: I want them to treat me, it hurts a lot, please.[64]

The District Court found that Martinez "had been shot in the face, both eyes were injured, he was screaming in pain, and coming in and out of consciousness while being repeatedly questioned about details of his encounter with the police."[65]

Martinez survived and filed a lawsuit in Federal District Court alleging that Chavez's interrogation had violated his constitutional rights under the Fifth Amendment's "privilege against self-incrimination" and the Fourteenth Amendment's prohibition against depriving "any person of life, liberty, or property, without due process of law." Martinez won his case in the Federal District Court on both claims, and his victory was upheld by the Ninth Circuit Court of Appeals.

Sergeant Chavez appealed, arguing that he had not violated Martinez's constitutional rights. The result was a fractured decision by the Supreme Court, traceable to different interpretations of the requirements of the Fifth and Fourteenth amendments. Most interesting are the justices' sensibilities in characterizing Chavez's persistent grilling.

A bare majority supported his claim that he had not violated Martinez's Fifth Amendment rights. Although Martinez had been placed under arrest, Chavez had not given *Miranda* warnings to Chavez. Citing *Brown v. Mississippi*, Justice Thomas acknowledged that "statements compelled by police interrogations may not be used against a defendant at trial . . . But in this case, Mr. Martinez was not even charged with a crime."

A more expansive vision of the Fifth Amendment's self-incrimination privilege was offered by several dissenters, most notably by Justice Kennedy, who wrote: "To tell our whole legal system that when conducting a criminal investigation police officials can use severe compulsion or even torture with no present violation of the right against compelled self-incrimination can only diminish a celebrated provision in the Bill of Rights."[66] And he goes on to say, regarding Martinez's Fourteenth Amendment claim: "It seems to me a simple enough matter to say that the use of torture or its equivalent in an attempt to induce a statement violates an individual's fundamental right to liberty of the person."

Justice Thomas did not interpret Chavez's behavior as "torture." Neither did he find it "conscience shocking" or "egregious." Justice Thomas argues that Chavez didn't "intentionally" interfere with Martinez's medical treatment, ceasing "his questioning to allow tests and other procedures to be performed." Chavez, he maintains, was simply doing his job of investigating "whether there had been police misconduct . . . evidence that would have been lost if Martinez had died without the authorities hearing his side of the story." To me, as a longtime observer of police practices, this motive seems plausible. But given that Martinez was in severe pain during the questioning, he felt as if he was being tortured into responding. Whatever Chavez's motive, his persistent questioning in the face of agonized requests to stop seems to me to qualify as torture. Besides, Chavez might also have had more than one motive. He might have been seeking to record an incriminating admission that could be used to challenge Martinez's claims of innocence if he was to recover, be tried for assaulting the police with a knife, and take the witness stand in his own defense.[67]

Justice Souter was the swing vote, siding with Justices Thomas, Rehnquist, Scalia, and O'Connor in denying Martinez's Fifth Amendment claim; and with Justices Kennedy, Stevens, Breyer, and Ginsburg in upholding Martinez's Fourteenth Amendment claim. The case was remanded to the Ninth Circuit to address the issue of possible liability for a substantive due process violation under the Fourteenth Amendment.

When one reads the decisions in this case, they reflect quite different doctrinal commitments, but more than that, they mirror fundamental differences in perspective and empathy. The "conservative" judges support the managerial obligations of Chavez as a supervisor and reject the depiction of his interrogation as "torture" or as "conscience shocking." The "liberal" vision, by focusing on the persistence of the interrogation, the pain already suffered by Martinez from the police shooting, and his repeated requests to be left alone in his pain, views the interrogation (as I do) as a form of "torture." Martinez's rights to compensation under the Constitution will succeed or fail with a jury on such viscerally conflicting responses.

Conclusion

I have tried to make two central arguments in this essay. The first maintains that while the concept "torture" evokes—at its core—images of interrogators in chambers furnished with implements of pain, our contemporary understanding has broadened the concept to include severe pain inflicted with the complicity of public officials. I proposed that the lynchings and whippings of African Americans in the Jim Crow South qualify because they were justified by three widely shared understandings: (1) that blacks are a race of people inferior to any white person, hence should be segregated; (2) that blacks deserve severe punishment—even whippings and public death—for alleged crimes, especially the allegation of having raped a white woman; and (3) that participants in the lynchings were not punished—indeed police were often accomplices.

The other argument is positive or empirical. Here I have maintained that the rise of racial equality norms, coupled with those of procedural jurisprudence, have virtually eliminated interrogatory torture in the United States, *where the interrogator's goal is a criminal conviction.*

With the revelations of "third degree" practices by the Wickersham Commission, and especially following the case of *Brown v. Mississippi,* judicial oversight began to provide normative standards ("due process" "voluntariness") for police to consider when contemplating custodial interrogation to produce evidence that would be acceptable in a trial. *Miranda v. Arizona* introduced an additional measure of constitutional protection grounded in the privilege against self-incrimination.

As the Supreme Court has become more conservative, and as American voters have become more concerned with controlling crime (the two developments are of course connected), the post-*Miranda* privilege against self-incrimination has been weakened. Detectives strategically interrogate suspects, using all the tactics the law allows, and some that are at the edge. Yet Sergeant Chavez's questioning of a suspect in a hospital, while the suspect was in immediate and severe pain, although not unheard of, scarcely typifies contemporary American police interrogation.[68]

The Supreme Court is slated to review a case in its current term that most closely illustrates current practices.[69] When a second-degree murder suspect, Patricia Seibert, was arrested in St. Louis County, she was put in a small interview room for fifteen or twenty minutes to "give her a little time to think about the situation." Without giving her a *Miranda* warning, Officer Hanrahan questioned her for about thirty to forty minutes. After she acknowledged her complicity in an arson and murder, she was given a twenty-minute break and was offered coffee and a cigarette. She was advised of her rights under *Miranda* only after she made incriminating admissions. She agreed to sign a waiver, and voluntarily repeated her incriminating statements into a tape recorder, which were recorded and played at her trial.

Officer Hanrahan testified that he was trained by his department, as well as one he had worked for previously, "to withhold *Miranda* warnings hoping to get an admission of guilt." Contemporary police interrogation manuals, we learn from this case, teach that the first admission, no matter how small, is the "breakthrough" or "the beachhead, " leading to a full confession.[70] This case, featuring deception and an assault on Miranda rights— but not the hidden pressures of the "third degree"—typifies much of contemporary American police interrogation practice.

Will "breakthrough" questioning be allowed by the Supreme Court, or will it accept the warning of Judge Michael A. Wolff of the Supreme Court of Missouri? "Were police able to use this 'end run' around *Miranda* to secure the all-important 'breakthrough' admission," he writes, "the requirement of a warning would be meaningless." The decision in *Missouri v. Seibert* will either undermine *Miranda* or affirm its significance as the embodiment of the privilege against self-incrimination. Whatever the outcome, it will powerfully influence police interrogation practices across the United States.

The case also reminds us that the domestic American interrogation issue is not about police torture—the "third degree" or whippings—as it was in the 1930s. The question has for some years been the meaning of *Miranda* rights in police interrogation rooms, especially the limits of police trickery and deception for producing evidence. I cannot prove a negative, but I feel confident in maintaining that there is no longer any torture by American police detectives who are seeking evidence to be introduced at a trial. And when the police are not seeking evidence, as presumably Sergeant Chavez was not when he questioned Oliviero Martinez, civil remedies are available to citizens of the United States who claim that they have been "tortured" by American police.

Notes

1. Gunnar Myrdal, *An American Dilemma: The Negro Problem and Modern Democracy* (New York: Harper, 1944), chap. 27.

2. Ibid., 541.

3. 325 U.S. 91 (1945).

4. Lillian Smith, *Strange Fruit* (New York: Harcourt Brace Jovanovich, 1992; originally published 1944). The title *Strange Fruit* comes from the song written by Abel Meeropol under the pseudonym Allan Lewis and made famous by Billie Holliday.

5. Nicholas Lemann, *The Promised Land: The Great Black Migration and How It Changed America* (New York: Knopf, 1991), 34–35.

6. Myrdal, *American Dilemma*, chap. 27.

7. 242 U.S. 540 (1932).

8. E. M. Beck, James L. Massey, and Stewart E. Tolney, "The Gallows, the Mob and the Vote: Lethal Sanctioning of Blacks in North Carolina and Georgia, 1882–1930," *Law and Society Review* 23 (1989): 329.

9. *Brown v. Mississippi*, 297 U.S. 278 (1936).

10. Richard C. Cortner, *A "Scottsboro" Case in Mississippi: The Supreme Court and Brown v. Mississippi* (Jackson: University Press of Mississippi, 1986), 8. Much of the discussion of the case in this article is based on this book.

11. *Brown v. Mississippi*, 281–282.

12. Ibid., 284.

13. See generally Cortner, *A "Scottsboro" Case*.

14. *Brown v. Mississippi*, 286.

15. Cortner, *A "Scottsboro" Case*, 153.

16. 384 U.S. 436 (1966).

17. *Dickerson v. U.S.*, 530 U.S. 428, 433.

18. 123 S. Ct. 1994 (2003).

19. John H. Langbein, *Torture and the Law of Proof: Europe and England in the Ancient Regime* (Chicago: University of Chicago Press, 1977), 4–5.

20. Michel Foucault, *Discipline and Punish: The Birth of the Prison*, trans. Alan Sheridan (1995; originally published 1977), 37–38.

21. Ibid., 40.

22. Elaine Scarry, *The Body in Pain* (New York: Oxford University Press, 1989), 29.

23. Winston P. Nagan and Lucie Atkins, "The International Law of Torture: From Universal Proscription to Effective Application and Enforcement," *Harvard Human Rights Journal* 14 (2001): 88.

24. Scarry, *Body in Pain,* 38–45.

25. Ibid., 1.

26. John Conroy, *Unspeakable Acts, Ordinary People: The Dynamics of Torture* (Berkeley: University of California Press, 2000).

27. Nagin and Atkins, *International Law of Torture,* 115.

28. *Supreme Court of Israel,* H.C.5100/94 (Sept. 6, 1999).

29. Bruce Hoffman, "A Nasty Business," *Atlantic Monthly,* January 2002, 4.

30. Stephen Erlanger and Chris Hedges, "A Nation Challenged: The Trail: Terror Cells Slip through Europe's Grasp," *New York Times,* December 28, 2001, P1.

31. The actual number is unknown. But as of August 2002, somewhere between twenty-seven and thirty were reported. Extrapolating to August 2003, there have been fifty to sixty or more. Helen and Harry Highwater, "US officials Are Lying about Suicide Attempts at Guantanamo Prison," *Unknown News,* August 15, 2003, available online at: www.unknownnews.net/suicides.html.

32. Leonard W. Levy, *Origins of the Fifth Amendment: The Right against Self-Incrimination* (New York: Oxford University Press, 1968).

33. *Dickerson v. U.S.,* 433.

34. George W. Wickersham, "Report on Lawlessness in Law Enforcement," *National Commission on Law Observance and Enforcement* (Washington, D.C.: U.S. Government Printing Office, 1931).

35. Richard Sylvester, "A History of the 'Sweat Box' and the 'Third Degree,'" in *The Blue and the Brass: American Policing 1890–1910* (Gaithersburg, Md.: IACP Press, 1976), 71–72.

36. Ernest Jerome Hopkins, *Our Lawless Police: A Study of the Unlawful Enforcement of the Law* (New York: Viking; Reprint: De Capo, 1972), 191–192.

37. Ibid., 192.

38. *Ashcraft v. Tennessee,* 322 U.S. 143 (1944).

39. *Malinski v. New York,* 324 U.S. 401 (1945).

40. *Rogers v. Richmond,* 365 U.S. 534 (1961).

41. *Lynumn v. Illinois,* 372 U.S. 528 (1963).

42. *Ward v. Texas,* 316 U.S. 547 (1942).

43. *Leyra v. Denno,* 347 U.S. 556 (1954).

44. *Rochin v. California,* 342 U.S. 165 (1952) 43.

45. Yale Kamisar, Wayne R. LaFave, and Jerold H. Israel, *Modern Criminal Procedure,* 8th ed. (St. Paul, Minn.: West, 1994), 454.

46. *Miranda v. Arizona,* 479.

47. *Dickerson v. U.S.,* 444.

48. Paul G. Casell, "Miranda's Social Costs: An Empirical Reassessment," in *The Miranda Debate: Law, Justice and Policing,* ed. Richard A. Leo and George C. Thomas (Boston: Northeastern University Press, 1996), 175–190.

49. Stephen Schulhofer, "Miranda's Practical Effect: Substantial Benefits and Vanishingly Small Social Costs," in Leo and Thomas, *Miranda Debate,* 191–207.

50. Jerome H. Skolnick, "Deception by Police," *Criminal Justice Ethics* (summer/fall 1982): 40–54.

51. Irene M. Rosenberg and Yale L. Rosenberg, "A Modest Proposal for the Abolition of Custodial Confessions," in Leo and Thomas, *Miranda Debate,* 142–152.

52. Richard J. Ofshe and Richard Leo, "The Decision to Confess Falsely: Rational Choice and Irrational Action," *Denver University Law Review* 74, 4 (1997): 979–1122.

53. *Harris v. New York,* 401 U.S.222 (1971); Charles D. Weisselberg, "Deterring Police from Deliberately Violating Miranda: In the Stationhouse after Dickerson," *Michigan Law Review* 99 (2001): 1121.

54. Jerome H. Skolnick and Richard A. Leo, "The Ethics of Deceptive Interrogation," in *Issues in Policing: New Perspectives,* ed. J. Bizzack (Lexington, Ky.: Autumn House, 1993), 75–91.

55. Richard A. Leo, "*Miranda* and the Problem of False Confessions," in Leo and Thomas, *Miranda Debate,* 271–282.

56. Jerome H. Skolnick and James J. Fyfe, *Above the Law: Police and the Excessive Use of Force* (New York: Free Press, 1993).

57. City of New York: Commission to Investigate Allegations of Police Corruption and the Anti-Corruption Procedures of the Police Department, Milton Mollen, Chair, July 7, 1994; Report of the Rampart Independent Review Panel, City of Los Angeles, November 2000; Matt Lait and Scott Glover, "The Rampart Scandal; LAPD Probe Fades into Oblivion; The Investigation That Gripped the City Is All but Over, though Far from Done," *Los Angeles Times,* August 11, 2003, A1.

58. 365 U.S. 167 (1961).

59. *Maine v. Thiboutot,* 448 U.S. 1 (1980), 27 fn. 16, Justice Powell dissenting. Justice Powell had not yet been appointed to the Supreme Court when *Monroe* was decided.

60. *Monroe v. Pape,* 187–192.

61. *Monell v. Department of Social Services of the City of New York et al.,* 436 U.S. 658 (1978), 691.

62. Gail Diana Cox, "Who Ya Gonna Call? Copbusters!" *Los Angeles Magazine,* May 1991, 77.

63. *Chavez v. Martinez,* 123 S.Ct. 1994, 1999 (2003).

64. Ibid., 2010–2012.

65. Ibid., 2017.

66. Ibid., 2015.

67. *Harris v. New York.*

68. *Mincey v. Arizona,* 437 U.S. 385 (1978).

69. *Missouri v. Seibert,* Review Granted: 05/19/2003 (71 U.S.L.W. 3721). On June 28, 2004, the Court, in a 5–4 decision, rejected the Missouri procedure as a deliberate attempt to evade *Miranda.*

70. Ibid., 704. Weisselberg, "Deterring Police," details the history of this tactic in the police departments of California, n. 53.

Mark Osiel

The Mental State of Torturers
Argentina's Dirty War

7

Alfredo Astiz led one of the most effective and notorious death squads during Argentina's dirty war, during which at least eleven thousand persons were murdered. Like the far better known Adolf Eichmann, he never committed any significant wrong before or after the particular wars in which they committed their evils. Neither man displayed any malicious motives, defects of character (such as uncontrollable rage), or mental instability, whether before, during or after their crimes. It is even impossible to assert that either of these men lacked meaningful attachment to other people, leaving him incapable of empathy for human suffering. What was central to each is the occupation of a role that dictated that commands from superiors were never to be questioned, much less challenged. "I have the soul of a soldier," says Astiz. "And the first thing they taught me was to obey my superiors."[1] Eichmann said virtually the same, both on the stand and in his diaries. By temperament and training, both men were careerists and conformists. But colleagues judged neither to be obsequious.[2]

How, then, do we understand what goes through the minds of torturers when performing their deeds? Is it really conceivable that they think only that they are obeying (legitimate) orders and that nothing more need be said (or felt)? Just as much to the point, how well does the criminal law make sense of these mental states? It is an appalling truth that anyone seeking answers to these questions immediately discovers that courts and legal scholars have had virtually nothing to say about them. The questions have operated under the protection of a taboo barring their serious examination. The taboo is held in place not by mere squeamishness but by the law itself—specifically, the law of evidence and, more particularly, the *presump-*

tions that can be found within that law. Beginning with Roman law, for example, there has been a conclusive presumption that certain actions carry their wrongfulness on their face, so that a culpable mental state—that is, actual knowledge of the evil of one's (mis)conduct—may be inferred on the part of the perpetrator of the actions. Roman military law described such acts as "atrocious and abhorrent."[3] Today they are simply designated, in national military codes and international conventions, as "manifestly" illegal.[4]

The presumption is what the law calls "conclusive," which means that defendants are barred from introducing evidence that might overcome it. Thus the possibility that someone might commit the most heinous deeds without any awareness of doing wrong becomes unthinkable, literally unspeakable in court, unless one claims something like insanity. But the very point of an "insanity defense" is its acknowledgment that any "normal" person would indeed recognize the "manifest" evil and concomitant illegality of the conduct. This is comforting, because it enables us to preserve the conceptual apparatus on which we rely in distinguishing the torturer from the rest of us.

As already suggested, manifestly illegal acts are distinguished by the fact that their criminality is immediately obvious ("manifest") to anyone under all circumstances. For instance, a soldier who receives an order to shoot children playing innocently in a schoolyard will know, without need for thought or deliberation, that the order is unlawful. On this basis, the soldier is obligated to disobey such an order. One problem with any such analysis, sadly, is that history does not reveal a single timeless response to such examples. One need, for example, look only to the Bible itself to see the Israelites carrying out ostensibly divine commands to engage in the ruthless slaughter of those whom we would easily classify as moral innocents. Thucydides writes of similar actions by Athenians, actions seemingly defended (or at least not condemned) by at least some recent analysts who look to ancient history for wisdom as to contemporary international relations.[5]

Similarly, as John Langbein demonstrates in his contribution to this book, torture has scarcely been universally classified as manifestly illegal. In fact, as he notes, the practice was itself once integral to the criminal process, enshrined within and regulated by medieval rules of evidence. It is only during the late twentieth century, in part because of widespread ratification of the United Nations Convention against Torture, that the practice came to be generally regarded as among the few crimes to which the label "manifestly illegal" could be unequivocally applied. This conclusion was reinforced by the nonderogable nature of the treaty's prohibitions: no exceptions would be authorized. Thus today we are strongly inclined to say that torture is manifestly illegal. The main problem with this conclusion is simply that it is demonstrably, empirically false. There are many torturers, and other perpetrators of mass atrocity, who remain unaware of the criminal nature of their actions and who believe them to be legally permissible, even required.

This was the case with Adolph Eichmann, as Hannah Arendt described him, and is also true of Argentina's "dirty warriors," such as navy captain Alfredo Astiz, in their self-descriptions.[6] There is no reason to think these are isolated cases. In fact, where torture by military personnel occurs today, there is reason to believe its perpetrators continue to think their conduct justified or excused, in ways that courts should acknowledge. They generally believe their legal defense to rest on obedience to superiors' orders and on likely judicial acknowledgement of the threat to their country's security posed by violent opponents.

If this is true—if many torturers hold such beliefs—the presumption that their wrongdoing is knowing (and therefore culpable) cannot remain conclusive; it must be made rebuttable, so that evidence to the contrary might be admitted. Whether this evidence ultimately proves persuasive to a fact-finder in a given prosecution is another matter; that is not a question about what the law should allow. The conclusiveness of its presumption prevents criminal law even from entertaining the possibility that torture, like other atrocities, is often committed by people who are not vicious, insane, malicious, disconnected interpersonally, or coerced by a totalitarian state. Careful assessment of relevant data compels this conclusion. We therefore reach a point where the legal fiction becomes simply a lie.[7]

Like other soldiers of their time and place, Eichmann and Astiz were deeply sympathetic to the ruling ideas of their day; that is to say, they shared the official creeds of their respective regimes. But neither held such beliefs with an extraordinary or rabid intensity. In this sense, they could not be considered fanatical ideologues, however repellant their views. Surely, neither man would have taken serious action in furtherance of these beliefs had he not perceived it his professional duty to do so. Yet each performed this duty imaginatively, enthusiastically, even cheerfully. Each took particular pride in his technical proficiency and each had quite a successful military career, though neither's was stellar or meteoric. In these respects, they were ordinary men. Their greatest concern seemed to be that they might be deemed inadequate to their assigned tasks.

Neither Eichmann nor Astiz claimed to feel coerced by his superiors or by threat of legal penalty for disobedience to their orders. In anticipating criminal acts he was about to commit, each apparently felt a sober sense of responding to moral obligation, not of submitting to personal inclination or temptation. Both remained completely unrepentant years later, while nonetheless expressing respect, of a kind, for their adversary.

How was it possible that such men could have failed to apprehend the criminality of their conduct?

In theory, highly repressive states may codify their most wicked policies into national law, so that torture would become legally authorized. In theory, such states might mobilize their populace through mass movements in ways that disrupt the normal social relationships anchoring the "common sense" of ordinary people. Both of these scenarios were central to Hannah Arendt's explanation of Eichmann's "banality," his apparent inability to apprehend the wrongfulness of his acts.[8] Neither of these explanations, however, find much support in recent historical and social scientific scholarship on the Third Reich or Argentina during the Dirty War.[9]

To understand the mental state of Argentina's torturers, at least, requires examination of the Catholic Church's contribution to their view of the world. Church leadership viewed the military operations against the regime's opponents as a just war, warranting no qualms and requiring no apologies by those called to participate.[10] Many officers in the Dirty War drew powerful inspiration from such clerical counsel. One junta member observed of Bishop José Miguel Medina that "both the troops and command used to welcome him, avid to hear his preaching, the irreplaceable spiritual sustenance for keeping up the struggle and overcoming the lack of understanding. . . . His advice clearly pointed the military sword in the right direction."[11] The chief bishop for the army preached to the officers, for instance, that "the anti-guerrilla struggle is for the Argentine Republic, for its integrity, but for its altars as well. . . . This is a struggle to defend morality, human dignity, and ultimately a struggle to defend God. . . . Therefore I pray for divine protection over this 'Dirty War' in which we are engaged."[12]

Bishops also privately offered theological justifications, drawn from medieval thought, for the practice of torture. Navy officers returning from dropping victims into the sea received comfort from chaplains who would cite parables from the Bible about separating the wheat from the chaff. Special military chaplains, assigned to serve exclusively the men in arms, took confession from officers at all ranks of service. Regarding the content of such confessions, Jorge Novak, one of four Argentine bishops who opposed the Dirty War, observed: "One wonders about officials in the recent military government who suspended the constitution and at the same time participated in Masses, listened to the word of God, received communion, and professed their faith. They must have posed the moral issues involved, so someone must have been counseling them. One can draw the logical inferences."[13]

Several priests in the military chaplaincy were present during torture sessions, encouraging victims to confess and collaborate, for the good of their souls. One surviving victim later remarked that during his detention "Bishop Medina said Mass, and in the sermon he said that he knew what we were going through, but that all this was for the good of the country, . . . and we ought to tell everything we knew. For that purpose, he offered to hear confessions."[14] Padre Sabas Gallardo counseled that torture is sinful only if it endures more than forty-eight hours, the period of time before which a guerrilla cell—one of whose members has been abducted—disperses (and after which the information offered under torture is presumably useless).

Thus, many participants in the Dirty War, at low and intermediate levels, exhibited considerable awareness that the actions commanded of them were wrong, demanding special justification from moral authority. There is reason to doubt whether, without such reinforcement, many of these officers would have successfully suppressed their initial hesitations and mistaken their orders as legitimate. A vital point, though, is that even if they viewed what they were being asked to do as "presumptively" wrong, the presumption in this case was not conclusive but, rather, subject to being overridden by sufficiently strong arguments, especially if they emanated from trusted authorities.

One squad member who participated in torture sessions with Astiz recalled, for instance: "Once I asked Father Sosa, who worked in the [detention] camp, if this all seemed right to him, and he said, 'You have to think like a surgeon. If you have to amputate a disease, you can't think about how the patient will look.'"[15] Another officer acknowledged that he first had reservations about what he was ordered to do. "When we had doubts, we went to our spiritual advisers, who could only be members of the vicariate, and they put our minds at ease," he reported. "We had the backing of the

Church," confided a third officer. "Not that priests said, 'Go ahead and torture,' but that the Church said there were two groups here and we were the ones who were right. The military vicarate said we had to rid the country of guerrillas." A police officer who worked as a driver in several abductions acknowledged: "Father von Wernich talked to me in particular because of the impact these events had on me. The priest told me that what we were doing was necessary for the good of our country . . . that God knew that what was being done was for the good of the country."[16]

Such soldiers are anxious to assure us that they are not ethical monsters, that they possess a moral sense. "As a good Christian," one acknowledges, "I have a problem of conscience regarding torture. The day we stop condemning torture—though *we tortured*—the day we become insensitive to mothers who lose their guerrilla sons—although they *are* guerrillas—is the day we stop being human beings."[17] In its own way, this is an unusually eloquent acknowledgment of the evil of torture, yet, as is obvious, it was not enough to forestall the occurrence of torture. Instead, it made it all the more important to accept the justifications proffered for the torture or even to reassure oneself that even as a torturer, one was remaining within some kind of limits. Thus, referring to his dragging drugged victims into navy helicopters (from which he would soon toss them into the sea), Adolfo Scilingo professed: "I tried to do things as humanely as possible," acknowledging that "it is difficult for anyone who wasn't there to understand that."[18]

Like Eichmann in his more reflective moments, such men reveal an awareness of facing a moral conflict. They resemble most of the subjects of Stanley Milgram's classic experiment, which involved persons—initially college students but in later versions adults from the surrounding community—who were hired to participate in a (faked) experiment involving learning, in which the apparent subjects of the faked experiment would receive greater and greater electrical shocks upon their failure to remember the information being tested. The hapless (real) subjects of the experiments were told that the experiment "required" that they shock the persons (whose apparent screams could be vividly heard). What so startled Milgram is that he never imagined that ordinary people would in fact be willing to impose the electrical shocks "required" by the experiment. The original design of the experiment was to discover the "one-in-a-hundred (or less)" person with a "Nazi-like personality," Instead, almost all of Milgram's subjects proved willing to engage in what could only be described as the torture of another human being. To be sure, they administered shock only under protest and displaying revulsion at their task. But they did it, helped along by the white-coated scientist who blandly kept repeating what the experiment "required" of them.

It is wrong to see such people as occupying an entirely separate moral universe, one in which the ethical judgments of others have become entirely indifferent to them. Though Argentine officers are indeed cut off from contact with civilian society to a degree unimaginable in the United States, it would be a mistake to overestimate the gap between the moral universes of officers and civilians. The self-exculpatory implications of these officers' remarks cannot be discounted. Nevertheless, some of President Alfonsín's top legal advisers, who had spoken directly with such soldiers, considered their statements plausible enough to have required careful judicial evaluation. In fact, this plausibility was crucial in leading Alfonsín, in his proposal to Congress, to exempt entirely from prosecution those who had followed orders to abduct and even to torture, provided they had not "exceeded" such orders (suggesting motives other than obedience). Referring to this proposed legislation, Carlos Nino, a great Argentine human rights activist, readily admitted that

> [w]e allowed the due-obedience defense with torture. While it is true that due obedience is not a viable excuse when referring to abhorrent acts such as torture, we acknowledged that in this particular historical context, an exception should be made. Such abhorrent acts were being committed within a climate of . . . an intense propaganda campaign that aimed to legitimate the violence.[19]

Since the Argentina Congress did not ultimately accept this restriction on the scope of criminal trials, the issue was thrown into the courts. The legal question became whether the statements of junior officers, such as those quoted here, amounted to an awareness of wrongdoing sufficient to reject the defense of reasonable mistake about the legitimacy of superior orders. We must stress, in this connection, that in many legal systems (including our own) a defendant's awareness of wrongdoing cannot be inferred simply from his belief in the ultimate weakness of his legal position. Such an inference would be particularly inapt where the defendant had seriously inquired into the permissibility of his contemplated conduct.

Hannah Arendt would be right to observe that these men exhibit the mental state of neither the common criminal nor the totalitarian ideologue. They betray neither a knowing defiance of moral authority that they acknowledge to be binding nor a principled repudiation of such authority and a willful embrace of its antithesis.

Yet neither do the comments of these officers suggest the indifferent equanimity of Eichmann on the witness stand, the untroubled complacency of the order-following bureaucrat. If their claims are to be given any credence, we must grant that these men were very much aware of the "moral enormity" of their acts, even if ultimately persuaded of their necessity. The awareness of moral enormity denotes a mental state registering recognition that one's acts normally would clearly violate central moral principles but that other concerns may prove weightier under the circumstances, all things considered. Such awareness of gravity is perfectly consistent with great difficulty in correctly balancing the conflicting concerns at the moment when one must decide how to act. These Argentine officers, like Eichmann, clearly have a sense of moral obligation, but one that surpasses the "role morality" of the unreflective clerk, that is, the highly limited sense of moral duty that Arendt ascribed to Eichmann.

Does an awareness of the moral enormity of one's acts, in this sense, permit us to say that their wrongfulness had been manifest to these men? One could certainly conclude that these men displayed ample awareness that their conduct posed a particularly serious risk of grievous wrong. Hence both of the elements of criminal negligence appear abundantly evident. Yet one could equally conclude that an initially troubled conscience, assuaged by reliance on assurances by trusted moral authorities, supports a legal claim of "reasonable mistake" regarding the legitimacy of one's orders.

The soldier's adverting to the risks, however serious, does not vitiate the reasonableness of his reliance on the most disinterested and unimpeachable source of moral guidance his society provides him. These men do not reveal a "willful blindness," in any conventional sense of the term. They may be contrasted in this regard with several of the Nuremberg defendants, who wept when compelled to watch films of the death camps or even with the SS guard at Treblinka who confessed that "he didn't want to see anything . . . the most positive one could do was play possum."[20] Willful blindness would more accurately describe the mental state of much of the general populace, who accepted that military rulers would operate above the law, provided that messy details were kept at a comfortable distance from public awareness.

By contrast, the officers quoted earlier engaged in a search for spiritual counsel, suggesting awareness of the moral enormity of their conduct. These men do not display, if their words are to be given any credence, the moral myopia of the bureaucrat, whose place within the division of labor is remote enough from the ultimate harm to enable him to escape what David Luban calls "the telltale signs of awfulness." These soldiers had not, to be sure, banished all doubt as to the wrongfulness of their orders.

But the law of manifest illegality does not require that they do so. On the contrary, it requires obedience to orders unless the illegality of the order is virtually certain. Any doubts are to be resolved in favor of compliance. It would be difficult to deny that these men, after receiving unequivocal clerical reassurance, could have entertained some genuine doubt that their orders were wrongful.

Were such mistakes, however honest, also *reasonable* under the circumstances, that is, given the "atrocious and abhorrent" nature of the acts these men committed? Having expressed his reservations and received unqualified reassurance, could the officer who then acted in obedience to orders requiring commission of atrocities be excused for having reasonably relied on those charged with guiding him in precisely such matters?

The persuasiveness of a given soldier's defense of reasonable mistake would depend, of course, on the available evidence concerning several questions. Just how religious had the defendant been over an extended period? How authoritative was the source of his religious guidance: a priest of short acquaintance or one on whose moral counsel he had long relied? A recent initiate to the priesthood, or an archbishop? How far from the penumbra (or close to the core) of manifest illegality did the defendant's acts lie? How deep were the doubts he expressed to his spiritual counselor? How specifically did he describe to the priest the acts commanded of him? How unqualified were the pastor's reassurances as to the legitimacy of compliance with such orders?

The deeper the doubts expressed by the soldier, the more vigorous the moral reassurances must have been, to overcome the presumption that his conduct was manifestly wrongful. This is because any sincere expression of doubt by the soldier to his spiritual counsel bespeaks at least a tentative awareness of the wrongfulness of his conduct. That very awareness, how-ever prereflective, is evidence that the unlawfulness of his orders was al-ready provisionally manifest to him.

The soldier attempting such a defense thus faces a difficult dilemma. He must stress the depth and sincerity of his doubts in order to lend any credi-bility to his claim that his mistake was an *honest* one. An accused who ad-mits to having initially doubted the legitimacy of "manifestly illegal" orders is surely far more credible than one who denies ever having given a mo-ment's thought to the defensibility of the conduct they required. But the accused must also stress that despite the sincerity of his doubts, it was not mere indifference or cynical self-interest that led him to overcome them.

His doubts must have been directly confronted and assuaged, not merely suppressed or denied, if he is to credibly establish the *reasonableness* of his mistake. Spiritual reassurance that was only ambiguous or qualified would weaken any claim that his ensuing mistake was one a reasonable person in his situation would have made. Ambiguous reassurance may often be the only kind that churchmen are willing to offer, for anything more specific would expose them to criminal liability as accessories—a risk they can scarcely afford to ignore.

The very difficulty of proving *both* these claims—honest mistake, rea-sonably grounded—from the same set of facts should reassure us that few, if any, genuinely culpable defendants will be able successfully to rebut the presumption that the illegality of their atrocious acts was manifest to them. The several factual questions raised here are enormously difficult to resolve in actual cases, of course, and it is not surprising that the law has striven to keep clear of them entirely, resolutely insisting that certain acts are *always* manifestly illegal, come hell or high water. But the vexing questions raised earlier become inescapable once one concedes that there could, in prin-ciple, be *any* circumstances under which a soldier might have been reason-ably mistaken as to the legitimacy of superior orders on account of reliance on trusted religious authorities.

It will not do to say that Astiz and his comrades saw themselves as en-gaged in a form of civil disobedience: knowing violation of the law in ser-vice of "higher" aims acknowledged to be unrecognized by it. One engaged in civil disobedience, to be sure, does not and cannot defend himself on grounds of legal mistake. This is because "the issue of mistake of law does not arise where the defendant knew that his moral judgment and the view-point of the criminal law clashed."[21]

But an offender may not necessarily possess this knowledge of wrongdoing—that is, in the eyes of the law—when he inhabits a society embracing natural law discourse, such as Argentina under the juntas. In such a society, the seemingly simple distinction between law-abiding behavior and civil disobedience can become quite hazy, for "there is a fluid borderline between those who violate the criminal law in the name of some higher justice and those who believe that their moral judgment is presently reflected in the criminal law, or will be, if—as they expect—it is interpreted properly."[22] Such an expectation would be entirely appropriate in Argentina, for the country's constitution goes so far as to codify a "natural law exception" to all other positive law. Article 19 expressly proclaims that God is the supreme legislator and that therefore formal, positive law should be treated as valid only insofar as it remains consistent with natural law.

The counsel offered by churchmen apparently suggested that officers could expect such "proper" interpretation from the regime's courts, if evidence of their activities were ever brought to light. This had indeed occurred after prior military regimes, whose official actions had not been invalidated by their constitutional successors. The reasonableness of such reliance cannot be gainsaid by classifying clerical advice as "moral" in nature, hence irrelevant to an excuse of *legal* mistake. This is because, in a society infused with naturalism as its operative concept of law (to the extent of giving it express constitutional supremacy over conflicting enactments), any intention to "obey the law" necessarily incorporates the "motive" of behaving as morality requires. The conflation of law and morality at the conceptual level of legal validity, in fact, encourages citizens to conflate the two at the level of personal action.

A soldier who intends to "obey the law" in such a legal system *necessarily* also intends to obey codified enactments only to the extent that they comport with "higher" moral-religious doctrine. Moreover, he reasonably expects his nation's courts to interpret "the law" in exactly this same fashion, since natural law plays a prominent part in the doctrinal development and interpretive practice of positive law. He thus expects these courts to excuse any conduct by him that, though inconsistent with codified law, is morally required. This expectation would be partly based upon the conduct of Argentine courts during prior periods of de facto (i.e., extraconstitutional) rule.

Whatever criticism (considerable) should rightly be leveled at these men, however, they are in no way "banal," in Arendt's sense. They are not unthinking automatons whose ethics are confined to the single commandment of obeying orders from a military or bureaucratic superior. It is untrue that they utterly lack "the habit of examining whatever happens to come to pass or to attract attention"[23]—the habit that Arendt found crucial to "mak[ing] men abstain from evil-doing." Yet neither is it easy to characterize their evil as satanic or "radical," in Kant's sense, for they do not willfully embrace the opposite of what they know to be the right or good.

If criminal law—national and international—is ever to grapple satisfactorily with torturers, it must confront these disconcerting facts about their actual motivations and mental states. The cases against Argentina's dirty warriors have recently been reactivated, and as of this writing, nearly fifty defendants are incarcerated, held for domestic prosecution or extradition to Spain. The question discussed in this chapter about the culpability of their mental state is certain to arise in the course of their prosecution.

Notes

1. Alfredo Astiz, interview in *Trespuntos*, Argentina, January 1998, 9.

2. Supporting authorities for all assertions made regarding Astiz and Eichmann may be found in Mark Osiel, *Mass Atrocity, Ordinary Evil, and Hannah Arendt: Criminal Consciousness in Argentina's Dirty War* (2002), 4–5.

3. For sources on this early history, see Mark Osiel, *Obeying Orders: Atrocity, Military Discipline, and the Law of War* (1999), 2.

4. See, e.g., the Rome Statute of the International Criminal Tribunal, art. 33, authorizing a defense of obedience to orders only when "the order was not manifestly unlawful."

5. See, for example, Daniel Mendelsohn, "Theatres of War," *New Yorker*, January 12, 2004, reviewing Donald Kagan, *The Peloponnesian War* (2003), and an article by Victor Davis Hanson, "A Voice from the Past: General Thucydides Speaks about the War," which appeared in *National Review Online*.

6. See Osiel, *Mass Atrocity*, 105–131.

7. Osiel, *Mass Atrocity*, 154.

8. Hannah Arendt, *Eichmann In Jerusalem* (1963).

9. Osiel, *Mass Atrocity*, 62–103.

10. Supporting authorities for all assertions made regarding the Church's role in the Dirty War may be found in Osiel, *Mass Atrocity*, 105–148.

11. General Cristino Nicolaides, in Emilio Mignone, *Witness to the Truth: The Complicity of the Catholic Church and Dictatorship in Argentina* (1986), 8.

12. Bishop Victorio Bonamin, *La Nacion,* May 6, 1976.

13. Diario del Juicio (1985), in Mignone, *Witness to the Truth,* 25.

14. Testimony of Ernesto Reynaldo Saman to the National Commission on Disappeared Persons, in Mignone, *Witness to the Truth,* 8.

15. Raul Vilarino, in Tina Rosenberg, *Children of Cain: Violence and the Violent in Latin America* (1991), 87.

16. A co-officer of Artiz, identified as "Jorge," in Rosenberg, *Children of Cain,* 130.

17. Horacio Mayorga, in Rosenberg, *Children of Cain,* 125.

18. In Horacio Verbitsky, *El Vuelo,* (1996), 168.

19. Carlos Nino, *Radical Evil on Trial,* (1996), 64.

20. Quoted in John Kekes, *Facing Evil* (1990), 235.

21. Gunther Arzt, "Ignorance or Mistake of Law," *American Journal of Comparative Law* 24 (1976): 646.

22. Ibid.

23. Hannah Arendt, *The Life of the Mind,* vol. 1, *Thinking* (1978), 5.

Contemporary Attempts to
Abolish Torture through Law

John T. Parry

Escalation and Necessity
Defining Torture at Home and Abroad

In the new war on terrorism, we are told, tough measures are necessary to protect our security. "After 9/11," according to State Department counter-terrorism coordinator Cofer Black, "the gloves came off."[1] Black's comments dovetail with the actions of U.S. military and intelligence personnel in operations after September 11. Some U.S. officials have used "a little bit of smacky-face" to provide "extra encouragement" to Afghani prisoners during interrogations.[2] Others have "softened up" prisoners by beating them and throwing them into walls.[3] Prisoners released from Guantanamo Bay and Bagram air base in Afghanistan claim they were "forcibly injected, denied sleep and forced to stand or kneel for hours in painful positions."[4] Two Afghan men died in U.S. custody at Bagram, the victims of "blunt force trauma"—presumably inflicted by U.S. forces.[5]

Some commentators minimized this conduct. A national security official suggested that "our guys may kick them around a little bit in the adrenaline of the immediate aftermath," while a former CIA agent asserted that "[e]verybody in the world knows that if you are arrested by the United States, nothing bad will happen to you."[6] Others took a harsher tone, contending that "[i]f you don't violate someone's human rights some of the time, you probably aren't doing your job."[7]

Human rights groups said that these allegations, if true, proved the United States had engaged in torture.[8] The administration, in turn, insisted that the interrogations were "humane and . . . follow[d] all international laws and accords."[9] In June 2003, facing criticism over the conduct of U.S. forces in Afghanistan and Iraq, President Bush went further and called on "all governments to join with the United States and the community of law-abiding nations in prohibiting, investigating, and prosecuting all acts of torture." The United States, he claimed, was "leading this fight by example."[10]

In the spring of 2004, the Abu Ghraib scandal broke. Pictures, testimony, and news reports demonstrated that U.S. forces had abused and killed Iraqi detainees at Abu Ghraib prison in Baghdad. Few were willing to defend the administration in the face of these charges. At the same time, however, almost no one in the government was willing to admit that U.S. forces had engaged in torture or, if they had, that U.S. policy had authorized the conduct at issue. President Bush apologized for the mistreatment of detainees, but he also insisted that it was the conduct of a few and "does not represent the America that I know."[11]

Underneath the war of words, we know that U.S. forces have used coercive tactics in the treatment and interrogation of prisoners. But how do we describe this conduct? Is it torture, or something less severe? More important, does it matter what label we attach to these practices? One almost gets the impression from media accounts that the propriety of our actions turns on whether or not the label will attach—even as the definition of torture seems elusive.[12]

This essay explains what is at stake in the debate over the characterization of U.S. interrogation practices. I also examine possible definitions of torture and use those definitions to consider whether the United States is mistreating its prisoners. I rely in part on recent news reports, but I also broaden the focus to compare our conduct overseas with the actions of British forces in Northern Ireland and Israeli security forces fighting Palestinian terrorism, as well as with police conduct at home. Finally, I briefly consider the circumstances under which torture can be justified.

Defining Torture

Torture under International Law

International law provides a fairly precise definition of torture that separates illegal practices into two categories while also providing that not all mistreatment amounts to torture. Thus, the Convention against Torture and Other Cruel, Inhuman or Degrading Treatment or Punishment ("Convention") declares:

The term "torture" means any act by which severe pain or suffering, whether physical or mental, is intentionally inflicted on a person for such purposes as obtaining from him or a third person information or a confession, punishing him for an act he or a third person has committed or is suspected of having committed, or intimidating or coercing him or a third person, or for any reason based on discrimination of any kind, when such pain or suffering is inflicted by or at the instigation of or with the consent or acquiescence of a public official or other person acting in an official capacity. It does not include pain or suffering arising only from, inherent in or incidental to lawful sanctions.[13]

In addition to prohibiting torture, the Convention binds signatories to "undertake to prevent . . . other acts of cruel, inhuman or degrading treatment or punishment which do not amount to torture."[14] The Convention does not define "cruel, inhuman or degrading treatment or punishment," but the United Nation's Code of Conduct for Law Enforcement Officials says that the phrase "should be interpreted so as to extend the widest possible protection against abuses, whether physical or mental."[15]

International tribunals have given additional content to these definitions and to the distinctions between them. Thus, severe beatings that do not break bones or cause lesions but cause intense pain and swelling are "classic" forms of torture.[16] Torture also includes the combination of being made to stand all day for days at a time, beatings, and withholding food; beatings and being buried alive; electric shocks, beatings, being hung with one's arms behind one's back, having one's head forced under water until nearly asphyxiated, and being made to stand for hours.[17] Rape or threats of physical mutilation are torture as well.

Another series of cases has found that certain combinations of conduct are torture *and* cruel or inhuman treatment. Without sorting out which specific practices fell into which category, they include: being beaten, given electric shocks and then forced to stand, hooded, for long hours, where the victim then fell, broke his leg, and was denied medical treatment for a period of time; electric shocks, having one's hooded head put into foul water, having objects forced into one's anus, and being forced to remain standing, hooded and handcuffed, for several days; and enduring a fractured jaw while being kept hanging for hours by the arms, subjected to electric shocks, thrown on the floor, covered in chains connected to electric current, and kept naked and wet. In a third group of cases, the European Commission of Human Rights found that beatings and one or more instances of electric shock, mock execution, or refusal of food and water were either torture *or* inhuman treatment.

Few cases address the distinction between torture and inhuman treatment, probably because both are barred and claims of government necessity rarely arise. Perhaps beatings that are not severe or sustained, or an isolated practice—such as wall-standing (being forced to stand spreadeagled on one's toes with fingers on the wall above one's head, so that the body weight is on the toes and fingers)—would be inhuman treatment but not torture. Similarly, the line between inhuman and permissible treatment is not clear. One case suggests that slaps and blows after arrest do not amount to cruel or inhuman treatment, but the court's decision turned, in part, on a finding that "most detainees had 'tolerated . . . and even taken for granted . . . a certain roughness of treatment.'"[18] The troubling assertion that the victim's expectations can turn coercion into acceptable conduct creates a shifting and exploitable standard. More obviously, not all forms of psychological pressure—a staple of police interrogation worldwide—are inhuman treatment.

The most significant case to examine the difference between torture and cruel or inhuman treatment is *Ireland v. United Kingdom.* In the early 1970s, British forces subjected suspected Irish Republican Army (IRA) members to wall-standing for hours, hooding, continuous loud and hissing noise, sleep deprivation, and restricted food and water.[19] The European Commission of Human Rights found that these practices, used together, amounted to torture,[20] but the European Court of Human Rights reversed by a divided vote. The court found that the British practices were inhuman and degrading but were not torture. The court explained that the difference between the two "derives principally from a difference in the intensity of the suffering inflicted." Because torture is an "aggravated" form of inhuman treatment that carries "a special stigma," it should be reserved for practices that exhibit a "particular intensity and cruelty."[21] The court's decision received significant criticism from commentators and human rights groups who believe that the British practices were clearly torture, but it remains a significant precedent.

Israeli interrogation practices—including prolonged standing or uncomfortable sitting positions, tight hand or ankle cuffing, loud noise, sleep deprivation, hooding, cold rooms, and violent shaking[22]—have also been the subject of significant international dispute. The U.N. Committee against Torture and the Special Rapporteur on Torture concluded that these practices are torture.[23] With the exception of shaking, however, the conduct of Israeli interrogators was not much different from that of British forces in Northern Ireland. In fact, an Israeli commission investigated the use of these practices and concluded that they were legally authorized in advance by analogy to the necessity defense. The Commission specifically denied that these methods were torture and cautioned that interrogators would have to be careful not to cross the line from physical force to torture.[24]

The Supreme Court of Israel ultimately prohibited most of these forms of coercion because they were not authorized by law. The court described several of these practices as degrading, harmful, or unnecessary but never suggested that they were torture under Israeli or international law. Significantly, the court also made clear that a justification defense would be available in individual criminal prosecutions of interrogators for using these methods.[25]

The Israeli situation presents the potential importance under the Convention for determining the difference between torture and the lesser—but still illegal—category of cruel, inhuman, or degrading treatment. The Convention bars torture absolutely. "No exceptional circumstances whatsoever, whether a state of war or threat of war, internal political instability or any other public emergency, may be invoked as a justification of torture." By contrast, states that ratify the Convention must "undertake to prevent" cruel, inhuman, or degrading treatment, but the "no exceptional circumstances" provision does not apply.[26] Thus, if conduct similar to Israel's former practices would not be torture under the Convention, an exceptional circumstances justification could be available. Some commentators strongly disapprove of the idea that exceptional circumstances could justify the infliction of cruel, inhuman, or degrading treatment, but the text of the Convention clearly supports that interpretation.[27]

Another important issue under international law is the legal status of the person being interrogated or detained. The Geneva Conventions ban the use of "torture [or] any other form of coercion"—including threats, insults, or "unpleasant or disadvantageous treatment of any kind"—on prisoners of war.[28] A similar protection extends to civilians during hostilities or occupations.[29] The Conventions do not apply to illegal combatants, however, although the less specific protections of the Convention against Torture remain in force.[30] Thus, determinations about status, which are a matter of controversy with respect to many of the people held in custody by U.S. forces, could have an impact on a prisoner's right to be free of at least some coercive practices.

Torture under U.S. Law

In the course of consenting to the Convention, the United States Senate restricted the definition of torture by requiring specific intent "to inflict severe physical or mental pain or suffering" and narrowing the concept of mental harm.[31] The Senate also tried to give clearer content to the category of cruel, inhuman, or degrading treatment. According to the Senate, "the United States considers itself bound by the obligation . . . to prevent 'cruel, inhuman or degrading treatment or punishment,' only insofar as the term . . . means the cruel, unusual and inhuman treatment or punishment prohibited by the Fifth, Eighth, and/or Fourteenth Amendments to the Constitution of the United States."[32] In other words, the Senate declared that the Convention bans conduct that is already unconstitutional.

The State Department attempted to explain the difference between torture and cruel, inhuman, or degrading treatment by insisting that "[t]orture is an extreme form of cruel and inhuman treatment and does not include lesser forms of cruel, inhuman or degrading treatment or punishment."[33] More broadly, the State Department has asserted that torture is illegal in the United States under any circumstances:

> Torture is prohibited by law throughout the United States. It is categorically denounced as a matter of policy and as a tool of state authority. . . . No official of the government, federal, state or local, civilian or military, is authorized to commit or to instruct anyone else to commit torture. Nor may any official condone or tolerate torture in any form. No exceptional circumstances may be invoked as a justification for torture. U.S. law contains no provision permitting otherwise prohibited acts of torture or other cruel, inhuman or degrading treatment or punishment to be employed on grounds of exigent circumstances (for example, during a "state of public emergency") or on orders from a superior officer or public authority.[34]

Whether this categorical statement still holds after the September 11 attacks remains to be seen. Indeed, some Bush administration officials have advanced controversial arguments about executive power to interrogate that contradict the State Department's earlier position.[35]

Notably, the Senate's statement that the definition of cruel, inhuman, or degrading treatment or punishment must be tied to the Fifth, Eighth, and Fourteenth Amendments gives federal courts the ultimate power to define our international obligations. A series of cases assessing the voluntariness of confessions under the due process clause suggests that these obligations could be broad.[36] But if the Court limits the applicability of these cases or changes course and determines that a particular practice is constitutional, then that practice is permitted under international law as well, at least as the United States understands it.

The Supreme Court's recent decision in *Chavez v. Martinez* provides a particularly powerful example. A police officer interrogated Olivero Martinez for forty-five minutes while doctors attempted to treat him for life-threatening wounds inflicted by other officers. Martinez sued the officer for damages. In an amicus brief opposing Martinez's claim, the solicitor general suggested a need for flexibility in the face of "imminent threats."[37] The possibility of a "necessity exception" for coercive interrogations was an issue at oral argument as well.[38] A badly divided Court held that Martinez had no Fifth Amendment self-incrimination claim but might have a substantive due process claim. On the Fifth Amendment claim, four justices asserted that "mere coercion does not violate the text of the Self-Incrimination Clause absent use of the compelled statements in a criminal case against the witness."[39] Two concurring justices agreed that there could be no Fifth Amendment damages claim in most cases involving coercive interrogations, but they held out the possibility that exceptional cases could support such a claim.[40] For substantive due process, three justices applied the "shocks the conscience" test, which considers whether the conduct at issue was "'unjustifiable by any government interest.'" They declared that "the need to investigate whether there had been police misconduct constituted a justifiable government interest given the risk that key evidence would have been lost if Martinez had died [without telling] his side of the story."[41]

The *Chavez* Court diminished the constitutional importance of coercive interrogation claims, and a plurality explicitly embraced the idea that the constitutionality of a coercive interrogation turns in part on the necessity for obtaining the information. Critically, because of the way in which the Senate gave its consent to the Convention, the holdings of *Chavez* and its progeny will define the obligations of the United States under international law.

Expanding the Definition

The legal definitions of torture and cruel, inhuman, or degrading treatment or punishment are carefully negotiated compromises that do not exhaust the questions of what torture is or how it operates. For example, the traditional connection between torture and the quest for information provides a formal motive for violence that, in Elaine Scarry's words, "enables the torturer's power to be understood in terms of his own vulnerability and need" and thus "deflect[s] the natural reflex of sympathy away from the actual sufferer" and toward the torturer.[42] When employed as punishment, torture risks becoming a ritual, a social and even aesthetic experience that exists for its own sake and for the sake of those consciously performing or observing the rite.[43] Yet if torture sometimes reflects the torturer's own claims of vulnerability and even functions as a ritualized and impersonal practice, then legal definitions aimed at official state policies and goals cannot capture its full scope or meaning.

Further, the impulse to torture may derive from the identification of the torture victim with a larger challenge to social order or values.[44] This possibility takes on greater salience amid claims that the threat of terrorism requires aggressive self-defense in a post–September 11 world. More generally, gathering information or inflicting punishment may be the stated motives for torture, but they may not be its only purpose. Rather, torture

> is designed to demonstrate the end of the normative world of the victim—the end of what the victim values, the end of the bonds that constitute the community in which the values are grounded. . . . The torturer and the victim do end up creating their own terrible "world," but this world derives its meaning from being imposed upon the ashes of another. The logic of that world is complete domination, though the objective may never be realized.[45]

In other words, at times when social order is threatened, especially by people seen as outsiders or subordinates, torture may function as a method of individual or collective assertion that creates a perhaps illusory sense of overcoming vulnerability by the thorough domination of others.

The domination effected by torture plays out in several ways. Intense pain warps and destroys human perception and personality. Even more, torture uses, inverts, and destroys the trappings of civilization. Thus, torture mocks the law, using punishment to gather evidence to justify the punishment already inflicted, rather than using evidence already gathered to justify punishment.[46] When torture becomes an official policy, the victims' suffering and pain lose legal relevance, and they become further isolated just when they most need the law's protections.

Torture is also "world-destroying" in its ability to invert and degrade the ideas of agency, consent, and responsibility that help shape our ideas of self and of self-government. The process is perversely straightforward. Once torture begins, the result is always the product of the victim's "choice." If the victim provides information, then he or she is weak, perhaps even a betrayer—but in either event a person who has chosen to talk. Yet these words unfairly ascribe agency and responsibility to the victim and conceal the destruction and pain caused by the torturer. If, on the other hand, the victim resists, then he or she will be tortured again, but again the victim is responsible. According to the logic of torture, if the victim talks, the pain will cease; by failing to talk, the victim consents to more torture.[47]

The logic of "consent" and "responsibility" suggests an important but often overlooked characteristic of torture: escalation. The victim's resistance leads to more and greater pain, to greater destruction of the victim's normative world, and to more complete domination. Importantly, however, escalation is not just about greater pain over time but also about beginning with a relatively milder amount of pain or coercion combined with the possibility of more. Torture can encompass this continuum; it can include not just the most intensely painful practices but also all the practices that use pain to punish or gather information, upend the victim's worldview, and express the domination of the state and the torturer. Escalation, in other words, is another way of describing the total power of the torturer and the corresponding powerlessness of the victim. Indeed, the victim's knowledge of the torturer's ability to escalate the pain at will is an important component of torture's dominating, world-destroying capacity.

In short, a victim who "breaks" at the beginning of coercive or inhuman treatment has still been tortured if he or she reasonably believes that progressively worse treatment would follow. The purposeful infliction of severe pain, whether or not accompanied by the threat of escalation, is torture. But so too is a practice that lasts relatively briefly and causes less than severe pain, if it does so against a background of total control and potential escalation that asserts the state's dominance over the victim. The difference between wall-standing and the rack is a matter of degree, not of kind.

Thus, torture is not merely the infliction of severe pain to gather information or punish. Rather, torture is also the infliction of potentially escalating pain for purposes that include dominating the victim and ascribing responsibility to the victim for the pain incurred. This definition broadens the Convention's carefully negotiated definition of torture and deliberately blurs the uneasy distinction between torture and cruel, inhuman, or degrading treatment or punishment.[48] Because this definition provides a more complete account of torture, it will help us assess reports that the United States is engaged in unduly coercive interrogation.

Torture at Home and Abroad

Overseas Interrogations

Recent news reports suggest that the United States has adopted a range of interrogation practices that are illegal under domestic and international law. Detainees in Afghanistan have been slapped and beaten. Some were "kept standing or kneeling for hours, in black hoods or spray-painted goggles [or] held in awkward, painful positions and deprived of sleep with a 24-hour bombardment of lights." At least one suspect who was suffering from gunshot wounds was given pain-killing drugs "selectively" to make him talk. Psychological tactics are also common. The same and worse conduct has been inflicted on detainees in Iraq. Finally, an unknown number of those who do not cooperate are sent to other countries, such as Jordan, Egypt, Morocco, and Syria, "whose practice of torture has been documented by the U.S. government and human rights organizations."[49]

Compared to the cases in which courts or commissions have found torture, most of these methods, considered individually, do not unequivocally rise to the level of torture under international law, although the beatings allegedly meted out by U.S. Special Forces could qualify as torture in the form of inflicting severe pain for the purpose of interrogation or intimidation. Similarly, the more extreme practices used against Iraqis are clearly torture. Withholding medical treatment may also qualify as torture, depending on the severity of the wounds and the length of time treatment was withheld, although the Supreme Court's decision in *Chavez* casts some doubt on that claim. Most psychological tactics do not raise serious questions of torture or cruel, inhuman, or degrading treatment.[50] Some tactics, however—such as exploiting a prisoner's phobias, making threats to use specific methods of torture, or threatening to send him to another country for the purpose of having him tortured[51]—may cause significant mental anguish and thus cross the line between permissible and impermissible conduct. Importantly, whether or not individual U.S. interrogation practices are torture, most of them probably qualify as cruel, inhuman, or degrading treatment.

Considered as a group, the more routine practices may be torture. Yet with the exception of beatings and the withholding of medical treatment, the interrogation methods adopted by U.S. forces are strikingly similar to those employed in the past by Britain and Israel, and a strong argument exists that these actions are cruel, inhuman, or degrading treatment, not torture. In sum, many of the methods used by U.S. forces to interrogate suspected terrorists violate the Convention, but relatively few of them are torture, perhaps not even when used together.

The similarity to British and Israeli methods may be purposeful. If obtaining information is the primary goal, more severe methods may be ineffective because the victim becomes useless as a source of information or simply provides false information in an effort to end the pain. British and Israeli "precedents" provide methods that have been successful in some instances.[52] Policymakers may also be attempting to observe the ban against torture while giving latitude to interrogators in the fight against terrorism. With an eye on the international community, they may be seeking to avoid the stigma of engaging in "torture." Perhaps even the theoretical availability of a necessity defense (even if only in the court of public opinion) to charges of cruel, inhuman, or degrading treatment—but not torture—has played a role.

Under the broader definition of torture I sketched earlier, however, beatings and the withholding of medical treatment are clearly torture, as are most of the other methods that U.S. officials are using (at least when used as a group)—just as they were when practiced by British and Israeli forces. In each instance, coercive practices routinely and purposefully inflicted pain on prisoners.[53] Indeed, the creation of a coercive routine makes it more likely that escalating pain or discomfort—or the threat of escalation—is part of the interrogation. Less painful tactics such as hooding, continuous noise, and extreme temperatures seek to bewilder, disorient, and control the victim—that is, to upend his worldview and to dominate him thoroughly.

Moreover, U.S. interrogation practices take place against a background of terrorism directed at the United States and its citizens, which has created a sense of vulnerability and social upheaval. In the British and Israeli contexts, the high stakes of the struggle sharpened already raw differences between Catholics and Protestants and between Israelis and Palestinians. In the U.S. context, the collective horror from the September 11 attacks fosters indifference toward detainees captured outside the United States who are of a different culture than our dominant cultures and who share the Middle Eastern origin of the September 11 terrorists (and, of course, who may themselves be terrorists). Taken together, one would not be surprised to learn that interrogators in each country use or used pain for the purpose of dominating particular suspects in addition to seeking information from them.

Domestic Practices

Although most interrogations of suspected terrorists occur overseas, the conduct of domestic law enforcement officials is relevant both to determining the range of circumstances in which the United States could be accused of torturing and to considering the ways in which definitions of torture apply in ordinary as well as extraordinary situations.

The most obvious places to look for torture are police interrogation and prison conditions. The voluntariness of a confession under the due process clause depends on a totality of the circumstances test that encompasses but goes well beyond torture. In the prison context, torture is a form of cruel and unusual punishment under the Eighth Amendment.[54] Within this framework, reports frequently arise of brutality that clearly amounts to cruel, inhuman, and degrading treatment and sometimes rises to the level of torture. Recent examples include the Area Two scandal in Chicago, the Rampart scandal in Los Angeles, and the torture of Abner Louima by New York police.[55] *Chavez v. Martinez* confirms that remedies for this kind of conduct may be limited and highlights the idea of government necessity. Although the Court insisted that damages remain available for torture, the plurality left the term undefined.[56]

Consider, too, the policy that authorized the use of chokeholds by Los Angeles police whenever an officer felt there was a threat of violence.[57] To the extent this policy allowed officers to base their actions on subjective fears and gut reactions, racial stereotypes—whether conscious or unconscious—almost certainly played a role in the decision whether to use a chokehold.[58] The policy may also have created an incentive for officers to use force to overcome fear by dominating the person "responsible" for creating it. Moreover, studies indicate that African Americans endure a disproportionate share of police violence.[59] That finding played out in Los Angeles. In at least one case, officers used a chokehold against a cooperative African American male who was not under suspicion of any significant offense. Chokeholds killed sixteen people in Los Angeles, twelve of whom were African American males, a ratio clearly disproportionate to the relevant population.[60]

Seen in this way, chokeholds resonate powerfully with other forms of state-sanctioned violence that historically functioned to enforce white dominance over blacks. Similarly, coercive treatment of suspected Palestinian, IRA, or al-Qaeda terrorists resonates powerfully as a symbol of the uncertain threats posed by terrorism and the efforts by dominant groups to maintain supremacy against a background of hostility and violence—an effort sometimes accompanied by a claim of justification. A state's ability to maintain order is intimately connected to its power to use violence across a continuum in which coercion risks sliding into torture, and the risk increases when torturer and victim have different racial, ethnic, religious, or cultural identities.

Chokeholds are similar to torture for an additional reason. One of the characteristics of torture is the way responsibility for the pain flips from the torturer to the victim. In *City of Los Angeles v. Lyons,* the victim's responsibility for his injuries emerged from subsequent cases, in which courts suggested that his status as a lawbreaker—driving with a broken taillight—was crucial to the Supreme Court's decision that he could not seek an injunction against chokeholds.[61] The Court thus performed the double trick of erasing race-based domination from the case while ascribing responsibility for intentional police violence to the victim of that violence. If Lyons was responsible for his injuries even though he offered no resistance, the responsibility of other victims of police violence who resisted even slightly or engaged in conduct that would allow a police officer to fear resistance follows *a fortiori*. And the responsibility of enemy combatants and accused terrorists is obvious.

In short, the actions at issue in police violence cases—whether or not involving interrogation—have much in common with the treatment of suspected terrorists. Both commonly involve the purposeful infliction of potentially escalating pain in order to dominate the victim, combined with the ascription to the victim of responsibility for that pain. Notably, the search for information provides a basis for masking and perhaps even seeking to justify the nature of the interrogation practices underway overseas, but that rationale is lacking in many police violence cases.

Domestic cases also reveal that claims of torture do not arise only on the international stage or at times of extraordinary threats. Most torture is inflicted by law enforcement or security officials on residents of their own country, and the tensions that contribute to the torture can be relatively mundane. The ongoing problem of police violence also highlights the fact that we have long had a law of torture in the United States. We should be careful about repeating in other countries the practices we have sought to root out here, and we should recognize that our actions abroad have uncomfortable resonances with recurring practices at home.

Necessity

Although torture is an awful practice, terrorist attacks against civilians who have no meaningful connection to the terrorists' grievances are equally wrong.[62] Moreover, preventing terrorism has become one of the most significant tasks for modern governments, even as protecting individual rights and liberties is at least as important. Against this background, we cannot completely reject the evil of torture as a method of combating terrorism, regardless of what international law provides. If torture provides the last remaining chance to save lives in imminent peril, the necessity defense should be available to justify the interrogators' conduct. The possibility of justification, in other words, is part of the definition of torture.[63]

If this approach is correct, then we must ask whether U.S. practices in Afghanistan, Iraq, and other places are justified. The answer, to date, is fairly clear. First, our conduct has purposes that go beyond foiling future acts of terrorism, such as learning who was involved in or provided support for past attacks, destroying entities that support terrorism, and intimidating or pacifying our prisoners. These purposes cannot justify torture unless we are willing to embrace a policy of mistreating people who may have knowledge (or perhaps just guilty knowledge) of terrorist activity in general or who are hostile to us. The same is true of cruel, inhuman, or degrading treatment. Although the level of necessity would be lower for what international law defines as a lesser harm, general claims of need are not sufficient. Indeed, if such claims were to justify cruel, inhuman, or degrading treatment abroad, we would have trouble preventing the same claims from justifying it at home. The necessity argument should attain meaningful weight only when we have information about a specific attack.

Second, even where the purpose of our interrogations is to prevent future attacks, physical mistreatment does not receive a blanket justification. The future almost surely will bring more terrorist attacks on the United States, but necessity claims usually require imminent peril.[64] Without firm suspicion that a particular individual has specific knowledge about specific, imminent attacks, coercive interrogation should not be an option. For that reason, current U.S. practices are unjustified. U.S. forces appear to have adopted a policy of physical coercion that applies to large numbers of detainees who almost certainly lack specific knowledge of future attacks. To be justifiable, torture must be the exception, not the norm. Yet accounts of our practices suggest, at least, that cruel, inhuman, or degrading treatment is the norm. Here, too, we see the significance of the plurality opinion in *Chavez,* which relied on necessity as a justification for otherwise unconstitutional interrogation in less than exigent circumstances.

Third, the argument from necessity is inadequate in one significant way. Even if torture could be justified in a specific case as a matter of criminal law, we still must ask if it is wise. The focus of the necessity defense is narrower than the focus of the policymaker, and using torture or cruel, inhuman, or degrading treatment may not be wise from that broader perspective even if it is justified as a matter of law.

The detention of high-level members of al-Qaeda puts this reasoning to its strongest test so far, because they are the most likely to have specific knowledge of future attacks. But that probability alone cannot justify coercive interrogation. Just as escalation is part of the definition of torture, so too is it part of necessity. Except under the most extreme circumstances, coercion must be a last resort, not a routine practice, even with people as little deserving of our sympathy and as likely to have specific knowledge as the leaders of al-Qaeda.

Here, then, is the dilemma posed by a complete definition of torture. Technical legal terms cannot mask or limit torture's evil. The seemingly eternal human urge to torture requires our vigilance and broad condemnation. Yet torture may be a legitimate option—the lesser of two evils—in rare circumstances. In theory, we can admit an exception to an otherwise universal prohibition without undermining the values that gave rise to that prohibition. But what of practice—is there such a thing as principled torture? Even if such a thing exists, reports of U.S. practices suggest that adhering to those principles is difficult indeed.

Notes

For earlier elaborations of the ideas of developed here, see John T. Parry, "What Is Torture, Are We Doing It, and What If We Are?" *University of Pittsburgh Law Review* 64 (2003): 237, and John T. Parry and Welsh S. White, "Interrogating Suspected Terrorists: Should Torture Be an Option?" *University of Pittsburgh Law Review* 63 (2002): 743.

1. Mark Bowden, "The Dark Art of Interrogation," *Atlantic Monthly,* October 2003, 51, 56, quoting testimony Black gave to Congress.

2. Jess Bravin and Gary Fields, "How Do U.S. Interrogators Make a Captured Terrorist Talk?" *Wall Street Journal,* March 4, 2003, B1.

3. Dana Priest and Barton Gellman, "U.S. Decries Abuse but Defends Interrogations," *Washington Post,* December 26, 2002, A1.

4. Tania Branigan, "Ex-Prisoners Allege Rights Abuses by U.S. Military," *Washington Post,* August 19, 2003, A2.

5. Barbara Starr, *Afghan Detainees' Deaths Ruled Homicides,* available online at: www.cnn.com/2003/US/03/05/?detainee.homicides/index.html (March 5, 2003); see also "Two Inmate Deaths at U.S. Base Ruled Homicides," *Los Angeles Times,* March 6, 2003, sec. 1, 14.

6. See Priest and Gellman, "U.S. Decries Abuse," quoting the national security official; Bowden, *Dark Art,* 56, quoting the former agent.

7. Priest and Gellman, "U.S. Decries Abuse," quoting an official who supervised the detention of accused terrorists.

8. See *Amnesty International Criticizes U.S. Handling of Terror Suspects,* available online at: www.cnn.com/2003/US/?03/05/terror.amnesty.internat/index.html (March 5, 2003); Human Rights Watch, *Reports of Torture of Al-Qaeda Suspects* (December 27, 2002), available online at www.hrw.org/press/2002/12/US1227.htm.

9. Bravin and Fields, *U.S. Interrogators.*

10. See Peter Slevin, "U.S. Pledges Not to Torture Terror Suspects," *Washington Post,* June 27, 2003, A1.

11. Elizabeth Bumiller and Eric Schmitt, "President Sorry for Iraq Abuse," *New York Times,* May 7, 2004, A1; Richard W. Stevenson, "Bush, on Arab TV, Denounces Abuse of Iraqi Captives," *New York Times,* May 6, 2004.

12. See Bowden, *Dark Art,* 56, 70–71, suggesting the administration and human rights groups are using different definitions of "torture."

13. Convention against Torture and Other Cruel, Inhuman or Degrading Treatment or Punishment, pt. 1, art. 1, par. 1 (1984) (hereafter Convention), available online at: www.un.org/documents/ga/res/39/a39r046.htm and reprinted in relevant part as the appendix to Sanford Levinson's introductory essay herein.

14. Convention, pt. 1, art. 16, par. 1. The International Covenant on Civil and Political Rights also distinguishes between torture and cruel, inhuman, or degrading treatment but does not define torture. See International Covenant on Civil and Political Rights, art. 7 (1966) (hereafter International Covenant), available online at: www.unhcr.ch/html/menu3/b/a_ccpr.htm. The European Convention on Human Rights makes a similar distinction. See Nigel S. Rodley, *The Treatment of Prisoners Under International Law,* annex 9c, 2nd ed. (1999), 468. The Inter-American Convention to Prevent and Punish Torture (hereafter Inter-American Convention) does not distinguish between torture and other prohibited conduct, but its definition of torture is broader than the Convention's, most notably because it does not require that the "physical or mental pain or suffering" be severe. See annex 2b, 402.

15. G.A. Res. 169, U.N. GAOR, 34th Sess., supp. no. 46, art. 5, cmt. c, U.N. Doc. A/RES/34/169 (1979), available online at: www.un.org/documents/ga/res/34/a34res169.pdf. See J. Herman Burgers and Hans Danelius, *The United Nations Convention Against Torture* (1988), 149; "while the concept of torture could be defined in reasonably precise terms, it was impossible to draft a precise definition of other cruel, inhuman or degrading treatment or punishment."

16. Rodley, *Treatment of Prisoners,* discussing the 1969 "Greek case," 77.

17. The cases discussed in this and the following two paragraphs are described in greater detail in ibid., 86–90, 95–96, 101–105.

18. See ibid., 103–104, quoting the "Greek case."

19. Ibid., 91.

20. See *Ireland v. United Kingdom,* 1976 Y.B. Eur. Conv. on H.R. 512 (European Commission of Human Rights), 792–794.

21. *Ireland v. United Kingdom,* app. no. 5310/71, 2 Eur. H.R. Rep. 25 (European Court of Human Rights), 79–80.

22. See Rodley, *Treatment of Prisoners,* 94–95, describing the techniques; John T. Parry, "Judicial Restraints on Illegal State Violence: Israel and the United States," *Vanderbilt Journal of Transnational Law* 35 (2002): 73, 88, n. 75, same.

23. See Rodley, *Treatment of Prisoners,* 95.

24. See Report of the Commission of Inquiry into the Methods of Investigation of the General Security Service Regarding Hostile Terrorist Activity (1987), excerpted in *Israel Law Review* 23 (1989): 146, 167–176.

25. H.C. 5100/94, *Public Committee Against Torture in Israel v. The State of Israel,* 53(4) P.D. 817 (1999) (hereafter *Public Committee*), reprinted in *International Legal Materials* 38 (1999): 1471, 1478, 1480–1486. For extensive analysis of *Public Committee,* see Parry, *Judicial Restraints.*

26. Compare Convention, pt. 1, art. 2, par. 2, and pt. 1, at. 16, par. 1. See Committee on International Human Rights, *The Convention against Torture and Other Cruel, Inhuman or Degrading Treatment of Punishment, Rec. of the Ass'n of the B. of the City of N.Y.* 42 (1987): 235, 240, noting this distinction.

27. Compare Rodley, *Treatment of Prisoners,* 81–82, 84, noting and appearing to endorse the view of the European Commission of Human Rights that exceptional circumstances justifications could support the reduction of the torturer's sentence, with Burgers and Danelius, *United Nations Convention,* 124, suggesting the Convention should be read together with the International Covenant to include an absolute ban on cruel, inhuman, or degrading treatment. The International Covenant, also ratified by the United States, declares that neither torture nor cruel, inhuman, or degrading treatment can be justified by a "public emergency." See International Covenant, art. 4. Similarly, the Inter-American Convention—which the United States has neither signed nor ratified—does not allow emergency justifications for violating its broader ban on torture. See Inter-American Convention, art. 5. The documents are clearly in tension, but the Convention is the more specific and significant source of international law on issues relating to interrogation.

28. See Convention Relative to the Treatment of Prisoners of War, August 12, 1949, arts. 3, 13, and 17, avalable online at: www.hri.ca/uninfo/treaties/92.shtml.

29. See Convention Relative to the Protection of Civilian Persons in Time of War, August 12, 1949, arts. 3 and 4, available online at: www.hri.ca/uninfo/treaties/93.shtml.

30. See George H. Aldrich, "The Taliban, al Qaeda, and the Determination of Illegal Combatants," *American Journal of International Law* 96 (2002): 891, 892–893.

31. Resolution of Advice and Consent to Ratification of the Convention against Torture and Other Forms of Cruel, Inhuman or Degrading Treatment or Punishment: Reservations, Declarations, and Understandings, part II(1)(a), 136 Cong. Rec. S17491 (daily ed. October 27, 1990).

32. Ibid., part I(1).

33. 22 C.F.R. sec. 95.1(b)(7) (2002).

34. U.S. Department of State, *Initial Report of the United States of America to the U.N. Committee against Torture* (1999).

35. See Working Group Report on Detainee Interrogations in the Global War on

Terrorism: Assessment of Legal, Historical, Policy, and Operational Considerations (March 6, 2003).

36. See Parry and White, *Interrogating Suspected Terrorists,* 748–751.

37. Brief for the United States as Amicus Curiae Supporting Petitioner, *Chavez v. Martinez,* 123 S. Ct. 1994 (2003) (no. 01-1444), 24–25.

38. Transcript of Oral Argument (December 4, 2002), *Chavez v. Martinez,* 123 S. Ct. 1994 (2003) (no. 01-1444), 34–35, 45–46.

39. *Chavez v. Martinez,* 123 S. Ct. 1994, 2002 (2003), plurality opinion.

40. See ibid., 2007, J. Souter concurring in the judgment.

41. Ibid., 2005–2006, plurality opinion, quoting *County of Sacramento v. Lewis,* 523 U.S. 833, 849 (1998). Five justices voted to remand the substantive due process claim, but only three justices explicitly contested the plurality's discussion of substantive due process.

42. Elaine Scarry, *The Body in Pain* (1985), 58.

43. See Michel Foucault, *Discipline and Punish: The Birth of the Prison,* trans. Alan Sheridan (New York: Vintage Books, 1999), 3–16, 28–29, 32–57; Alan Hyde, *Bodies of Law* (1997), 187–191; Kate Millet, *The Politics of Cruelty: An Essay on the Literature of Imprisonment* (1994), 107–108.

44. See, e.g., Millet, *Politics of Cruelty,* 101, 108–109.

45. Robert Cover, "Violence and the Word," *Yale Law Journal* 95 (1986): 1601, 1603, reprinted in *Narrative, Violence, and the Law: The Essays of Robert Cover,* ed. Martha Minow, (1993), 203, 205–206.

46. See Franz Kafka, "In the Penal Colony," in *The Complete Stories* trans. Willa Muir and Edwin Muir (New York: Schocken, 1976), 140, 145: "There would be no point in telling him [his sentence]. He'll learn it on his body."

47. See Henry Shue, chapter 2 herein, assessing this logic; see Barbara Maria Stafford, "Difficult Content, or the Pleasures of Viewing Pain," in *Good Looking: Essays on the Virtue of Images* (1996), describing the manufacture of a "voyeuristic fiction that the object [of vivisection] agreed to its exhibition," 168, 182.

48. In the language of the Convention, a victim's awareness of potential escalation could be relevant to determining whether he endured mental suffering at a level of severity amounting to torture. My discussion also can be described as elaborating on the "intimidation" aspect of the Convention's definition of torture.

49. Priest and Gellman, "U.S. Decries Abuse." The Convention forbids sending detainees to other countries where they will be tortured, although it is less clear about sending them to places where they will be subjected to cruel, inhuman, or degrading treatment. See Parry, *What Is Torture?,* 245 n. 42.

50. For example, officials may seek to convince a prisoner that he is being held by a country that employs torture. See Priest and Gellman, "U.S. Decries Abuse." Although obviously designed to cause anguish, this tactic is probably permissible un-

less the deceit includes specific threats of torture. Other tactics include feigned friendship, respect, or sensitivity (see Priest and Gellman, *U.S. Decries Abuse*) or the use of female interrogators on devout Muslims (see Dale Van Natta, Jr., "Questioning Terror Suspects in a Dark and Surreal World," *New York Times,* March 9, 2003, 1.

51. See Bravin and Fields, "U.S. Interrogators."

52. See Van Natta, "Questioning Terror Suspects," 1, discussing information obtained from al-Quaeda members; see also *Ireland v. United Kingdom,* App. No. 5310/71, 2 Eur. H.R. Rep. 25, 60, finding that British interrogators obtained "a considerable quantity of intelligence information" through coercive interrogations; Jason S. Greenberg, "Torture of Terrorists in Israel: The United Nations and the Supreme Court of Israel Pave the Way for Human Rights to Trump Communitarianism," *ILSA Journal of International and Comparative Law* 7 (2001): 539, 546, noting similar methods had some success in Israel.

53. See Parry, *Judicial Restraints,* 88–90, discussing Israel; *Ireland,* 2 Eur. H.R. Rep. at 59–60, discussing Britain.

54. See *Hudson v. McMillian,* 503 U.S. 1, 6–9 (1992).

55. See Susan Bandes, "Patterns of Injustice: Police Brutality in the Courts," *Buffalo Law Review* 47 (2000): 1275, discussing the Area Two scandal and other police brutality cases; Parry, *Judicial Restraints,* 31, discussing several police brutality cases.

56. See *Chavez,* 123 S. Ct., 2004. Injunctions against torture will rarely if ever be available under federal law. See Parry, *Judicial Restraints,* 97–100.

57. See *City of Los Angeles v. Lyons,* 461 U.S. 95 (1983); Parry, *Judicial Restraints,* 84.

58. See Jody D. Armour, "Race Ipsa Loquitur: Of Reasonable Racists, Intelligent Bayesians, and Involuntary Negrophobes," *Stanford Law Review* 46 (1994): 781, 784–785, 793–796; Charles R. Lawrence, III, "The Id, the Ego, and Equal Protection: Reckoning with Unconscious Racism," *Stanford Law Review* 39 (1987): 317, 330–344.

59. See Parry, *Judicial Restraints,* 77 n. 14 (collecting citations).

60. See *Lyons,* 461 U.S., 95, 99, 100; 116–117, J. Marshall, dissenting; Parry, *Judicial Restraints,* 82 n. 33.

61. See *Spencer v. Kemna,* 523 U.S. 1, 15 (1998); *Hodgers-Durgin v. de la Vina,* 199 F.3d 1037, 1041 (9th Cir. 1999).

62. For a discussion of collective responsibility issues in the context of terrorism, see John T. Parry, "Collective and Individual Responsibility for Acts of Terrorism," in *Understanding Evil: An Interdisciplinary Approach,* ed. Margaret Sönser Breen (2003).

63. See Parry and White, *Interrogating Suspected Terrorists,* 763–765.

64. See *United States v. Aguilar,* 883 F.2d 662, 693 (9th Cir. 1989).

Supreme Court of Israel

Judgment Concerning the Legality of the General Security Service's Interrogation Methods (September 6, 1999)

Background

1. The State of Israel has been engaged in an unceasing struggle for both its very existence and security, from the day of its founding. Terrorist organizations have established as their goal Israel's annihilation. Terrorist acts and the general disruption of order are their means of choice. In employing such methods, these groups do not distinguish between civilian and military targets. They carry out terrorist attacks in which scores are murdered in public areas, public transportation, city squares and centers, theaters and coffee shops. They do not distinguish between men, women and children. They act out of cruelty and without mercy.

2. The facts presented before this Court reveal that one hundred and twenty one people died in terrorist attacks between 1.1.96 to 14.5.98. Seven hundred and seven people were injured. A large number of those killed and injured were victims of harrowing suicide bombings in the heart of Israel's cities. Many attacks—including suicide bombings, attempts to detonate car bombs, kidnappings of citizens and soldiers, attempts to highjack buses, murders, the placing of explosives, etc.—were prevented due to the measures taken by the authorities responsible for fighting the above described hostile terrorist activities on a daily basis. The main body responsible for fighting terrorism is the GSS.

In order to fulfill this function, the GSS also investigates those suspected of hostile terrorist activities. The purpose of these interrogations is, among others, to gather information regarding terrorists and their organizing methods for the purpose of thwarting and preventing them from carrying out these terrorist attacks. In the context of these interrogations, GSS investigators also make use of physical means. The legality of these practices is being examined before this Court in these applications. . . .

The Physical Means

8. . . . The decision to utilize physical means in a particular instance is based on internal regulations, which requires obtaining permission from various ranks of the GSS hierarchy. . . . Different interrogation methods are employed depending on the suspect, both in relation to what is required in that situation and to the likelihood of obtaining authorization. The GSS does not resort to every interrogation method at its disposal in each case.

Shaking

9. A number of applicants claimed that the shaking method was used against them. Among the investigation methods outlined in the GSS' interrogation regulations, shaking is considered the harshest. The method is defined as the forceful shaking of the suspect's upper torso, back and forth, repeatedly, in a manner which causes the neck and head to dangle and vacillate rapidly. According to an expert opinion submitted in one of the applications, the shaking method is likely to cause serious brain damage, harm the spinal cord, cause the suspect to lose consciousness, vomit and urinate uncontrollably and suffer serious headaches.

The State entered several countering expert opinions into evidence. It admits the use of this method by the GSS. To its contention, there is no danger to the life of the suspect inherent to shaking; the risk to life as a result of shaking is rare; there is no evidence that shaking causes fatal damage; and medical literature has not to date listed a case in which a person died directly as a result of having been only shaken. In any event, they argue, doctors are present in all interrogation compounds, and instances where the danger of medical damage presents itself are investigated and researched.

All agree that in one particular case the suspect in question expired after being shaken. According to the State, that case constituted a rare exception. . . .

In addition, the State argues in its response that the shaking method is only resorted to in very particular cases, and only as a last resort. The interrogation directives define the appropriate circumstances for its application and the rank responsible for authorizing its use. The investigators were instructed that in every case where they consider resorting to shaking, they must probe the severity of the danger that the interrogation is intending to prevent; consider the urgency of uncovering the information presumably possessed by the suspect in question; and seek an alternative means of preventing the danger. Finally, the directives respecting interrogation state, that in cases where this method is to be used, the investigator must first provide an evaluation of the suspect's health and ensure that no harm comes to him. According to the respondent, shaking is indispensable to fighting and winning the war on terrorism. It is not possible to prohibit its use without seriously harming the GSS' ability to effectively thwart deadly terrorist attacks. Its use in the past has lead to the thwarting of murderous attacks.

Waiting in the "Shabach" Position

10. This interrogation method arose in numerous applications. . . . [A] suspect investigated under the "Shabach" position has his hands tied behind his back. He is seated on a small and low chair, whose seat is tilted forward, towards the ground. One hand is tied behind the suspect, and placed inside the gap between the chair's seat and back support. His second hand is tied behind the chair, against its back support. The suspect's head is covered by an opaque sack, falling down to his shoulders. Powerfully loud music is played in the room. According to the affidavits submitted, suspects are detained in this position for a prolonged period of time, awaiting interrogation at consecutive intervals.

The aforementioned affidavits claim that prolonged sitting in this position causes serious muscle pain in the arms [and] the neck and headaches. The State did not deny the use of this method before this Court. They submit that both crucial security considerations and the investigators' safety require tying up the suspect's hands as he is being interrogated. The head covering is intended to prevent contact between the suspect in question and other suspects. The powerfully loud music is played for the same reason.

The "Frog Crouch"

11. This interrogation method appeared in one of the applications. . . . This refers to consecutive, periodical crouches on the tips of one's toes, each lasting for five minute intervals. The State did not deny the use of this method. . . . Prior to hearing the application, however, this interrogation practice ceased.

Excessive Tightening of Handcuffs

12. In a number of applications before this Court, various applicants have complained of excessive tightening of hand or leg cuffs. To their contention, this practice results in serious injuries to the suspect's hands, arms and feet, due to the length of the interrogations. The applicants invoke the use of particularly small cuffs, ill fitted in relation to the suspect's arm or leg size. The State, for its part, denies any use of unusually small cuffs, arguing that those used were both of standard issue and properly applied. They are, nonetheless, prepared to admit that prolonged hand or foot cuffing is likely to cause injuries to the suspect's hands and feet. To the State's contention, however, injuries of this nature are inherent to any lengthy interrogation.

Sleep Deprivation

13. In a number of applications applicants have complained of being deprived of sleep as a result of being tied in the "Shabach" position, being subjected to the playing of powerfully loud music, or intense nonstop interrogations without sufficient rest breaks. They claim that the purpose of depriving them of sleep is to cause them to break from exhaustion. While the State agrees that suspects are at times deprived of regular sleep hours, it argues that this does not constitute an interrogation method aimed at causing exhaustion, but rather results from the prolonged amount of time necessary for conducting the interrogation.

Applicants' Arguments

14. . . . In principle, all the applications raise two essential arguments: *First,* they submit that the GSS is never authorized to conduct interrogations.

Second, they argue that the physical means employed by GSS investigators not only infringe upon the human dignity of the suspect undergoing interrogation, but in fact constitute criminal offences. These methods, argue the applicants, are in violation of International Law as they constitute "Torture," which is expressly prohibited under International Law. . . . Furthermore, the "necessity" defence which, according to the State, is available to the investigators, is not relevant to the circumstances in question. In any event, the doctrine of "necessity" at most constitutes an exceptional *post factum* defence, exclusively confined to criminal proceedings against investigators. It cannot, however, by any means, provide GSS investigators with the preemptory authorization to conduct interrogations *ab initio.* . . .

We asked the applicants' attorneys whether the "ticking time bomb" rationale was not sufficiently persuasive to justify the use of physical means, for instance, when a bomb is known to have been placed in a public area and will undoubtedly explode causing immeasurable human tragedy if its location is not revealed at once. This question elicited a variety of responses from the various applicants before the Court. There are those convinced that physical means are not to be used under any circumstances; the prohibition on such methods to their mind is absolute, whatever the consequences may be. On the other hand, there are others who argue that even if it is perhaps acceptable to employ physical means in most exceptional "ticking time bomb" circumstances, these methods are in practice used even in absence of the "ticking time bomb" conditions. The very fact that, in most cases, the use of such means is illegal provides sufficient justification for banning their use altogether, even if doing so would inevitably absorb those rare cases in which physical coercion may have been justified. Whatever their particular views, all applicants unanimously highlight the distinction between the ability to potentially escape criminal liability *post factum* and the granting of permission to use physical means for interrogation purposes *ab initio.*

The State's Arguments

15. . . . With respect to the physical means employed by the GSS, the State argues that these do not violate International Law. Indeed, it is submitted that these methods cannot be qualified as "torture," "cruel and inhuman treatment" or "degrading treatment," that are strictly prohibited under In-

ternational Law. Instead, the practices of the GSS do not cause pain and suffering, according to the State's position.

Moreover, the State argues that these means are equally legal under Israel's internal (domestic) law. This is due to the "necessity" defence outlined in article 34(11) of the Penal Law (1977). Hence, in the specific cases bearing the relevant conditions inherent to the "necessity" defence . . . In support of their position, the State notes that the use of physical means by GSS investigators is most unusual and is only employed as a last resort in very extreme cases. Moreover, even in these rare cases, the application of such methods is subject to the strictest of scrutiny and supervision, as per the conditions and restrictions set forth in the [*Report of the Commission of Inquiry Regarding the GSS' Interrogation Practices with Respect to Hostile Terrorist Activities* headed by (ret.) Justice M. Landau, 1987—hereinafter *Commission of Inquiry Report*]. This having been said, when the exceptional conditions requiring the use of these means are in fact present, the above described interrogation methods are fundamental to saving human lives and safeguarding Israel's security.

The Commission of Inquiry's Report

16. The GSS' authority to employ particular interrogation methods, and the relevant law respecting these matters were examined by the *Commission of Inquiry*. . . . Following a prolonged deliberation, the *Commission* concluded that the GSS is authorized to investigate those suspected of hostile terrorist acts, even in absence of express statutory regulation of its activities, in light of the powers granted to it by specific legislation and the government's residual (prerogative) powers. . . . Another part of the *Commission of Inquiry's Report* deals with "the investigator's potential defences" (defences available to the investigator). With regards to this matter, the *Commission* concluded that in cases where the saving of human lives necessarily requires obtaining certain information, the investigator is entitled to apply both psychological pressure and "a moderate degree of physical pressure." Thus, an investigator who, in the face of such danger, applies that specific degree of physical pressure, which does not constitute abuse or torture of the suspect, but is instead proportional to the danger to human life, can avail himself of the "necessity" defence, in the face of potential criminal liability. The *Commission* was convinced that its conclusions to this effect

were not in conflict with International Law, but instead reflect an approach consistent with both the Rule of Law and the need to effectively safeguard the security of Israel and its citizens.

The *Commission* approved the use of "a moderate degree of physical pressure" with various stringent conditions including directives that were set out in the second (and secret) part of the Report, and for the supervision of various elements both internal and external to the GSS. The *Commission's* recommendations were duly approved by the government. . . .

The Authority to Interrogate

18. . . . An interrogation inevitably infringes upon the suspect's freedom, even if physical means are not used. Indeed, undergoing an interrogation infringes on both the suspect's dignity and his individual privacy. In a state adhering to the Rule of Law, interrogations are therefore not permitted in absence of clear statutory authorization. . . .

[Although the Court concludes, after considering a number of arguments, that "A specific statutory provision authorizing GSS investigators to conduct interrogations does not exist," it nonetheless holds that a provision of the Criminal Procedure Statute can legitimately be interpreted to authorize "GSS investigators to conduct interrogations regarding the commission of hostile terrorist activities."]

The Means Employed for Interrogation Purposes

22. An interrogation, by its very nature, places the suspect in a difficult position. "The criminal's interrogation," wrote Justice Vitkon over twenty years ago, "is not a negotiation process between two open and fair vendors, conducting their business on the basis of maximum mutual trust" (Cr. A 216/74 *Cohen v The State of Israel*) 29(1) P.D. 340 at 352). An interrogation is a "competition of minds," in which the investigator attempts to penetrate the suspect's thoughts and elicit from him the information the investigator seeks to obtain. . . .

In crystallizing the interrogation rules, two values or interests clash. *On the one hand,* lies the desire to uncover the truth, thereby fulfilling the public interest in exposing crime and preventing it. *On the other hand,* is the wish to protect the dignity and liberty of the individual being interrogated. This having been said, these interests and values are not absolute. A democratic, freedom-loving society does not accept that investigators use any means for the purpose of uncovering the truth. . . . At times, the price of truth is so high that a democratic society is not prepared to pay it. To the same extent however, a democratic society, desirous of liberty seeks to fight crime and to that end is prepared to accept that an interrogation may infringe upon the human dignity and liberty of a suspect provided it is done for a proper purpose and that the harm does not exceed that which is necessary. . . .

Our concern, therefore, lies in the clash of values and the balancing of conflicting values. . . .

23. . . . The "law of interrogation" by its very nature, is intrinsically linked to the circumstances of each case. This having been said, a number of general principles are nonetheless worth noting:

First, a reasonable investigation is necessarily one free of torture, free of cruel, inhuman treatment of the subject and free of any degrading handling whatsoever. There is a prohibition on the use of "brutal or inhuman means" in the course of an investigation. Human dignity also includes the dignity of the suspect being interrogated. This conclusion is in perfect accord with (various) International Law treaties—to which Israel is a signatory—which prohibit the use of torture, "cruel, inhuman treatment" and "degrading treatment." These prohibitions are "absolute." There are no exceptions to them and there is no room for balancing. Indeed, violence directed at a suspect's body or spirit does not constitute a reasonable investigation practice. The use of violence during investigations can potentially lead to the investigator being held criminally liable. *Second,* a reasonable investigation is likely to cause discomfort; it may result in insufficient sleep; the conditions under which it is conducted risk being unpleasant. Indeed, it is possible to conduct an effective investigation without resorting to violence. Within the confines of the law, it is permitted to resort to various machinations and specific sophisticated activities which serve investigators today (both for Police and GSS); similar investigations—accepted in the most progressive of societies—can be effective in achieving their goals. In the end result, the legality of an investigation is deduced from the propriety of its purpose and from its methods. Thus, for instance, sleep deprivation for a prolonged period, or sleep deprivation at night when this is not necessary to the investigation time wise may be deemed a use of an investigation method which surpasses the least restrictive means.

From the General to the Particular

24. We shall now turn from the general to the particular. Plainly put, shaking is a prohibited investigation method. It harms the suspect's body. It violates his dignity. It is a violent method which does not form part of a legal investigation. It surpasses that which is necessary. Even the State did not argue that shaking is an "ordinary" investigation method which every investigator (in the GSS or police) is permitted to employ. The submission before us was that the justification for shaking is found in the "necessity" defence. That argument shall be dealt with below. . . .

25. It was argued before the Court that one of the investigation methods employed consists of the suspect crouching on the tips of his toes for five-minute intervals. The State did not deny this practice. This is a prohibited investigation method. It does not serve any purpose inherent to an investigation. It is degrading and infringes upon an individual's human dignity.

26. The "Shabach" method is composed of a number of cumulative components: the cuffing of the suspect, seating him on a low chair, covering his head with an opaque sack (head covering) and playing powerfully loud music in the area. Are any of the above acts encompassed by the general power to investigate? Our point of departure is that there are actions which are inherent to the investigation power. Therefore, we accept that the suspect's cuffing, for the purpose of preserving the investigators' safety, is an action included in the general power to investigate. Provided the suspect is cuffed for this purpose, it is within the investigator's authority to cuff him. The State's position is that the suspects are indeed cuffed with the intention of ensuring the investigators' safety or to prevent fleeing from legal custody. Even the applicants agree that it is permissible to cuff a suspect in similar circumstances and that cuffing constitutes an integral part of an interrogation. Notwithstanding, the cuffing associated with the "Shabach" position is unlike routine cuffing. The suspect is cuffed with his hands tied behind his back. One hand is placed inside the gap between the chair's seat and back support, while the other is tied behind him, against the chair's

back support. This is a distorted and unnatural position. The investigators' safety does not require it. Therefore, there is no relevant justification for handcuffing the suspect's hands with particularly small handcuffs, if this is in fact the practice. The use of these methods is prohibited. As was noted, "Cuffing causing pain is prohibited." Moreover, there are other ways of preventing the suspect from fleeing from legal custody which do not involve causing the suspect pain and suffering.

27. This is the law with respect to the method involving seating the suspect in question in the "Shabach" position. We accept that seating a man is inherent to the investigation. This is not the case when the chair upon which he is seated is a very low one, tilted forward facing the ground, and when he is sitting in this position for long hours. This sort of seating is not encompassed by the general power to interrogate. Even if we suppose that the seating of the suspect on a chair lower than that of his investigator can potentially serve a legitimate investigation objective (for instance, to establish the "rules of the game" in the contest of wills between the parties, or to emphasize the investigator's superiority over the suspect), there is no inherent investigative need for seating the suspect on a chair so low and tilted forward towards the ground, in a manner that causes him real pain and suffering. Clearly, the general power to conduct interrogations does not authorize seating a suspect on a forward tilting chair, in a manner that applies pressure and causes pain to his back, all the more so when his hands are tied behind the chair, in the manner described. All these methods do not fall within the sphere of a "fair" interrogation. They are not reasonable. They impinge upon the suspect's dignity, his bodily integrity and his basic rights in an excessive manner (or beyond what is necessary). They are not to be deemed as included within the general power to conduct interrogations.

28. We accept that there are interrogation related considerations concerned with preventing contact between the suspect under interrogation and other suspects and his investigators, which require means capable of preventing the said contact. The need to prevent contact may, for instance, flow from the need to safeguard the investigators' security, or that of the suspects and witnesses. It can also be part of the "mind game" which pins the information possessed by the suspect, against that found in the hands of his investigators. For this purpose, the power to interrogate—in principle and according to the circumstances of each particular case—includes preventing eye contact with a given person or place. In the case at bar, this was the explanation provided by the State for covering the suspect's head

with an opaque sack, while he is seated in the "Shabach" position. From what was stated in the declarations before us, the suspect's head is covered with an opaque sack throughout his "wait" in the "Shabach" position. It was argued that the sack (head covering) is entirely opaque, causing the suspect to suffocate. The edges of the sack are long, reaching the suspect's shoulders. All these methods are not inherent to an interrogation. They do not confirm the State's position, arguing that they are meant to prevent eye contact between the suspect being interrogated and other suspects. Indeed, even if such contact should be prevented, what is the purpose of causing the suspect to suffocate? Employing this method is not connected to the purpose of preventing the said contact and is consequently forbidden. Moreover, the statements clearly reveal that the suspect's head remains covered for several hours, throughout his wait. For these purposes, less harmful means must be employed, such as letting the suspect wait in a detention cell. Doing so will eliminate any need to cover the suspect's eyes. In the alternative, the suspect's eyes may be covered in a manner that does not cause him physical suffering. For it appears that at present, the suspect's head covering—which covers his entire head, rather than eyes alone—for a prolonged period of time, with no essential link to the goal of preventing contact between the suspects under investigation, is not part of a fair interrogation. It harms the suspect and his (human) image. It degrades him. It causes him to lose sight of time and place. It suffocates him. All these things are not included in the general authority to investigate. In the cases before us, the State declared that it will make an effort to find a "ventilated" sack. This is not sufficient. The covering of the head in the circumstances described, as distinguished from the covering of the eyes, is outside the scope of authority and is prohibited.

29. Cutting off the suspect from his surroundings can also include preventing him from listening to what is going on around him. We are prepared to assume that the authority to investigate an individual equally encompasses precluding him from hearing other suspects under investigation or voices and sounds that, if heard by the suspect, risk impeding the interrogation's success. Whether the means employed fall within the scope of a fair and reasonable interrogation warrant[s] examination at this time. In the case at bar, the detainee is found in the "Shabach" position while listening to the consecutive playing of powerfully loud music. Do these methods fall within the scope or the general authority to conduct interrogations? Here too, the answer is in the negative. Being exposed to power-

fully loud music for a long period of time causes the suspect suffering. Furthermore, the suspect is tied (in place) in an uncomfortable position with his head covered (all the while). The use of the "Shabach" method is prohibited. It does not fall within the scope of the authority to conduct a fair and effective interrogation. Powerfully loud music is a prohibited means for use in the context described before us.

30. To the above, we must add that the "Shabach" position includes all the outlined methods employed simultaneously. Their combination, in and of itself gives rise to particular pain and suffering. This is a harmful method, particularly when it is employed for a prolonged period of time. For these reasons, this method does not form part of the powers of interrogation. It is an unacceptable method. . . .

A similar—though not identical—combination of interrogation methods were discussed in the case of *Ireland v. United Kingdom* (1978) 2 EHRR 25. In that case, the Court probed five interrogation methods used by England for the purpose of investigating detainees suspected of terrorist activities in Northern Ireland. The methods were as follows: protracted standing against the wall on the tip of one's toes; covering of the suspect's head throughout the detention (except during the actual interrogation); exposing the suspect to powerfully loud noise for a prolonged period and deprivation of sleep, food and drink. The Court held that these methods did not constitute "torture." However, since they treated the suspect in an "inhuman and degrading" manner, they were nonetheless prohibited.

31. The interrogation of a person is likely to be lengthy, due to the suspect's failure to cooperate or due to the information's complexity or in light of the imperative need to obtain information urgently and immediately. Indeed, a person undergoing interrogation cannot sleep as does one who is not being interrogated. The suspect, subject to the investigators' questions for a prolonged period of time, is at times exhausted. This is often the inevitable result of an interrogation, or one of its side effects. This is part of the "discomfort" inherent to an interrogation. This being the case, depriving the suspect of sleep is, in our opinion, included in the general authority of the investigator. . . .

The above described situation is different from those in which sleep deprivation shifts from being a "side effect" inherent to the interrogation, to an end in itself. If the suspect is intentionally deprived of sleep for a prolonged period of time, for the purpose of tiring him out or "breaking" him—it shall not fall within the scope of a fair and reasonable investigation. Such means harm the rights and dignity of the suspect in a manner surpassing that which is required.

32. . . . There is no statutory instruction endowing a GSS investigator with special interrogating powers that are either different or more serious than those given the police investigator. From this we conclude that a GSS investigator, whose duty is to conduct the interrogation according to the law, is subject to the same restrictions applicable to a police interrogation.

Physical Means and the "Necessity" Defence

33. . . . As noted, an explicit authorization permitting GSS to employ physical means is not to be found in our law. An authorization of this nature can, in the State's opinion, be obtained in specific cases by virtue of the criminal law defense of "necessity," prescribed in the Penal Law. The language of the statute is as follows: (Article 34 (1)):

> A person will not bear criminal liability for committing any act immediately necessary for the purpose of saving the life, liberty, body or property, of either himself or his fellow person, from substantial danger of serious harm, imminent from the particular state of things [circumstances], at the requisite timing, and absent alternative means for avoiding the harm.

The State's position is that by virtue of this "defence" to criminal liability, GSS investigators are also authorized to apply physical means, such as shaking, in the appropriate circumstances, in order to prevent serious harm to human life or body, in the absence of other alternatives. The State maintains that an act committed under conditions of "necessity" does not constitute a crime. Instead, it is deemed an act worth committing in such circumstances in order to prevent serious harm to a human life or body. . . . Not only is it legitimately permitted to engage in the fighting of terrorism, it is our moral duty to employ the necessary means for this purpose. This duty is particularly incumbent on the state authorities—and for our purposes, on the GSS investigators—who carry the burden of safeguarding the public peace. . . . From this flows the legality of the directives with respect to the use of physical means in GSS interrogations. In the course of their argument, the State's attorneys submitted the "ticking time bomb" argument. . . .

34. We are prepared to assume that—although this matter is open to debate—(See A. Dershowitz, *Is it Necessary to Apply "Physical Pressure" to Terrorists—And to Lie About It?* [1989] 23 Israel L. Rev. 193; Bernsmann, *Private Self-Defence and Necessity in German Penal Law and in the Penal Law Proposal—Some Remarks,* [1998] 30 Israel L. Rev. 171, 208–210)—the "necessity" defence is open to all, particularly an investigator, acting in an organizational capacity of the State in interrogations of that nature. Likewise, we are prepared to accept—although this matter is equally contentious—(see M. Kremnitzer, *The Landau Commission Report—Was the Security Service Subordinated to the Law or the Law to the Needs of the Security Service?* [1989] 23 Israel L. Rev. 216, 244–247)—that the "necessity" exception is likely to arise in instances of "ticking time bombs," and that the immediate need ("necessary in an immediate manner" for the preservation of human life) refers to the imminent nature of the act rather than that of the danger. Hence, the imminence criteria is satisfied even if the bomb is set to explode in a few days, or perhaps even after a few weeks, provided the danger is certain to materialize and there is no alternative means of preventing its materialization. In other words, there exists a concrete level of imminent danger of the explosion's occurrence.

Consequently we are prepared to presume, as was held by the *Inquiry Commission's Report,* that if a GSS investigator—who applied physical interrogation methods for the purpose of saving human life—is criminally indicted, the "necessity" defence is likely to be open to him in the appropriate circumstances Israel's Penal Law recognizes the "necessity" defence.

35. Indeed, we are prepared to accept that in the appropriate circumstances, GSS investigators may avail themselves of the "necessity" defence, if criminally indicted. This however, is not the issue before this Court. . . . We are dealing with a different question. The question before us is whether it is possible to infer the authority to, in advance, establish permanent directives setting out the physical interrogation means that may be used under conditions of "necessity." . . . .

36. In the Court's opinion, a general authority to establish directives respecting the use of physical means during the course of a GSS interrogation cannot be implied from the "necessity" defence. The "necessity" defence does not constitute a source of authority, allowing GSS investigators to make use physical means during the course of interrogations. The reasoning underlying our position is anchored in the nature of the "necessity" de-

fence. This defence deals with deciding those cases involving an individual reacting to a given set of facts; it is an ad hoc endeavour, in reaction to a event. It is the result of an improvisation given the unpredictable character of the events. Thus, the very nature of the defence does not allow it to serve as the source of a general administrative power. The administrative power is based on establishing general, forward looking criteria, as noted by Professor Enker:

> Necessity is an after-the-fact judgment based on a narrow set of considerations in which we are concerned with the immediate consequences, not far-reaching and long-range consequences, on the basis of a clearly established order of priorities of both means and ultimate values. . . . The defence of Necessity does not define a code of primary normative behaviour. Necessity is certainly not a basis for establishing a broad detailed code of behaviour such as how one should go about conducting intelligence interrogations in security matters, when one may or may not use force, how much force may be used and the like (Enker, "The Use of Physical Force in Interrogations and the Necessity Defense," in *Israel and International Human Rights Law: The Issue of Torture* 61, 62 (1995)). . . .

Moreover, the "necessity" defence has the effect of allowing one who acts under the circumstances of "necessity" to escape criminal liability. The "necessity" defence does not possess any additional normative value. In addition, it does not authorize the use of physical means for the purposes of allowing investigators to execute their duties in circumstances of necessity. . . . The lifting of criminal responsibility does not imply authorization to infringe upon a human right. . . .

37. . . . If the State wishes to enable GSS investigators to utilize physical means in interrogations, they must seek the enactment of legislation for this purpose. This authorization would also free the investigator applying the physical means from criminal liability. This release would flow not from the "necessity" defence but from the "justification" defense which states:

> A person shall not bear criminal liability for an act committed in one of the following cases:

> (1) He was obliged or authorized by law to commit it (Article 34(13) of the Penal Law). . . .

Endowing GSS investigators with the authority to apply physical force during the interrogation of suspects suspected of involvement in hostile terrorist activities, thereby harming the latters' dignity and liberty, raise[s] basic questions of law and society, of ethics and policy, and of the Rule of Law and security. These questions and the corresponding answers must be determined by the Legislative branch [and not implied from the presence of "necessity" as a defence to certain criminal charges]. This is required by the principle of the Separation of Powers and the Rule of Law, under our very understanding of democracy.

38. Our conclusion is therefore the following: According to the existing state of the law, neither the government nor the heads of security services possess the authority to establish directives and bestow authorization regarding the use of liberty infringing physical means during the interrogation of suspects suspected of hostile terrorist activities, beyond the general directives which can be inferred from the very concept of an interrogation. Similarly, the individual GSS investigator—like any police officer—does not possess the authority to employ physical means which infringe upon a suspect's liberty during the interrogation, unless these means are inherently accessory to the very essence of an interrogation and are both fair and reasonable.

An investigator who insists on employing these methods, or does so routinely, is exceeding his authority. His responsibility shall be fixed according to law. His potential criminal liability shall be examined in the context of the "necessity" defence, and according to our assumptions (see paragraph 35 *supra*), the investigator may find refuge under the "necessity" defence's wings (so to speak), provided this defence's conditions are met by the circumstances of the case. Just as the existence of the "necessity" defence does not bestow authority, so too the lack of authority does not negate the applicability of the necessity defense or that of other defences from criminal liability.

A Final Word

39. This decision opens with a description of the difficult reality in which Israel finds herself security wise. We shall conclude this judgment by readdressing that harsh reality. We are aware that this decision does not ease dealing with that reality. This is the destiny of democracy, as not all means

are acceptable to it, and not all practices employed by its enemies are open before it. Although a democracy must often fight with one hand tied behind its back, it nonetheless has the upper hand. Preserving the Rule of Law and recognition of an individual's liberty constitutes an important component in its understanding of security. At the end of the day, they strengthen its spirit and its strength and allow it to overcome its difficulties. This having been said, there are those who argue that Israel's security problems are too numerous, thereby requiring the authorization to use physical means. If it will nonetheless be decided that it is appropriate for Israel, in light of its security difficulties to sanction physical means in interrogations (and the scope of these means which deviate from the ordinary investigation rules), this is an issue that must be decided by the legislative branch which represents the people. We do not take any stand on this matter at this time. It is there that various considerations must be weighed. The pointed debate must occur there. It is there that the required legislation may be passed, provided, of course, that a law infringing upon a suspect's liberty "befitting the values of the State of Israel," is enacted for a proper purpose, and to an extent no greater than is required. (Article 8 to the Basic Law: Human Dignity and Liberty.)

40. Deciding these applications weighed heavy on this Court. True, from the legal perspective, the road before us is smooth. We are, however, part of Israeli society. Its problems are known to us and we live its history. We are not isolated in an ivory tower. We live the life of this country. We are aware of the harsh reality of terrorism in which we are, at times, immersed. Our apprehension is that this decision will hamper the ability to properly deal with terrorists and terrorism, [which] disturbs us. We are, however, judges. Our bretheren require us to act according to the law. This is equally the standard that we set for ourselves. When we sit to judge, we are being judged. Therefore, we must act according to our purest conscience when we decide the law. . . .

Miriam Gur-Arye

Can the War against Terror Justify the Use of Force in Interrogations?
Reflections in Light of the Israeli Experience

In 1987, after the public in Israel found out that the Israeli General Security Services (GSS) had used force in interrogating Palestinians suspected of "hostile terrorist activity,"[1] a commission of inquiry chaired by former Supreme Court president Moshe Landau (hereinafter the Landau Commission) was established. The Commission held that the use of moderate force by the GSS in interrogating terrorist's suspects is permissible by virtue of the criminal law defense of necessity.[2] A special Public Committee against Torture in Israel was established following the Landau Commission report. The Committee, as well as other human rights groups in Israel, consistently publicized detailed reports on the GSS' methods of interrogations, and challenged the legality of these methods before the Israeli Supreme Court. In 1999 the Israeli Supreme Court ruled that the coercive methods used by the GSS following the Landau Commission's recommendations are illegal.[3] The Israeli Supreme Court ruling should be read as a response to the ongoing protests against the Landau Commission's conclusion permitting the use of moderate force in interrogating suspects of terrorist activities.

In this article I present the debate invoked by the Landau Commission report and analyze the Supreme Court ruling in light of that debate. I offer a distinction between official-power and criminal-law defenses and argue that officials ought never be empowered to use force in interrogation; nonetheless, in rare situations the use of interrogational force may be justified under the limited boundaries of self-defense rather than necessity. Although some readers may object to the potential toleration of interrogational force at all, my proposal would absolutely forbid such methods against those who did not directly cause the potential danger in the first place, unlike some arguments that, if taken to their logical conclusions, would seem to allow torture of truly innocent persons (e.g., the family of suspected terrorists) if deemed "necessary" to encourage the terrorist to disclose essential information. I note, incidentally, that I am referring to the general use of force in interrogation designed to break the suspect's refusal to reveal information, whether or not we classify such force as "torture"[4] or as "cruel, inhuman or degrading treatment or punishment,"[5] both of which, after all, are prohibited by international convention.

The Landau Commission's Holding and Its Response

The Landau Commission held that the use of moderate force in interrogating suspects of hostile activities is permissible by virtue of the criminal law defense of necessity. The main assumptions that led to that conclusion were as follows.

1. Interrogating suspects of terrorist activities is not primarily designed to elicit confession and secure convictions; the primary goal is rather "to protect the very existence of society and the State against terrorist acts directed against citizens, to collect information about terrorists and their modes of organization and to thwart and prevent preparation of terrorist acts whilst they are still in a state of incubation."[6]

2. It is impossible to achieve that goal "without the use of pressure, in order to overcome an obdurate will not to disclose information and to overcome the fear of the person under interrogation that harm will befall him from his own organization, if he does reveal information."[7]

3. The necessity defense, applying to cases where legitimate interests were sacrificed to prevent danger to other legitimate interests, is based on the concept of lesser evil. "The decisive factor is not the element of time"; that is, it does not depend on the immediacy of the danger to be prevented. The decisive factor is rather "the comparison between . . . the evil of contravening the law as opposed to the evil which will occur sooner or later."[8]

4. In balancing the interests involved in the use of force in interrogating suspects of terrorist activities, "[t]he alternative is: are we to accept the offense of assault entailed in slapping a suspect's face, or threatening him, in order to induce him to talk and reveal a cache of explosive materials meant for use in carrying out an act of mass terror against civilian popula-

tion, and thereby prevent the greater evil which is about to occur? The answer is self-evident."[9]

Scholars of law and philosophy, both within and outside Israel, criticized the conclusion of the Landau Commission and the assumptions that led to it.[10] It was argued that the Commission should have focused on "general strategy in the fight against terrorism and the alternative means of . . . information-gathering" rather than on "individual suspects and alternative means of extracting information from them"[11] (the first assumption). In waiving the need for immediacy from the necessity defense (the third assumption), the Landau Commission ignored the unique nature of the defense as an emergency measure aimed at preventing concrete and actual danger.[12] In balancing the interests at stake (the fourth assumption) "one must take into account the special weight assigned to individual autonomy and human dignity,"[13] as well as the danger to the whole legal system that would result from the precedent of permitting the use of force in the course of interrogations.[14] To limit this latter danger the Commission should have at least imposed a ban on using the confession obtained by coercive methods in criminal proceedings (in the light of its first assumption).[15]

The main criticism of the Landau Commission focused on its conclusion. By its very nature, it was argued, necessity cannot serve as a source for governmental authority. It is an ad hoc defense applied to an individual confronted with imminent danger; it is not a basis "for weighing policy by state agency faced with long-term systemic problems."[16] In a democratic state it is the legislature that should decide on the methods of conducting intelligence interrogations in the war against terrorism.[17] Some went further, arguing that even if morally there are rare cases in which the use of force in interrogation might be justified as the lesser of two evils, legally, there should be an absolute ban on using force in the course of interrogations.[18]

In the classified section of its report, the Landau Commission "formulated a code of guidelines for GSS interrogators," which it commended be taken up "annually for reappraisal before a small Ministerial Committee."[19] In the years to follow, the GSS employed coercive methods of interrogation established by the special Ministerial Committee. The main methods were described in the opinion of the Israeli Supreme Court (reprinted herein): "shaking of the suspect's upper torso"; "[w]aiting in the 'shabach' position," in which the suspect is seated on a small, low chair, the seat of which is tilted forward, his hands are tied, his head is covered by an opaque sack, and powerfully loud music is played in the room; the 'Frog Crouch' on the tips of one's toes; excessive tightening of hand or leg cuffs; and sleep deprivation." Petitions challenging the legality of these methods were repeatedly brought before the Israeli Supreme Court, which rejected them without taking an explicit stand on the legality of the methods of interrogation. Finally, in 1999 the Supreme Court changed its attitude, took a stand on the merits, and ruled that the coercive methods used by the GSS are illegal.

The Israeli Supreme Court Ruling

Three different premises underlie the Supreme Court ruling that says that the coercive methods used by the GSS in interrogating suspects of terrorist activities are illegal.[20]

The first premise relates to the GSS general power to interrogate. According to the Court, the GSS has a power to interrogate suspects of terrorist activities similar to that of the "ordinary police force."[21] The interrogation, which necessarily causes discomfort to the suspect, ought to be fair and reasonable. The methods used by the GSS were unfair and unreasonable, and therefore are not included within the general power to interrogate.[22]

It should be noted that the Court avoided classifying the methods used by the GSS explicitly as "torture" or as "cruel inhuman and degrading treatment." Such a classification was, however, implicit in the Court's ruling. The Court clarified that

> a reasonable investigation is necessarily one free of torture, free of cruel, inhuman treatment of the subject and free of any degrading handling whatsoever. . . . This conclusion is in perfect accord with (various) International Law treaties—to which Israel is a signatory—which prohibit the use of torture, "cruel, inhuman treatment" and "degrading treatment." . . . These prohibitions are "absolute." There are no exceptions to them and there is no room for balancing. *Indeed, violence directed at a suspect's body or spirit* does not constitute a reasonable investigation practice. (Emphasis added)[23]

In ruling that the various methods used by the GSS "do not fall within the sphere of a 'fair' interrogation," the Court in fact described the various methods in a manner that meets the Court's characteristics of torture or at least cruel inhuman and degrading treatment. According to the Court, the various methods used by the GSS were unreasonable and unfair because, "[used] in a manner that applies *pressure and cause pain* . . . [t]hey impinge upon the *suspect's dignity, his bodily integrity and his basic rights in an excessive manner*" (emphases added).[24] Similarly, "if the suspect is intentionally deprived of sleep for a prolonged period of time, for the purpose of tiring him out or *'breaking' him*—it shall not fall within the scope of a fair and reasonable investigation. Such means *harm the rights and dignity of the suspect*" (emphasis added).[25]

The second premise underlying the Supreme Court ruling focuses on the need for an explicit legislative authorization to use force in interrogations. "This is required by the principle of the separation of powers and the rule of law, under our very understanding of democracy."[26] The Court explicitly held, in contrast to the Landau Commission, that "[t]he necessity defense does not constitute a source of authority, allowing GSS investigators to make use physical means during the course of interrogation."[27] The second premise was crucial to the Court's ruling, inasmuch as the lack of explicit authority invalidated the coercive methods used by the GSS. It should be noted that the Court did not impose a general ban on using force during interrogations. The Court rather left it to the legislator to decide whether "it is appropriate for Israel, in light of its security difficulties, to sanction physical means in interrogations."[28]

The third premise touches upon the criminal law defense of necessity. The Court left open the "necessity" defense with regard to particular episodes and persons accused of the use of excessive force. "Just as the existence of the "necessity" defense does not bestow authority, so too the lack of authority does not negate the applicability of the necessity defense or that of other defenses from criminal liability."[29]

Reactions to the Supreme Court's judgment varied. Some praised it,[30] even as others criticized it for not going far enough, arguing that the Court should have ruled out the necessity defense and imposed an absolute ban on using force in interrogation rather than leaving it to the legislature to decide whether to legalize the use of force in interrogations.[31] I agree with the critics, that the legislature ought never to empower officials to use force in interrogation, though I shall offer an alternative approach to the relationship between official empowerment and criminal law defenses emphasizing "self-defense" rather than "necessity" in specific instances.

Criminal Law Defenses versus Official Power to Interrogate

Criminal law defenses may be classified as either justifications or excuses. Justifications negate the wrongfulness of the conduct, whereas excuses negate only the culpability of the actor for her wrongful conduct. Excuses are personal; they are granted because it would be unfair to blame the actor for her wrongful conduct, for example because she was insane or because she acted under extreme psychological pressure (duress). The defense of necessity—available, according to the Israeli Supreme Court, to an individual interrogator—can also be classified as either a justification or an excuse.

In discussing the notion of necessity the Supreme Court said: "the necessity defense has the effect of allowing one who acts under the circumstances of necessity to escape criminal liability. The necessity defense does not posses any additional normative value."[32] By denying necessity normative value, the Court rejected the notion of necessity as a justification. The Court rather emphasized the personal nature of the necessity, as in the notion of excuse, by ruling that the necessity defense might apply to individual investigators who "claim to have acted from *a feeling of necessity*" (emphasis added).[33]

On the face of it, the notion of excuse in the context of force in interrogation is attractive. It enables us to declare that the use of force in interrogations is wrong and yet to release the individual interrogator from criminal liability on the grounds that it would be unfair to blame an interrogator who, under a pressure to prevent terrorist attack, has used force in interrogating those who might have useful information. However, I believe that necessity should not excuse an individual interrogator who has used force in interrogating terror suspects. The rationale of necessity as an excuse is that, due to the pressure stemming from imminent danger and in view of the need for self-preservation, it would be unfair to require an individual to avoid protecting her interests by sacrificing those of another person, even when the sacrifice of the other person's interests is wrong. From governmental officials, on the other hand, we can and should demand that they overcome pressures and avoid committing wrongs while carrying out their duty. Once society is committed in its law to the view that it is wrong to use force in interrogations in order to reveal information necessary to prevent terrorist attacks, the interrogators should be required to overcome the pressure to use such force and to turn to other techniques of information gathering.

Unlike excuses, criminal law justifications imply that, under the specific circumstances, performing the conduct was right. On the face of it, there is no reason to deny justifications, as opposed to excuses, from officials who have made the "right" choice. Can justifications serve, therefore, as a source of official power? In what follows I shall assume that in rare situations criminal law justification may legitimate the use of force in interrogation (I shall discuss that assumption later), and I offer a distinction between official empowerment and justifications applied to officials.

When the legislature empowers governmental officials to carry out certain duties, the individual official is relieved of the need to deliberate, each time she performs her duty, on whether or not carrying out that duty is right. The legislature weighed the conflicting policies/interests and struck a balance between them, and the officials are entitled to assume that the balance struck was the right one.[34] All they have to do is ensure that the conditions for doing their duty exist in each individual case. Granting such power for handling routine tasks is necessary in order to relieve individual officials from deliberating daily on the justifications underlying that routine. That conclusion is simply a reflection of the rule of law consideration that the legislature must be the one to decide on long-term policies.

Justifications provide reasons for doing what would otherwise have been breaking the law. In defining justifications the legislator provides only a framework for when "breaking the law" might be justified by clarifying guidance for the balance of the interests involved. To justify her concrete conduct, the individual must deliberate on the balance between the beneficial and harmful results of breaking the law in the concrete circumstances. Allowing justifications to apply to official conduct is necessary in those exceptional cases where the values at stake are crucially important and it is therefore in society's interest that the individual official be particularly cautious. The official should not rely solely on the abstract balance struck by the legislator in defining justifications; she should rather deliberate before acting whether in the concrete circumstances the balance indeed justifies breaking the law.

To clarify the distinction between official empowerment and the justifications just offered, take the example of a prison guard. The guard has the power to keep convicts in prison, and to see to it that they behave according to prison rules. She does not have to deliberate as to the justifications of holding convicts in prison, or as to the justification of prison rules (provided that those rules were laid down by an authorized body). Let us now assume that one of the convicts succeeds in getting a knife and threatens to kill another convict. In such a case, the prison guard may be justified in using deadly force to defend the other convict by virtue of "self-defense."[35] We may and should, however, expect her to deliberate before using the deadly force. She should not use the force unless she has reasons to believe that the convict is indeed able to kill the other convict with the knife; that there is no other less harmful way to stop the convict from using the knife; and that stopping the convict from using the knife will not have worse results. The deliberation on the last issue requires "moral knowledge."[36] She must consider what the right balance between the potential harms involved is.

The distinction between power and justifications offered here provides us with a useful legal tool for dealing with the use of force in interrogation. To demonstrate this, let me discuss the view that even if the use of force in interrogation may be morally justified in rare situations, legally there should be an absolute ban on using such force. According to Shue, "An act of torture ought to remain illegal so that anyone who sincerely believes such an act to be the least available evil is placed in a position of needing to justify his or her act morally in order to defend himself or herself legally."[37] A somewhat similar view led Sanford Kadish to distinguish "between what is morally permitted for a state to do officially and to proclaim by its law, and what is morally permitted for an individual to do." According to him:

> Individuals, even individuals who happen to be state officials, may take it upon themselves to use such [coercive] methods, and they may turn out to have been morally justified. But the state itself in what it legally authorizes, in contrast to what individual officials may take upon themselves to do, may not. . . .
>
> The individual official would have to make his own decision whether the circumstances are so utterly powerful in their moral weight that even legal and moral ban must give.[38]

In contrast to the Israeli Supreme Court's assumption, and in a similar spirit to that of Kadish, I believe that the state ought never to empower officials to use force in interrogations. The absence of such power will prevent the use of force as a matter of routine. Even limited power to use force in interrogation in exceptional situations ought not to be granted: individual officials should not be able to be relieved of the burden of deliberating on the justification of using force in the specific case. However, in those exceptional situations where the use of force is *morally* justified, a criminal law justification may apply. Making justification available will not relieve the individual official from the burden, as Kadish puts it, "to make his own decision whether the circumstances are so utterly powerful" as to justify the use of force in interrogation. Justifications, based on moral evaluation, will, in Shue's words, place the individual official "in a position of needing to justify his or her act morally in order to defend himself or herself legally."

Necessity versus Self-Defense

The necessity defense, being the focus of the debate invoked in Israel following the Landau Commission report, is too broad a justification. The use of interrogational force may only be justified under the more limited boundaries of self-defense.

Necessity as a justification derives from consequential moral theories, according to which wrongful actions may be morally deemed by the goodness of their consequences. It justifies the sacrifice of legitimate interests to protect other interests of substantially higher value. It does not grant the individual "a license to determine social utility."[39] It is rather limited to emergency cases in which there is an imminent and concrete danger to an interest recognized by the legal system. In the context of this discussion, such an emergency exists in the "ticking bomb" situation, in which a bomb has been set to explode imminently and innocent people are likely to be killed.[40] The only hope for saving their lives is to get information about the location of the bomb in order to defuse it. Should necessity justify the use of force in an attempt to coerce the person under interrogation to reveal such information?

The justification of necessity rests on the balance between interests of innocent persons. The sacrifice of an innocent person's interests is justified when necessary to save those of another, when that other person's interests have a higher value. Therefore, if necessity is to apply to ticking bomb situations it will justify the use of interrogational force against the *innocent*. Taken to an extreme, necessity might prima facie justify the use of force against a terrorist's child in order to force the terrorist to reveal the information about the location of a bomb he has planted. Even to consequentialists the use of force against the child might seem "morally repugnant. No one should torture innocent children—even when done to produce a sizeable gain in aggregate welfare."[41]

To rule out necessity in the case of the terrorist's child, we can introduce a limitation into necessity, similar to that in the German penal code, according to which necessity "applies only if the act is an appropriate means to avert the danger."[42] However, since the basic premise of necessity is that it is justified to sacrifice an innocent person's interests of a lesser value, necessity will not rule out the use of force against the innocent in less extreme situations; that is, when force is used in interrogating a bystander who happens to have the necessary information about the location of the bomb.[43]

The argument that the use of force in interrogating bystanders is justified may rest on the moral principle that prohibits attacking the defenseless. Unlike the terrorist's child, who is indeed defenseless, the bystander who knows of the location of the bomb may escape the use of force by compliance: she can reveal the information concerning the location of the bomb.

The very nature of the use of force in interrogation makes the foregoing claim unrealistic.[44] In the real world, it is doubtful whether "the interrogators 'know' with any reasonable degree of certainty that the suspect being questioned has accurate and reliable information that is immediately useful."[45] The person under interrogation might have only partial information. Even when she reveals all the information she has under interrogation, the interrogator might not be persuaded that she does not hold more useful details. In such cases there is nothing she can do to avoid using force against her. She is defenseless, and is entirely at the interrogator's mercy.

The one person who is not defenseless in ticking bomb situations is the terrorist who has planted the bomb. He has full information, and the interrogators, having him in their hands, can know with reasonable certainty that he indeed holds the necessary information required for defusing the bomb. It is true that, even with regard to the terrorist, we cannot always expect a high degree of certainty: the interrogators may not be certain that the suspect in their hands is indeed the terrorist. However, there is a significant difference between the uncertainties involved.

When a bystander, suspected of having useful information, is under interrogation, the uncertainty focuses on the suspect's inner world. Even when there is reasonable cause to believe that she has been at the scene or that she is related to a terrorist, one cannot draw conclusions from those external events regarding the extent of her knowledge: Does she hold useful information? Has she revealed the full information she holds to her interrogators? When the person under interrogation is suspected to be the terrorist, on the other hand, the uncertainty has to do with his external acts: Is he indeed the one who has planted a bomb? Once a reasonable degree of certainty is obtained with regard to the suspect being the terrorist who has planted the bomb, we may assume, with a high degree of certainty, that he has the full information regarding the location of the bomb.

Moreover, the intrusion inherent in inquiring whether the suspect is a terrorist who has been planted a bomb rests on stronger justifications than those involved in inquiring whether a bystander has information about a location of a bomb. If the suspect is indeed the terrorist who has endangered innocent peoples' lives, fairness dictates that he will be the one to pay the costs for dealing with that danger;[46] that is, he is the one to be coerced to reveal the information necessary to defuse the bomb and save the lives of innocent people. Fairness, however, does not justify coercing an innocent bystander who happens to have the necessary information to reveal that information. To demonstrate why, let me discuss Michael Moore's contrasting view.[47]

Moore claims that a bystander who refuses, for no good reason,[48] to reveal useful information re the location of a ticking bomb is a Bad Samaritan, who therefore "becomes part of the threat to be defended against, and should be treated accordingly."[49] There might be good reasons to treat everyone who happens to know of the location of a bomb in a ticking bomb situation and refuses to reveal the information as a Bad Samaritan. Such reasons can justify imposing a *legal* duty to reveal the information, either within the general Good Samaritan duty to come to the aid of endangered persons (imposed only rarely in common law legal systems) or as a more limited duty to inform the authorities of the location of the bomb (which will require creating a specific legal duty).[50] Violating this duty will result in criminal liability, imposed on proving that the defendant indeed knew of the location of the bomb and refused to reveal it. Being a Bad Samaritan violating a criminal-law duty does not, however, justify the use of force in the course of interrogation. It is important to note that even in legal systems imposing a Good Samaritan legal duty (mainly in Europe), the Bad Samaritan who violates the duty by failing to come to the aid of an endangered person is not held liable for the consequences that she could have prevented. Unlike Moore, those legal systems do not see the Bad Samaritan as part of the threat to the person endangered.

To ensure that in ticking bomb situations force will be used only against the terrorist who planted the bomb, we may turn to another possible justification, that is, that of self-defense, which justifies the use of force against an unlawful attack. Self-defense is not limited to defending one's own self; it applies also when third parties are being attacked. Like necessity, the use of force seeks to prevent an imminent danger to legitimate interests. Unlike necessity, preventing the danger in cases of self-defense does not involve the sacrifice of innocent people's interests. The self-defender repels the attack by using force—at times even deadly force—against the attacker who has unlawfully created the danger. The moral basis for self-defense is, therefore, stronger than that of necessity. The use of force is not directed at the defenseless but rather at the person who has unlawfully created the danger and is able to avoid the need to sacrifice her interests by ceasing the attack.

Strictly speaking, the use of force in interrogation does not fall within the justification of self-defense. The question is whether it is close enough to the typical version of self-defense to justify extending self-defense to include the use of interrogational force. To clarify this matter, let me invoke the following example. A law enforcement agent using deadly force to prevent a terrorist from planting a bomb set to explode is justified by virtue of self-defense. Let us now assume that the terrorist is captured only after planting the bomb (a ticking bomb situation). May the official agent (the interrogator) use force in order to coerce the terrorist to reveal information required for defusing the bomb?

As noted, in cases of self-defense, the attacker—who unlawfully has created the danger—is not defenseless: he can avoid the need to sacrifice his interests by ceasing the attack. In both versions of our example, the terrorist can indeed avoid the use of force against him. However, the way to avoid it is different. In the typical version of self-defense, the terrorist can cease the attack and refrain from planting the bomb; whereas in the second version of the example, he can reveal the information necessary for defusing the bomb. The difference is like that between act and omission. In the typical version of self-defense, the force is used against the attacker because his *act* (planting the bomb) creates the danger to other people lives; in the second version, the force is used because the terrorist refrains from revealing the information—*omission.*

The difference between act and omission within legal systems is indeed significant; imposing criminal liability for omission is generally thought to require special justification.[51] However, unlike Good Samaritan legal duties requiring special justification to demand that a bystander come to the aid of endangered strangers, being linked to the dangerous situation provides a more common justification. Most legal systems tend to treat equally those whose acts have harmed other persons and those whose acts have created only a danger of harm but who later refrained from intervening to save other persons from being harmed. Similarly, legal systems may treat equally the two versions of my example: self-defense will justify the use of force both against a terrorist who did not refrain from planting the bomb (and thereby created the danger) and against a terrorist who refused to reveal the information necessary to defuse the bomb he had planted (did not intervene to avoid the danger he had created).

Concluding Remarks

Security services should not be authorized to use force in interrogations as a general strategy in the fight against terror. They should rather develop alternative means of information gathering. The use of force in interrogation, which severely violates the suspect's human dignity and autonomy, may only be justified in limited cases of an imminent threat of a concrete terrorist attack—ticking bomb situations in its narrow sense—when it is impossible to turn to more general means of collecting information. Only in such cases can self-defense, the right to repel an unlawful concrete attack, justify the use of interrogational force. A preemptive use of force, as well as the use of force in the aftermath of the attack, cannot be justified by self-defense or by any other justification; nor should the use of force be justified against a bystander who happens to know the location of the bomb.

Notes

1. See "Experts of the Report of the Commission of Inquiry into the Methods of Investigation of the General Security Service Regarding Hostile Terrorist Activity," *Israel Law Review* 23 (1989): 149–154 (hereafter "Experts of the Report").

2. Ibid., 167–176.

3. H. C. 5100/94 Public Committee against Torture in Israel and Others v. The State of Israel, The General Security Services and Other, 53(4) PD 817 (1999) (hereafter the Judgment), reprinted herein, chapter 9.

4. Torture, according to its various definitions, "is not just an issue of pain itself. It is an issue of who is doing it and for what purpose." The pain is inflicted "to break a person's will for the purpose of the captor"; Nigel S. Rodley, *The Prohibition of Tor-*

ture and How to Make It Effective, in Center for Human Rights, Hebrew University of Jerusalem, *Symposium on Israel and International Human Rights Law: The Issue of Torture* (1995), available online at: http:/humrts.huji.ac.il/rodley.htm at p. 3. See also John Parry, chapter 8 herein.

5. Article 16 of the Convention against Torture and Other Cruel, Inhuman or Degrading Treatment or Punishment (United Nation General Assembly 39/46 of December 10, 1984). Similar formulations are to be found in various international conventions. See Nigel S. Rodley, The Treatment of Prisoners under International Law (1999), 46–74.

6. "Experts of the Report," 157.

7. Ibid., 184.

8. Ibid., 174.

9. Ibid., 174.

10. The *Israel Law Review* devoted an issue to a written international academic symposium on the Landau Commission report. See *Israel Law Review* 23 (1989).

11. Mordechai Kremintzer, "The Landau Commission Report—Was the Security Service Subordinated to the Law, or the Law to the 'Needs' of the Security Service? *Israel Law Review* 23 (1989): 229.

12. Alan M. Dershowitz, "Is It Necessary to Apply 'Physical Pressure' to Terrorists—and to Lie About It?" *Israel Law Review* 23 (1989): 198; Kremnitzer, "Landau Commission Report," 243–247.

13. Kremnitzer, "Landau Commission Report," 248.

14. Paul H. Robinson, letter to the editor, *Israel Law Review* 23 (1989): 189.

15. Adrian A. S. Zuckerman, "Coercion and the Judicial Ascertainment of Truth," *Israel Law Review* 23 (1989): 363–369.

16. Dershowitz, "Is It Necessary," 198.

17. Arnold Enker, *The Use of Physical Force in Interrogations and the Necessity Defense,* in Center for Human Rights, Hebrew University of Jerusalem, *Symposium,* 6.

18. Sanford H. Kadish, "Torture, the State, and the Individual," *Israel Law Review* 23 (1989): 35–355.

19. "Experts of the Report," 185.

20. For alternative possible readings of the judgment, see Amnon Reichman and Tsvi Kahana, "Israel and the Recognition of Torture: Domestic and International Aspects," in *Torture as Tort: Comparative Perspectives on the Development of Transnational Human Rights Litigation,* ed. C. Scott (2001), 631.

21. The Judgment, para. 32.

22. Ibid., para. 31.

23. Ibid., para. 23.

24. Ibid., para. 27.

25. Ibid., para. 31.

26. Ibid., para. 37.

27. Ibid., para. 36.

28. Ibid., para. 39.

29. Ibid., para. 38.

30. See, e.g., Johan T. Parry, "Judicial Restraints on Illegal State Violence: Israel and the United States," *Vanderbilt Journal of Transnational Law* 35 (2002): 74.

31. See, e.g., Mordechai Kremnitzer and Re'em Segev, "The Legality of Interrogational Torture: A Question of Proper Authorization or a Substantive Moral Issue? *Israel Law Review* 34 (2000): 522–528; Barak Cohen, "Democracy and the Mis-Rule of Law: The Israeli Legal System's Failure to Prevent Torture in the Occupied Territories," *Indiana International and Comparative Law Review* 12 (2001): 75.

32. The Judgment, para. 36.

33. Ibid., para. 38.

34. For the purpose of this argument we may ignore immoral laws.

35. The term "self-defense" usually applies to the use of force to protect both oneself and others.

36. Michael S. Moore, "Torture and the Balance of Evils," *Israel Law Review* 23 (1989): 286.

37. Henry Shue, *Torture*, chapter 2 herein, p. **xx**.

38. Kadish, "Torture, the State, and the Individual," 354.

39. As was suggested by David Cohen, "Development of the Modern Doctrine of Necessity," in *Justification and Excuse, Comparative Perspectives,* ed. Albin Eser and George Fletcher (1987), 991.

40. The term "ticking bomb" is a metaphor for all cases "in which a captured terrorist who knows of an imminent large-scale threat refuses to disclose it"; Alan M. Dershowitz, "Is There a Torturous Road to Justice?" *Los Angeles Times,* November 8, 2001, at part 2, 19. For an example of a "ticking bomb" situation, in which there was no "bomb," that occurred in Israel, see Eyal Benvenisti, "The Role of National Courts in Preventing Torture of Suspected Terrorists." *European Journal of International Law* 8 (1997): 600.

41. See Moore, "Torture and the Balance of Evils," 292.

42. See section 34 of the German Penal Code, 1975.

43. It should, however, be noted that in most discussionsn of ticking bomb situations the assumption is that "the interrogee is, in some way, responsible for the creation of the danger itself (and not only has the information regarding the way to prevent the realization of this danger)"; Kremnitzer and Segev, "Legality," 549.

44. See Shue, chapter 2 herein.

45. Enker, *Use of Physical Force,* 13.

46. Moore, "Torture and the Balance of Evils," 322.

47. Ibid., 325–326.

48. A good reason not to speak, according to Moore, might be "a death threat by the terrorist organization." Ibid., 325.

49. Ibid.

50. I have elaborated on a similar issue in Miriam Gur-Arye, "A Failure to Prevent Crime—Should It Be Criminal?" *Criminal Justice Ethics* 20 (2001): 127.

51. See Joel Feinberg, *Harm to Others* (1984), 126–186; Steven J. Heyman, "Foundation of the Duty to Rescue," *Vanderbilt Law Review* 47 (1994): 673.

Oona A. Hathaway

The Promise and Limits
of the International Law of Torture

The Convention against Torture and Other Cruel, Inhuman or Degrading Treatment or Punishment is regularly celebrated as one of the most successful international human rights treaties.[1] Its adoption by the United Nations in 1984 culminated an effort to outlaw torture that began in the aftermath of atrocities of World War II. Nations that ratified the Convention consented not to intentionally inflict "severe pain or suffering, whether physical or mental," on any person to obtain information or a confession, to punish that person, or to intimidate or coerce him or a third person.[2] Today, with a membership of over 130 countries, the Convention stands as a symbol of the triumph of international order over disorder, of human rights over sovereign privilege.

Yet while the Convention and its regional counterparts are indisputably remarkable achievements, events of the post–September 11 era have given reason for pause. Torture, we have learned, is not just a practice of the past. As the United States prepared to go to war in Afghanistan, the Bush administration repeatedly drew attention to the Taliban's use of torture to maintain a semblance of control. And no one who followed the news during the following year could not be aware that Saddam Hussein's regime survived for so long in no small part by instilling a paralyzing fear in the population through the widespread use of torture and killing of those it deemed a threat.

Even more troubling, it has become apparent that our enemies in the war on terrorism are not the only ones who have made use of what had previously been seen as unthinkable practices. As noted in Sanford Levinson's introduction, it is an open secret that many of the suspects caught by the

United States in the course of the war on terrorism have been turned over to Saudi, Egyptian, Syrian, and Jordanian officials, who are suspected of using torture in the course of their subsequent questioning. Indeed, even before the scandal over the treatment of prisoners held by the United States at the Abu Ghraib prison in Iraq erupted, it was well known that the United States has itself used "stress and duress" techniques that skirt and perhaps sometimes cross the line dividing legal interrogation from torture.[3]

These revelations pose not only a moral challenge, which the earlier chapters in this book have explored, but also a challenge to those who believe in the power of international law to impose global order. All of the nations mentioned earlier, except Iraq and Syria, have ratified the Convention against Torture and thereby made an international legal commitment not to use torture. Yet they are known to have continued, if not expanded, its use. Recent events thus leave exposed the dark underbelly of the international legal regime against torture: it is not so clear that it really works.

In this chapter, I explore the place of international law in efforts to bring an end to the practice of torture. The debate over whether international law "works" has until now been highly polarized. On the one hand, skeptics of international law claim that international law is mere window dressing. States don't give up the right to engage in torture unless they have no intention of using it anyway. And once they join treaties like the Convention against Torture, states will act no differently from if they had not done so.

On the other side of the debate are those who reject this dismissive view of international law. They argue that states do not simply join treaties that are in their material interests. Rather, states will join a treaty if they are committed to the ideas and goals it embodies, even if doing so may be costly. And once states join, believers in international law argue, they will abide by their international legal commitments "most of the time."[4]

I, by contrast, argue that international law has a real effect, but not one that either friends or foes of international law would expect. In short, neither advocates nor skeptics of international law examine the whole picture. Both fail to consider the role of internal enforcement of international treaties on countries' willingness to join and abide by them. Moreover, both ignore almost completely the indirect effects of treaties on countries' decisions to accept international legal limits on their behavior and then to violate or abide by them. Recognizing these dynamics creates a broader perspective on the role that international law plays in shaping how states actually behave and hence provides a more accurate picture of both the potential and the limits of international law.

Who Joins the Treaties Prohibiting Torture and What Effect Do They Have?

Let us begin by examining the facts. Which states commit to the Convention against Torture and thereby agree not to take advantage of this possibly useful (if horrific) tool? Do states that do so actually improve their practices as a result?

My examination of the practices of over 160 nations over the course of forty years provides some answers to these questions. The evidence supports several key findings. First, countries that ratify treaties outlawing torture do not always have better torture practices than those that do not. Second, democratic countries are more likely overall to make the legal commitment not to use torture than nondemocratic countries. Third, democratic nations that use torture more frequently are less likely to join the Convention against Torture than those that engage in less. Fourth, nondemocratic nations that use more torture are more likely to join the Convention against Torture than those that use it less. Finally, and perhaps most surprising, not only does it appear that the Convention does not always have the intended effect of reducing torture in countries that ratify, but, in some cases, the opposite might even be true.

I begin by examining which nations make the legal commitment not to engage in torture. Do countries that sign and ratify treaties that outlaw torture have better torture practices than do those that do not?[5] Contrary to the predictions of both critics and advocates of international law, the answer is no. Indeed, countries with worse torture ratings are *slightly more likely* to ratify the Convention against Torture than those with better ratings.[6] Even more striking, states that have ratified the regional conventions prohibiting torture have *worse* practices on average than those that have not, or that did so only after letting several years pass.[7] On the other hand, the opposite is true of articles 21 and 22 of the Convention against Torture (which have stronger enforcement provisions that countries can separately agree to accept). Countries with better torture ratings have committed to articles 21 and 22 at four times the rate of those that have worse torture ratings.[8]

Table 11.1. Who Accepts Limits on Torture?

	Countries that Torture Less	Countries that Torture More
Convention against Torture	41%*	47%*
Articles 21 and 22	22%*	6%*

*Indicates pairs for which the difference is statistically significant at the 99% level.

The story becomes even more interesting when we compare the willingness of democratic and nondemocratic nations to accept international legal limits on their torture practices, as revealed in tables 11.2 and 11.3.[9] First, it is apparent that democratic nations are more likely, on the whole, to join the Convention against Torture. That, perhaps, is not all that surprising, particularly given that democratic nations are less likely to torture than nondemocratic nations.[10] What is surprising, however, is that *non*democratic nations that reportedly use torture frequently are *more* likely to join the Convention than nondemocratic nations that reportedly use torture infrequently.[11] For example, Afghanistan, Cameroon, and

Table 11.2. Comparing Democracies and Nondemocracies

		Better Torture Ratings	Worse Torture Ratings
Nondemocratic	Ratified Convention:	24%*	40%*
		(776)	(383)
	Signed Convention:	35%*	50%*
		(776)	(383)
	Joined articles 21 and 22:	4%	6%
		(776)	(383)
Democratic	Ratified Convention:	57%	62%
		(790)	(201)
	Signed Convention:	76%	74%
		(790)	(201)
	Joined articles 21 and 22:	40%*	6%*
		(790)	(201)

Note: The number of observations appears in parentheses.

*Indicates pairs for which the difference is statistically significant at the 95% level or higher.

Table 11.3. Comparing Democracies and Dictatorships

Torture Rating:		1 (No Verified Allegations of Torture)	2	3	4	5 (Torture Is "Prevalent" or "Wide-spread")
Dictatorship	Ratified	7%	14%	35%	41%	43%
	Convention:	(73)	(218)	(410)	(218)	(109)
	Signed	7%	22%	40%	47%	53%
	Convention:	(94)	(259)	(487)	(247)	(125)
	Joined	1%	1%	5%	2%	6%
	articles 21 and 22:	(94)	(259)	(487)	(247)	(123)
Democracy	Ratified	69%	76%	53%	50%	60%
	Convention:	(221)	(279)	(223)	(115)	(43)
	Signed	85%	83%	67%	64%	68%
	Convention:	(264)	(300)	(236)	(121)	(47)
	Joined	49%	34%	20%	10%	11%
	articles 21 and 22:	(264)	(600)	(236)	(121)	(47)

Note: The number of observations apperas in parentheses.

Egypt—all of which have well-documented histories of using torture—ratified the treaty almost immediately after it opened for signature, whereas Oman and the United Arab Emirates, with their comparatively good records, have yet to ratify. These patterns are found across the board. As table 11.3 demonstrates, as democracies' torture ratings grow worse, they are increasingly less likely to make legal commitments that prohibit them from engaging in torture. Again, the opposite is true of dictatorships: those with worse reported torture practices are *more* likely to join the Torture Convention than those with better reported practices.

All of these results hold up in a more sophisticated statistical analysis that holds states' economic and political characteristics constant. Looking at the group of states as a whole (grouping together democratic and non-democratic states), I find that states that reportedly engage in more torture are no less likely to commit to the Convention against Torture or to articles 21 and 22 than states that reportedly engage in less torture. But again, if we look at democratic regimes alone, we find that they differ from the nondemocratic states in two interesting ways. First, they are simply more likely to join the Convention against Torture and articles 21 and 22. Second, even though they are more likely on the whole to join the Convention and articles, the more torture they use, the less likely they are to join—a pattern exactly opposite of that seen among nondemocratic regimes.

We now know something about which states join the Convention against Torture. But whether states will actually abide by international legal commitments once they are made is, of course, another issue altogether. Again, the empirical evidence holds some surprises for traditional accounts. My research indicates that human rights treaties do not always have the effects their proponents intend. A state's ratification of the Convention against Torture provides no guarantee that its actions will improve. Egypt, Cameroon, and Mexico were among the earliest to ratify the Convention against Torture, yet they continued to have some of the worse torture practices well into the 1990s. Indeed, if one compares states that share otherwise similar economic and political characteristics, it turns out that—if anything—those that ratify the Convention against Torture are reported to engage in *more* torture than those that have not ratified.

Accounting for the Evidence

As the foregoing evidence amply demonstrates, traditional accounts of international law that see it as either almost wholly effective or almost wholly ineffective are simply wrong. States do not only agree to the Convention against Torture if it requires them to do what they are already doing, as critics contend. They actually join it even it commits them to do something more. Yet, at the same time, states that ratify the Convention might sometimes have practices that are actually worse than those of states that have not ratified. Advocates of international law are equally at a loss to explain the empirical results. States with poor torture records commit so readily to the Convention against Torture that it would not be unreasonable to conclude that they do so only because they do not take the commitment seriously. More troubling for advocates of international law, however, is the evidence suggesting that countries that ratify the Convention against Torture and articles 21 and 22 do not engage in less torture as a result. In fact, some countries that ratify might possibly torture their citizens more!

Hence neither side of the existing debate provides a convincing account of the facts. In what follows, I argue that their failure to do so is due to their common oversight of important parts of the broad landscape that defines the role and effect of international law in modern society. More specifically, both fail to consider the role that domestic institutions play in shaping states' willingness to join and to comply with international legal rules. Both also ignore almost completely the role that concern about reputation plays in states' decisions to commit to and abide by international legal rules.[12] These two dynamics have long been overlooked in international law scholarship; yet both, I will show, are central to understanding state choices to commit to and abide by international law.

Domestic Institutions and Self-Enforcement

Often ignored in the celebrations of the Convention against Torture is the fact that while it is quite strong in substance, it is remarkably weak in enforcement. The central enforcement procedure in the treaty is a requirement that states submit reports to the Committee against Torture, an international body created by the treaty to oversee the Convention.[13] But failure to abide by even this minimal commitment is frequently ignored.[14] Stronger enforcement procedures are available but wholly optional: countries can agree to allow states and individuals to file complaints against them with the Committee against Torture, but they are not required to do so in order to join the treaty.[15] Consequently, only about 30 percent of those who have joined the Convention have accepted these additional procedures. According to the skeptical view of international law, these weak enforcement provisions mean that states will never change their behavior to obey the Convention.

Unquestionably, it is true that fear of enforcement is an important reason that states follow international rules. Thus the absence of significant enforcement provisions in the Convention against Torture (and, indeed, in much of international law) certainly means that the Convention is less likely to be closely observed. Yet it does not mean, as some skeptics would argue, that the Convention will have no effect. Indeed, if enforcement were the only reason people followed the law, the world would be a much messier place. Individuals abide by the law for a complex mix of reasons, including, among others, fear of enforcement by private parties or of retribution by the wronged party, internalization of the legal rule, and concerns about the impact on their reputation if others learn of their wrongdoing. Hence, even if there is no chance that individuals will be punished for a legal transgression, there are still many reasons why they might abide by the law.

As advocates of international law are quick to point out, the same is true of states. There are many reasons other than enforcement that states can be expected to follow international law. Yet when it comes to specifying what those reasons are, the advocates of international law tend to fall short. They often fall back on the relatively imprecise claim that *pacta sunt servanda* is the central proposition of international law.[16] Or they argue that norms of international law are "internalized" by states, without giving much guidance as to when and why certain rules or propositions will be internalized and others will not.[17]

The notion of "self-enforcement"—the use of domestic institutions by domestic actors against the government to uphold international rules—provides more precise guidance. International law is not obeyed only when states fear that an international organization or other state actor will levy sanctions against those who disobey the law, as many skeptics assume. Much of international law is instead obeyed primarily because domestic institutions create mechanisms for ensuring that a state abides by its international legal commitments, whether or not particular governmental actors wish it to do so. In democratic nations, in particular, actors outside government can use litigation, media exposure, and political challenges to compel governments to abide by their international legal commitments. In states lacking these institutions, however, it is more difficult for domestic actors to pressure the government to live up to the commitments it has made. For this reason, the extent to which domestic institutions permit domestic actors to pressure the state to abide by international law can have an important influence on a state's record of compliance.

However, a perverse prediction arises from these claims. The more likely a state is to engage in self-enforcement, the more likely it is to expect to be required to change its practices to abide by an international treaty. And the more likely a state expects to change its practices to abide by a treaty, the more costly and hence less attractive membership will appear. States that are more likely to engage in self-enforcement of the terms of a treaty are therefore less likely to commit to the treaty in the first place. Put another way, the more likely the treaty is to lead to an improvement in a state's practices, the less likely the state will be to join it.

This is, of course, exactly what the evidence outlined earlier shows. This approach thus helps explain why the democratic nations that are reported to engage in more torture are less likely to ratify the Convention against Torture than those that reportedly engage in less (even though, on the whole, nations that reportedly engage in more torture are no less likely to ratify the Convention than those that reportedly engage in less). It also helps account for why nondemocratic nations actually appear to be substantially more likely to ratify the Convention if they have worse torture records than they are if they have better torture records.

The dynamic of self-enforcement described here enriches both skeptical and sanguine accounts of the role of international law. For skeptics, it has the effect of broadening the notion of enforcement to include internal enforcement efforts. For advocates, it gives a more detailed and precise mechanism to account for the process of internalization. To determine when and why some international rules will be internalized and some will not one can simply look to the treaty terms (is it self-executing?) and the domestic institutions of member states (can actors independent of the government compel it to abide by its international legal commitments?).

The Role of Reputation

Traditional accounts of international law not only tend to ignore the role of domestic institutions in enforcing international law. They have also, for the most part, turned a blind eye to the effects of states' concerns about their reputations. This is a serious oversight, for in many areas—particularly the international law of torture—reputational concerns often play a more significant role than do the much-studied sanctions imposed by a treaty in states' decisions to commit to international legal limits on their torture practices and then abide by or shirk them.

Simply put, states join treaties like the Convention against Torture in no small part to make themselves look good. In doing so, they may hope to attract more foreign investment, aid donations, international trade, and other tangible benefits. The consistent result is that those that do not engage in prohibited practices will be less likely to join treaties because they have little to gain (their reputation is already good) and something to lose. Conversely, those who are reported to engage in prohibited practices will be *more* likely as a result to join treaties because they stand to gain something and put very little at risk.

Concerns about reputation at home and abroad can also provide states with a powerful motivation to abide by their international legal commitments once they are made. Where violations are likely to be discovered (as is often true, for example, of international trade laws), states will be likely to follow international rules in order to foster a good impression among other members of the international community. But where violations of international commitments are difficult to detect—for example, torture—violations will probably be more common. Moreover, states that already possess good reputations are more likely to abide by their commitment under treaties than are those with poor reputations—again because they have more to lose. This, in turn, further reinforces the counterintuitive dynamic noted earlier: to the extent that those with good reputations expect to expend time and energy ensuring that their treaty commitment will be followed (thus protecting their strong reputations), the prospect of making a treaty commitment will be viewed as more costly, and hence the state will be more reluctant to commit in the first place. Thus, once again, states that are more likely to comply with a treaty's requirements will be less likely to agree to them in the first place as a consequence.

Once again, reference to the actions of states in the real world confirms these claims, some of which are deeply counterintuitive. To begin with, states that have better torture records (and better reputations) are *less*, not more, likely to join the Convention against Torture than states that have worse torture records (and worse reputations). This is particularly true among dictatorships (who do not face the countervailing pressure of self-enforcement discussed earlier). Dictatorships are not only more likely on the whole to join the Convention against Torture if their practices are worse than if they are better but also their likelihood of joining the Convention against Torture grows with each successive increment of worsening torture ratings. Moreover, it appears that the calculated risk that states with poor torture records (and reputations) take in joining the Convention may in fact pay off. The empirical evidence suggests that, if anything, states that join the Convention have *worse* practices than they would be expected to have had they not joined the Convention. This puzzling result may arise because states that ratify receive a boost in their reputations and consequently feel less incentive to make real improvements in their actual torture practices (improvements that would undoubtedly be more difficult and more expensive to achieve than the highly visible but potentially costless act of ratifying a treaty).

Lessons for the Future

What lessons can be drawn from the successes and shortcomings of the Convention against Torture? I will highlight three in particular here. First, while enforcement of international law by international actors is not essential to effective international law, it is far from irrelevant. Where international institutions do not put in place effective enforcement mechanisms, there is of necessity greater reliance on other methods of maintaining compliance, such as domestic enforcement and reputational incentives. But these other methods do not, as I have shown, always have the effects that are intended. In particular, the reliance on domestic enforcement to fill the gap left by weak international enforcement can produce a regime that is shunned by precisely those states who would be the best members. There is, therefore, a tradeoff between widespread participation in the regime and its effectiveness: the more effective the regime would be at changing a state's behavior, the more reluctant the state is to join it in the first place. Any modifications to the international legal torture regime must be made with an awareness of this tradeoff.

Second, the evidence presented here makes clear that strong domestic institutions are essential not only to domestic rule of law but also to international rule of law. Where international bodies are less active in enforcement of treaty commitments, it falls to domestic institutions to fill the gap. In some states, this reliance on domestic institutions is effective. In others, however, it is less so. Because the international torture regime relies so heavily on domestic rule of law institutions, strengthening those institutions could have a profound impact on compliance with the international legal torture regime.

Third, and finally, state reputation plays a central role in state decisions to participate in and comply with the international torture regime. This, again, sometimes produces unintended consequences. At present, membership in the Convention against Torture can confer a boost to a state's reputation, regardless of whether it actually abides by the Convention's requirements. This is possible because the international community does little to police the treaty requirements, leaving member states facing little risk of external exposure if they fail to abide by the Convention's requirements. As a consequence, states that engage in torture and have weak domestic rule of law institutions have every reason to join the Convention. However, simply monitoring the activities of treaty members could substantially improve the situation. If states' violations of the terms of the treaty were likely to be made public, states that do not intend to abide by the treaty would be substantially less likely to join.

The Convention against Torture has not brought an end to states' horrific abuse of their own citizens. Far from it. Each day we learn of new violations, even by states that joined the Convention in its earliest days. Violations of both the letter and spirit of the law are rampant. Yet while the Convention is not a panacea, neither is the problem of torture beyond the reach of international law. Although the Convention has not achieved its lofty goals, it has contributed to the now almost universal view that torture is an unacceptable practice. By facing up to the Convention's successes and its failures, we can begin to learn how to harness the real but limited power of international law to continue to change the world for the better.

Notes

1. This chapter draws on research conducted and data collected for Oona A. Hathaway, "Do Human Rights Treaties Make a Difference?" *Yale Law Journal* 111 (2002): 1935–2042 (hereafter Hathaway [2002]); and "The Cost of Commitment," *Stanford Law Review* 55 (2003): (hereafter Hathaway [2003]). Portions of the chapter are adapted from a forthcoming article, "Between Power and Principle: International Law and State Behavior," *Chicago Law Review* 72 (forthcoming 2005).

2. See John Parry, chapter 8 herein, for a full discussion of the various definitions of torture in international law.

3. See Dana Priest and Barton Gellman, "U.S. Decries Abuse but Defends Interrogations: 'Stress and Duress' Tactics Used on Terrorism Suspects Held in Secret Overseas Facilities," *Washington Post,* December 26, 2002, A1.

4. Louis Henkin, *How Nations Behave,* 2nd ed. (New York: Columbia University Press, 1979), 320–321.

5. The database I use in this article includes crossnational and time series data. Hence a single observation provides information only about a single country during

a single year—a "country-year." When discussing empirical results in this chapter, I refer to such "country-years" with the shorthand "country."

6. This difference is statistically significant at the 99 percent level.

7. For more on the method used to construct the ratings discussed herein, see Hathaway (2002), 1968–1976.

8. This difference is statistically significant at the 99 percent level.

9. The data for table 11.1 are drawn from Hathaway (2003). Table 11.2 is drawn from Hathaway (2003), 1850. Table 11.3 is drawn from James Raymond Vreeland, "CAT Selection: Why Governments Enter into the UN Convention against Torture," unpublished manuscript (2003), which tests arguments made in Hathaway (2002, 2003). It uses data on torture from Hathaway (2002) and data on democracy and dictatorship from a yet unpublished manuscript by Jennifer Gandhi and Adam Przeworski, "Dictatorial Institutions and the Survival of Dictators" (2002), whose definition of democracy and dictatorship differs in several ways from the data on democracy used in Hathaway (2002). This makes the coherence in results all the more striking.

10. Countries that reportedly torture the least (have a torture rating of 1) have an average democracy rating of 7.59; countries that reportedly torture the most (have a torture rating of 5) have an average democracy rating of 2.42. For more on the sources of data on torture and democracy, see Hathaway (2002), 1969–1972, 2029–2030.

11. Hathaway (2003), 1850. These differences are statistically significant at the 99 percent level.

12. My other work situates these dynamics within a broader framework that more fully describes the relationship between international law and state behavior. In that work, I demonstrate that international law gives rise to three contrasting and overlapping sets of incentives for countries to voluntarily accept limits on their actions and then abide by them. I place the incentives created by internal enforcement and state concerns about reputation within these broader categories. I will be elaborating this argument in forthcoming publications.

13. Article 40 of the International Covenant on Civil and Political Rights reads, in part: "The States Parties to the present Covenant undertake to submit reports on measures they have adopted which give effect to the rights recognized herein and on the progress made in the enjoyment of those rights." Article 19 of the Convention Against Torture and Other Cruel, Inhuman or Degrading Treatment or Punishment, reads, in part: "The States Parties shall submit to the Committee . . . reports on the measures they have taken to give effect to their undertakings under this Convention."

14. As of 2000, 71 percent of all state parties to human rights treaties had overdue reports, and 110 states had five or more overdue reports. Anne F. Bayefsky, *The UN Human Rights Treaty System: Universality at the Crossroads* (Ardsley, N.Y.: Transnational, 2001), 8. For descriptions and assessments of the intergovernmental human rights enforcement system, see Henry J. Steiner and Philip Alston, eds., *International*

Human Rights in Context: Law, Politics, Morals, 2nd ed. (New York: Oxford University Press, 2000), 592–704, as well as Philip Alston, ed., *The United Nations and Human Rights: A Critical Appraisal* (New York: Oxford University Press, 1992), and Philip Alson, *Final Report on Enhancing the Long-Term Effectiveness of the United Nations Human Rights Treaty System,* U.N. ESCOR, 53d Sess., Agenda Item 15, U.N. Doc. E/CN.4/1997/74, 1996, 37.

15. Articles 21 and 22 of the Convention provide for these additional enforcement mechanisms.

16. *Pacta sunt servanda* means "[a]greements (and stipulations) of the parties (to a contract) must be observed." *Black's Law Dictionary,* 6th ed., (1990), 1109.

17. For a more complete overview of this scholarship, see Hathaway (2002), 1955–1962, and Oona A. Hathaway and Harold Hongju Koh, *Foundations of International Law and Politics* (New York: Foundation Press, forthcoming 2004). Especially important are Abram and Antonia H. Chayes, *The New Sovereignty: Compliance with International Regulatory Agreements* (Cambridge, Mass.: Harvard University Press, 1995); Thomas M. Franck, *Fairness in International Law and Institutions* (New York: Oxford University Press, 1995); and Harold Hongju Koh, "Why Do Nations Obey International Law?" *Yale Law Journal* 106 (1997): 2599–2659; Koh, "The 1998 Frankel Lecture: Bringing International Law Home," *Houston Law Review* 35 (1998): 623–680; and Koh, "Is International Law Really State Law?" *Harvard Law Review* 111 (1998): 1824–1861.

Fionnuala Ní Aoláin

The European Convention on Human Rights and Its Prohibition on Torture

As is well known, the European Convention on Human Rights (ECHR) prohibits torture and inhuman and degrading treatment. The European Court is generally lauded for its extensive and detailed jurisprudence interpreting article 3 of the Convention, with the predictable caveat of academic and policy quibbles around individual decisions. The Court has moved from an early jurisprudential tentativeness to a liberal interpretation of the requirements of proof for torture and an expansion of multiple institutional and individual contexts in which the prohibition is applicable. Moreover, recent decisions suggest a significant move toward a "horizontal" application of the torture prohibition, which means that states are held responsible for a failure to curb or prevent the actions of private parties that lead to the experience of torture or inhuman or degrading treatment.

This brief essay does not purport to offer a comprehensive review of all case law under article 3; rather, it seeks to identify key strands of judicial thought on the prohibition of torture. Where relevant I link the development of the Court's thinking to identifiable influences that have shaped its judicial approach. I then go on to assess the uniqueness of the Court's approach in comparative terms. Part of this analysis is based on the fact that there exist in Europe a broader set of rights enforcement mechanisms that go beyond the development and enforcement of the ECHR or the more explicit European Convention for the Prevention of Torture and Inhuman or Degrading Treatment or Punishment. So while singling out the ECHR, the essay also affirms that any analysis of a European "view" on torture can only be fully understood in a much broader context of analysis, and situated in a specific cultural and political context. The obvious point is that this environment is not blandly transferable to other parts of the world. I then examine some of the problem areas of torture practices and jurisprudence in Europe.

The fundamental weakness in the European system is a structural and political inability to respond to systematic violations of human rights, as manifested particularly in the dealings of the Court with jurisdictions such as Turkey and Northern Ireland. Both have experienced long-term internal conflict mediated only to some degree by the application of the Convention. The European judiciary's failings are not simply due to the complexities of dealing with "problem" societies but rather reflect on a broader inability to respond to systemic human rights abuses committed by formally democratic states. I conclude by assessing the challenges posed to the prohibition of torture in Europe in the post–September 11 context.

Standards for Defining Torture under the Convention

Article 3 of the Convention prohibits torture in absolute terms: "No one shall be subjected to torture or to inhuman or to degrading treatment or punishment." No derogation is permitted from the rule, meaning that even where a state finds itself in the most acute situations of crisis it is not permitted to resort to any of the measures prohibited under article 3. The Court has been consistently strict in its emphasis on the nonviolable nature of article 3, leaving no loopholes for states to justify the use of any of the measures prohibited in the provision.

The Court has developed a three-tier hierarchy of proscribed forms of treatment or punishment corresponding to the terminology of the prohibition. Notably, the bulk of the cases coming before the Court have come under the degrading or inhuman treatment/punishment thresholds. In clarifying the standards the Court applies to each of these thresholds, a number of preliminary points need to be made. First, because the Court has substantially refined its criteria on each threshold over time, early jurisprudence of the Court under article 3 should not be taken as indicative of the standards the Court applies to cases it reviews currently. Second, there is a substantial degree of conceptual overlap between all three thresholds, and it is sometimes difficult to separate out the distinctions that form the basis of the Court's separation, particularly as between the standards of "degrading" treatment and "inhuman" treatment. Finally, the Court has laid extensive emphasis on the subjective experience and characteristics of the individuals alleging violations under article 3. Thus, while objective criteria can be identified in relation to the prohibition, the subjective element can significantly skew the identification and application of abstract standards per se.

The existence of a three-pronged hierarchy was confirmed by a 1969 case brought by Denmark and other states against the Greek military government.[1] Here, the now defunct Commission examined allegations of extensive ill-treatment against detainees, including "falanga" (beating the feet with a wooden or metal stick in a manner that leaves no skin lesions but causes intense pain), the application of electric shocks, hair-pulling from the head and pubic region,[2] intense noises and sleep deprivation, prolonged manacling, genital mutilation, and severe pain infliction. Each threshold represents a progression of seriousness, in which one moves progressively from forms of treatment that are "degrading" to those that are "inhuman" and then finally to "torture."[3] This formal typology suggests that that it is the seriousness or intensity of the experience alone that places treatment in one category or another. As the analysis hereafter reveals, this is not actually the case, and there are a complex set of factors that operate to place particular experiences of ill-treatment along the continuum of seriousness, as set out in the three-tier hierarchy.

In relation to degrading treatment or punishment, the threshold has been applied to a wide variety of situations, including prison and detention conditions, corporal punishment, gender-based discriminations (including the treatment of transsexuals), and racial discrimination. Generally, degrading treatment encompasses treatment or punishment that humiliates or demeans a person in a way that shows a lack of respect for his or her dignity and personhood. It is also characterized by the feelings it arouses in the victim, including inferiority, fear, anguish, and physical or mental suffering. The inflicted and experienced aspects of this come together when they operate to break an individual's moral and physical resistance. The treatment need not be public for the threshold to be reached. It is enough that the individual experiences humiliation for a violation to have taken place.[4] The cases also reveal that experiences of psychological anguish are a compelling feature for the degrading treatment threshold to be satisfied.[5] The Court's willingness to focus on the experienced nature of the incident(s) for the victim moves us some ways away from a fully objective set of criteria that might easily be transferable from one case to another.

The standards articulated by the Court in respect of inhuman treatment or punishment are also to be found across a range of contexts, including treatment when in state custody (e.g. prisons, custody in general, including medical institutions), through the process of extradition and immigration controls, and in schools through the use of punishments or controls on pupil behaviors. The difference in defining treatment as *inhuman* rather than *degrading* or as *torture* could be said to derive primarily from the intensity of the suffering experienced by the individual. The case that has served to illustrate this divide is the well-known case brought by the Republic of Ireland against the United Kingdom with regard to five particular interrogation techniques used by the British government against detainees held in prolonged custody in Northern Ireland during the early 1970s.[6] They included wall-standing, hooding, subjection to noise, and deprivation of sleep, food, and drink. While the European Commission was unanimously satisfied that all of these measures amounted to the use of torture against the detainees, the Court disagreed, categorizing them as inhuman treatment. The formal language of the decision suggests that it was the *degree of suffering* experienced by the detainees, in terms of its cruelty and intensity, that constituted the basis for the Court's finding of the lesser violation. The Court's standards have shifted over the intervening twenty-five years; were this case to appear on the Court's docket today, the outcome might well be a very different one. In the well-publicized case of *Selmouni v. France,* where the French state was found to have violated the torture prohibition, the Court said:

> [C]ertain acts which were classified in the past as "inhuman and degrading" as opposed to "torture" could be classified differently in the future. [T]he increasingly high standard being required in this area of the protection of human rights and fundamental liberties correspondingly and inevitably require greater firmness in assessing breaches of the fundamental values of democratic societies.[7]

The earlier case thus needs to be read in the context of its time as a highly sensitive political case—a leading Western democracy being accused of systematic torture, in the context of a fraught internal conflict in Northern Ireland to which the British government had committed its military forces. In such a context, the decision needs to be read as much in terms of its political weight as the practices being examined.

As regards *torture,* the threshold established by the Court makes clear that the term is reserved for treatment or punishment of the most serious form. Thus, in the recent case of *Askoy v. Turkey,* the Court confirmed that "the distinction [between torture and other forms of treatment] would appear to have been embodied in the Convention to allow the special stigma of 'torture' to attach only to deliberate inhuman treatment causing very serious and cruel suffering."[8] In the earlier Greek case, the Court had said that the word *torture* was often used "to describe inhuman treatment, which has a purpose, such as obtaining information or confessions, or the infliction of a punishment."[9] It is generally evident in the European torture cases that the elements of deliberation and objectives are highly significant. Thus, deliberation and intention on the part of the torturer are key to finding that the prohibition has been breached.[10] Torture can be either physical or psychological. In the Greek case, the Commission accepted that such acts as mock executions, threats to throw persons out of windows, the use of insulting language, being compelled to witness the torture, and inhuman or degrading treatment of others (particularly of family members or friends) all fell within the ambit of the prohibition. The Court has indicated that the motivation for the act of torture is irrelevant, that is, it need not be used as a means to gather information but can be an expression of sadism, and still constitute torture.

In highlighting the definitional features of article 3, the distinctions between *torture* and *inhuman* and *degrading* treatments or punishments would seem to center on the degree of pain or suffering inflicted or experienced. This view would suggest that there are objectives markers on the kinds of acts and experiences that would automatically fall into one category over another. In fact, the European Court has never held this to be the case. Rather, the categorization of violation has consistently been determined by reference to *all* the circumstances of a case, specifically taking into account the duration of the treatment, its physical and mental effects *on the person* experiencing or observing it, the age, sex, culture, and state of health of the victim and the gender or social status of the person inflicting the treatment. It is also clear that as the range and breadth of cases coming before the Court has expanded in recent years, the Court's greatest strength has been to maintain its flexibility and nuance. Thus, in the recent case of

Keenan v. United Kingdom the Court clearly accepted that severity of suffering is only one of the factors that it takes in account when applying the three-pronged choice offered by the language of article 3.

> While it is true that the severity of suffering, physical or mental, attributable to a particular measure has been a significant consideration in many of the cases decided by the Court under Article 3, there are circumstances where proof of the actual effect on the person may not be a major factor.

Finally, it is worth noting that the Court has moved in the direction of acknowledging state responsibility for the actions of private persons ("private" rather than "public" torture, as it were). Here the Court has focused on the responsibility of the state in terms of both its acts and omissions that could have functioned to prevent, punish, or remedy the actions of third parties.[11] This emerging stream of jurisprudence is a clear indication of the moving boundaries of protection against torture in the European context, and an increasingly extensive application of vertical human rights norms to a wide variety of horizontal contexts.

The Uniqueness of the Court's Approach

It follows from the foregoing brief survey that there are valid reasons to identify a uniquely European approach to the prohibition on torture. As compared with other international human rights systems, the scale of case law on torture and inhuman and degrading treatment in the European context is unparalleled. A number of commentators have also noted that despite the ratification and operationalization of the 1987 United Nations Convention against Torture and Other Cruel, Inhuman or Degrading Treatment or Punishment, the European Convention system continued to play a leading role in defining the legal terms of the international debate on standards prohibiting and defining acts of torture. In acknowledging this, it is also important to place the European Convention within a broader set of rights enforcement mechanisms in Europe, including, but not limited to, the development and enforcement of the European Convention for the Prevention of Torture and Inhuman or Degrading Treatment or Punishment. Moreover, the European Convention operates in a regional environment that is highly supportive, at least at the rhetorical political level, of human rights norms. The most recent evidence of this is the commitment by the European Union under the Nice Treaty to a human rights charter that would bind European states in their multilateral political and legal relationships within the Union's economic, political, social, and military context.[12] In addition, states (generally eastern European) seeking entry to the single European market understand that a key criteria for admissibility is a "human rights proofing" of their legal and political systems. In this environment, not only is there political validation for human rights norms but enforcement mechanisms such as the European Court also extend considerable influence on political structures outside their own obvious sphere of influence. It is in this broader context that the Court's development of article 3 jurisprudence must be viewed.

Equally, as the European Convention has embedded itself in the constitutional and legal systems of states, a process of circular reinforcement is evident. The Court's early tentativeness can easily be read as a deferential pose in a political context that was highly sensitive to external legal intrusion. As European states have become accustomed to external legal scrutiny, and their legal systems have accordingly bent to preempt and/or accommodate such review, it has become much easier for the Court to extend both the depth and breadth of its jurisprudence in the context of article 3. This also means that a step back from the high moral ground established by the Court in a post–September 11 climate is highly unlikely, at least in the short term.[13]

One of the clear advantages of the European system is that its approach has been seen as giving rise to a "preventative" approach to violations.[14] This can be identified in the Court and Commission's jurisprudence but also occurs as a result of the work of the European Committee on the Prevention of Torture (ECPT). While the ECPT is not a juridical body empowered to settle claims in any way, it is designed to prevent ill-treatment from occurring in the first place. It does so by having a preemptive approach, visiting states on a regular basis, and accessing places of detention during such visits. It also engages in ongoing conversations with states about how to practically and legally create the appropriate kinds of legal prohibitions, give the appropriate training to state agents, and upgrade physical locations of detention, which can assist in preventing torture or ill-treatment happening in the first place.

In conclusion, it is also useful to reflect on the language contained in article 3 itself. As one commentator has noted, "the laconic style in which article 3 is drafted leaves open a number of definitional elements of torture or other forms of ill-treatment."[15] The looseness of the drafting has left maximum flexibility to the Court and encouraged an open-ended and innovative approach. This has dovetailed with an increasingly receptive approach by European states to supranational legal oversight. In this context, the Court has exploited the political capacity of European states to absorb a shifting and evolving standard for democratic states. In short, the Court has effectively continued to raise the bar for democratic states, in respect of the levels of protection expected for human rights norms in general and with regard to the prohibition of torture in particular. An interesting aspect of state behavior in all this is that states have not rebelled. Rather, there is an obvious internalization of these norms at the domestic level and a willingness to acquiesce to the Court's jurisprudential expansionism.[16]

The Problem of Systematic Violations Involving Article 3

After offering a rosy assessment of the European Convention's performance, I now turn to examine some weaknesses in this system. Much of the intricacy and sophistication of the European Court's jurisprudence in the article 3 context has been developed in dealing with individual complaints. This is not surprising, in that the ECHR is a system primarily focused on individual litigants, and the strength of the system has traditionally been defined as its capacity to fine-tune its jurisprudence to individual circumstance. However, this individual capacity also demonstrates certain limitations, most obviously when gross and systematic violations of human rights are at issue. As many observers have noted, torture and other forms of inhuman and degrading treatment are by and large not sporadic occurrences within institutional settings; rather they are evidence of systemic problem indicating widespread resort to such measures by officials of the state. The European Convention faces two specific problems when dealing with allegations of gross and systematic violations of human rights and, more specifically, torture. First, the Convention system is structurally ill equipped to respond to such allegations by individuals or state parties. Its fact-finding capacity has been little used, and its jurisprudence has created conceptual and practical obstacles for litigants in proving that systemic violations are taking place within a state. Moreover, group rights are conceptually underdeveloped in the Convention jurisprudence.[17] As a result, widespread violations of human rights are difficult to confront procedurally. A further procedural complication is that the Convention contains no basis of standing for groups of cases alleging the same violation by the same state (though in such cases the registrar has the discretion to bind the cases together for the Court's review). Second, the perceived defamatory or negative implication of a torture finding for states is seen as especially sharpened when allegations of systematic violation are sustained by the Court. This has resulted in a self-imposed unwillingness by the Court (and the Commission before it) to develop the concept of administrative practice (the formal phrase used within the Convention system to describe gross and systematic violations of human rights) and to apply it to circumstances where arguably it is well grounded.[18]

The first formal recognition by the Court of administrative practice in an individual case came in *Donnelly v. United Kingdom*.[19] The case concerned allegations of brutality and ill-treatment following the introduction of detention without trial in Northern Ireland during the 1970s. The most significant part of the decision concerned whether or not the individuals alleging the violations were required to seek a domestic remedy before resorting to supranational oversight by the European Court (the treaty rule is termed "exhaustion of domestic remedies"). The Court had to decide whether, given the peculiar characteristics of administrative practice and the presumption of tolerance by the state of the acts alleged in such a context, an individual should be required to seek a domestic legal remedy. Following lengthy review the Commission found that if there was prima facie evidence of such tolerance, individuals could be exempted from the rule.[20] In such cases the Commission would examine the efficacy of the domestic remedies available as part of its substantive assessment. However, the drawback for the victim with this approach is that if the state's remedies are deemed retrospectively to have been operating effectively, her case may be deemed procedurally inadmissible, because she failed to access those remedies before looking outside the state for review. Despite these procedural limitations, it remains theoretically possible for any applicant to allege administrative practice. However, in practice its use has been extremely limited.

The *Donnelly* decision on administrative practice raises one more important issue. In its adjudication the Commission leaned to the view that administrative practice was defined only by tolerance at the highest levels of government. It seems that tolerance at the lower and middle levels of the state does not suffice to constitute administrative practice (even if that tolerance is frequently demonstrated) when governments take reasonable steps to prevent recurrence. The reasonableness of such steps is not defined. For the victims of systematic human rights violations, this threshold has proven very difficult to reach, and is probably one of the reasons why, despite compelling evidence and a plethora of cases, administrative practice has never been sustained against states like the United Kingdom (in Northern Ireland) and Turkey in the context of torture and right-to-life complaints.

Finally it is worth noting that there is a link between allegations of systematic human rights violations and the willingness of Convention states to use the interstate complaint mechanism. States will generally not take other states to public task for one-off violations of human rights but may do so if practices are widespread and blatantly egregious. For example, in the Greek Case, Denmark alleged, *inter alia,* that multiple violations of article 3 of the Convention had taken place, at multiple detention facilities.[21] In this case the European Commission did acknowledge that widespread practices of human rights violations had occurred, demonstrating that the European system is not incapable of naming multiple human rights violations as systemic political practices. However, the European system has been generally slow to name and shame states for systematic violations of human rights. This reluctance is likely to cause considerable difficulties when the Council of Europe is fully expanded to encompass the former Soviet states.

The reasons for the European Court's reluctance are manifold, but arguably to raise administrative practice is to undermine a central feature of the European self-definition of its rights identity. It is potentially destabilizing of the political support enjoyed by the Court (and previously the Commission). States are loath to admit human rights violations but are more graceful where the state violation can be explained away as an individual aberration, a one-off situation. That is to say, the consequences in political terms for a state of being deemed a gross violator of human rights may be quite extensive in political terms, when participation in international human rights structures is a defining feature (externally and internally) of its constitutionalism and democratic standing. Further, as membership of human regimes is increasingly deemed to be a precursor to the membership of the elite international economic communities, the significance of being found to breach the human rights rules may be augmented, as eastern European states' experience of the European Union's membership process has demonstrated.[22]

We should also note that for states who are found to be in violation of human rights norms, the political presentation of that fact is not without significance. This has two aspects. The first is the servicing of a domestic political audience, which may punish a democratic government electorally for its policy failures, or which may lose the confidence of significant communities within the state in governance. Second, alliances with the external political community of nations, on which both democratic and nondemocratic states depend, may be put in jeopardy. These complex relationships underpin state unwillingness to be categorized as a persistent violator of human rights. It is always easier for states to present a human rights violation as an aberration from the normal practices of good governance than to admit that violations are widespread and are defining of the experience of government for citizens.

To some extent *Ireland v. United Kingdom* demonstrates the point. Here the United Kingdom government accepted that ill-treatment occurred in a detention context and issued the public undertaking that the five techniques under Court and Commission review would be suspended and never employed again. There was a clear political benefit to that acknowledgment, which went hand in hand with the position that it was a unique situation that would not occur again.

However, the broader point I would make here is that the European human rights system has been complicit in hiding the extent of violations by certain states, and that this is specifically identifiable when analyzing the Court's approach to the issue of torture. The Court has played a game with states, treating each violation as if it were the sole violation ever to appear before it, even if the same state is appearing before it again and again in respect of the same types of violation. The perpetuation of similar kinds of violations is indicative of more rudimentary problems with the contracting state, which the Court has been reluctant to respond to. To legally entertain the political reality that systemic human rights' violations have been a feature of western European state experience would open up Pandora's box, requiring an assessment of whether there is a genuine commitment to human rights protection by leading democratic states. This is a place where the Court (as yet) has not been prepared to go.

Torture and Terrorists under the European Convention

The absolute nature of the prohibition against torture under the Convention is best illustrated by the Court's views on the use of torture or other forms of inhuman and degrading treatment against terrorist suspects. There is little sense of explicit or implicit latitude to the state's authorities when dealing with individuals in this category, an approach that has become even more evident in the Court's jurisprudence in the past decade. This stream of thinking has a parallel in the approach of the Court to the use of force endangering the life of alleged terrorist suspects. In this context, the Court has essentially said that a democratic society owes a burden of protection to suspected terrorists equal to what it owes to any citizen.[23]

The general approach to torture in the antiterrorism context can be gleaned from the Chahal case, a deportation case involving a suspected terrorist to a third state:

> Article 3 enshrines one of the most fundamental values of democratic society. The Court is well aware of the immense difficulties faced by States in modern times in protecting their communities from terrorist violence. However, even in these circumstances, the Convention prohibits in absolute terms torture or inhuman or degrading treatment or punishment, irrespective of the victim's conduct.[24]

The Court has persistently emphasized that article 3 enshrines one of the most fundamental values of a democratic society. While the Court has also affirmed its awareness of the immense difficulties faced by states in protecting their communities from terrorist violence, this has not deterred it from setting absolute prohibitions in the antiterrorism context. Even here the Court's jurisprudence prohibits torture irrespective of the victim's conduct.[25] The pertinent question may well be, as a result of the Court's unrelenting emphasis on the Convention as a "living" instrument, whether the long and increasingly ambitious "war" against terrorism will have a degrading effect on the level of protection currently afforded under article 3 over the medium to long term.

Conclusion

This brief reflection on the prohibition against torture and inhuman and degrading treatment contained in the European Convention on Human Rights emphasizes both the strengths and weaknesses of the European system. Comparatively the European Court measures up exceedingly well against other regional courts and international bodies in the scope and depth of its jurisprudence on torture. In recent years it has also demonstrated an increasingly robust approach to the behavior of state agents in democratic states, and shown that it is prepared to raise the standards of behavior that it expects democratic states and their agents to adhere to. It has also demonstrated unusual innovation in its willingness to hold states responsible for the behavior of ordinary individuals in what would, to date, have been described as private contexts of torture and inhuman and degrading treatment. All this bodes well for the extension of the torture prohibition, and has contributed to creating a political and legal climate in Europe where (at least officially) there is no tolerance for the use of torture, and there is little appetite for weakening the strength of the prohibition. However, the system has its weak points. The most notable of these is the unwillingness of the Court and the Council of Europe's political system to robustly confront systemic violations of human rights, including torture. To do this effectively, the legal thresholds must be procedurally accessible to and meaningful for vulnerable victims, and be reflective of the forms in which systemic violations present themselves within states. The challenges of these limitations loom large with a series of cases from Chechnya pending on the Court's docket. There is also little doubt that in a post–September 11 world, as European states have rushed to legislate in the antiterrorism field, human rights norms are under increasing pressure in Europe. The long war against terrorism may wield a pernicious and underestimated effect on both the general political climate within European states and the willingness of the Court to remain at the forefront in enforcing ever-higher standards for human rights protection on those same states.

Notes

1. See *Denmark et al. v. Greece*, (1976) 12 Yearbook.
2. See Malcolm D. Evans, "Getting to Grips with Torture," *International and Comparative Law Quarterly* 51 (2000): 370.

3. See *Tryer v. United Kingdom*, Judgment of 25 April 1978, A26, para. 32.

4. Thus, for example, in some recent cases involving disappearances of family members, the Court has said that the "severe mental distress and anguish" experienced by a close family member after a prolonged period would meet the level of "degrading" or even "inhuman" treatment. See *Kurt v. Turkey*, Judgment of 25 May 1988, paras. 133–134.

5. See *Ireland v. United Kingdom* (1978) 2 EHRR 25, para. 16.

6. See *Selmouni v. France*, Judgment 28 July 1999, 29 EHRR 403, para. 101. The case concerned the ill-treatment in France of an individual suspected of drug trafficking. The alleged acts included severe beatings, sexual violence and debasement, urination on the person by officials during the course of detention and interrogation, and ongoing mental suffering. See generally Neils Uidriks, "Police Torture in France," *Netherlands Quarterly of Human Rights* (1999): 411.

7. See *Askoy v. Turkey*, Judgment of 18 December 1996, 23 EHRR 553, para. 63.

8. *Denmark*, para. 186.

9. See *Aydin v. Turkey* (1997) 25 EHRR 251.

10. See *Keenan v. United Kingdom*, Judgment of April 3, 2001, para. 112.

11. See *D.P. & J.C. v. United Kingdom*, Judgment of 10 October, 2002. Here the Court was asked to determine whether the state was liable for its failure to protect the applicants, allegedly subject to child abuse by their stepfather during childhood.

12. Available online at: www.europarl.eu.int/charter/default_en.htm.

13. Early evidence of this has been the firm refusal of European states to extradite persons suspected of terrorist activity to the United States and other countries where they may be subject to the death penalty if charged and convicted of terrorist activity. This refusal is based on article 3 jurisprudence, where the European Court of Human Rights has defined the death row experience as constituting torture, inhuman, and degrading treatment under the Convention. See *Soering v. United Kingdom*, Judgment of 7 July 1989.

14. Evans, "Getting to Grips with Torture," 368.

15. See Yutaka Arai-Yokoi, "Grading Scale of Degradation: Identifying the Threshold of Degrading Treatment or Punishment under Article 3 ECHR," *Netherlands Quarterly on Human Rights* 21 (2003): 388.

16. An example of this internalization, and the setting of even higher domestic standards within states, based on article 3 of the Convention, is a series of cases concerning the use of force by state agents in Austria. Thus, the Austrian Constitutional Court has found that the use of physical force by state agents may constitute inhuman treatment when it shows disregard for the human dignity of the person so treated. See, e.g., Decision of 29 September 1992, Constitutional Cout of Austria, B.590/89; Decision of 10 June 1988, Constitutional Court of Austria, B. 483/86; Decision of 27 February 1987, Constitutional Court of Austria, 30 Yearbook (1987), 273.

17. While it is fair to say that domestic minorities have been protected as individu-

als by efficient use of procedural guarantees, there is no coherent theory of "the group" emerging from the Court. See generally *Golder v. United Kingdom* (1975) 1 E.H.R.R. 524; *Schonenberger & Durmaz v. Switzerland,* (1988) 11 E.H.R.R. 202. Nor has there been a carving out of special status for minorities and identifiable groups within member states' political structures arising from any such duty identified under the Convention.

18. The practical significance of finding administrative practice is twofold. First, at the stage of admissibility, the Commission has held that the rule requiring the exhaustion of domestic remedies does not apply in cases of administrative practices. This means that a litigant is not bound to seek a domestic remedy for the alleged violation prior to seeking an international remedy. Second, the finding of administrative practice means that official recognition and acceptance of the practice in question is clearly far more widespread and serious than an isolated incident of breach by a particular state official.

19. *Donnelly v. United Kingdom,* Application Nos. 5577/72-5533/72, *Collection of Decisions* (1973): 122. Decision on admissibility, April 5, 1973.

20. Thus, the Commission observed that "where there is a practice of non-observance of certain Convention provisions, the remedies prescribed will of necessity be sidestepped or rendered inadequate. Thus, if there were an administrative practice of torture or ill-treatment, judicial remedies prescribed would tend to be rendered ineffective by the difficulty of securing probative evidence, and administrative inquiries would either not be instituted, or if they were, would be likely to be half-hearted and incomplete."

21. *Denmark,* Report of the Commission, 12 Yearbook (1969), 194.

22. See generally Thomas M. Franck, "Legitimacy in the International System," *American Journal of International Law* 82 (1988): 705.

23. See *McCann and Others v. United Kingdom:* Fionnuala Ni Aolán, "Truth Telling, Accountability and the Right to Life," *European Human Rights Law Review* 5 (2002): 572.

24. *Chahal v. United Kingdom* (Application no. 22414/93), Judgment of 15 November 1996; (1997) 23 EHRR 413, para. 80.

25. Ibid., para. 80.

Oren Gross

The Prohibition on Torture
and the Limits of the Law

13

The debate about the moral and legal nature of the prohibition on torture is often conducted as if there is no middle ground. One may support an absolute ban on torture, a ban that applies in times of peace as well as in times of great calamity. Alternatively, one may believe that the duty not to torture, even if generally desirable and laudable, does not apply in certain exceptional circumstances, or, even if it does apply, is overridden, canceled, or trumped by competing values.

Absolutists—those who believe that an unconditional ban on torture ought to apply without exception regardless of circumstances—frequently base their position on deontological grounds, that is, they assess the intrinsic moral value of things independent of their consequences. For them, torture is inherently wrong. It is an evil that can never be justified or excused. It violates the physical and mental integrity of the person subjected to it, negates her autonomy and humanity, and deprives her of human dignity. It reduces her to a mere object, a body, from which information is to be extracted, while coercing her to act in a manner that may be contrary to her most fundamental beliefs, values, and interests.[1] Torture is also wrong because of its depraving and corrupting effects on individual torturers as well as on society at large. Hence, under no circumstances should such actions be morally acceptable or legally allowed.

Others support an absolutist view of the ban on torture by arguing that the social costs of permitting the use of torture, even in narrowly defined exceptional circumstances (assuming that those exceptional circumstances lend themselves to such narrowly tailored definitions), would always outweigh the social benefits that could be derived from applying torture. Hence, there can be no point in any act of balancing on a case-by-case basis with respect to the question of torture, since a correctly calibrated cost-benefit analysis must always lead to the same conclusion, namely, that torture should not be allowed regardless of any specific context. Any analysis that leads to a contrary conclusion is based on miscalculation, which is the result of distorted focus on isolated cases while ignoring long-term and systemic implications of particular courses of action.

In its purest form, the absolutist point of view does not accept the permissibility or the usefulness of talking about the possibility of using torture in exceptional circumstances or of discussing moral and legal dilemmas that are invoked by such cases as the "ticking bomb" scenario.[2] Indeed, even attempting to conduct a rational conversation about torture may be deemed wrong, as it can undermine the commitment to a general absolute prohibition. Torture is impermissible, and that is all there is to it.

It is easy to see why this uncompromising point of view is castigated by its opponents as utopian, naive, or even outright hypocritical. The case of the ticking bomb is used by those who advocate the position that use of coercive interrogation methods may be justified in certain—albeit exceptional and extraordinary—circumstances. Under this position, which can be termed the "conditional ban" approach, there seems to be no place for a comprehensive, absolute, a priori prohibition on the use of torture.

The most prevalent arguments in support of the conditionality of the prohibition on torture are consequentialist claims comparing costs and benefits on a case-by-case basis. Consequentialists measure the worth of any thing by its ultimate consequences. A thing is worthy if it increases the overall "good." Such an approach may lead to the conclusion that, at least in some cases, the social benefits of torture exceed the social costs that attach to such practices.[3] Aside from the important question of what constitute good (and bad) consequences, people who are willing to engage in this sort of analysis are often charged with being biased toward immediate consequences while discounting (or ignoring entirely) long-term consequences of the use of torture as well as with treating the use of torture, in and of itself, as morally neutral, since all that really matters are the results. These failings result in too much, rather than too little, torture.

One attempt to escape both sets of criticisms calls for the use of what Charles Black coined "orders of magnitude" assessment. Thus, even if a straightforward cost-benefit analysis leads to the conclusion that, in a given case, the benefits from use of torture outweigh the costs involved, torture is not to be used unless the magnitude of the threat to society (which may be prevented or minimized as a result of resorting to torture) is of a particularly large scale (e.g., the "nuclear weapon in a suitcase in the middle of a major metropolis" scenario). Under this approach, the prohibition on torture sets out a strong presumption against the use of torture. That presumption is, however, rebuttable. Yet to refute it in any given case a showing must be made of the exceptional magnitude of the risk involved. Only in such extreme cases may the fundamental presumption against the use of torture be refuted. In all other cases, torture is banned.[4]

A third set of arguments put forward by the conditionalists suggests that the prohibition on torture cannot be defensible as a moral absolute. The prohibition on torture, it is conceded, is an important and fundamental principle, but it is not the only value in play in extreme circumstances. Thus, for example, when the choice is between the physical integrity and dignity of a suspected terrorist, on the one hand, and the lives of a great many innocent persons (e.g., those who are highly likely to be killed or be seriously injured should the ticking bomb actually go off), on the other hand, an absolute ban on torture cannot be morally defensible.[5] Indeed, the fact that all but unabashed Kantians recognize the difficulties presented by extreme cases to any absolutist position is taken as further evidence that an absolutist position with respect to the ban on torture is untenable.

Interestingly enough, most absolutists and conditionalists share at least one common, if unstated, theme. While the former regard such scenarios as the ticking bomb case as irrelevant, the latter often focus precisely on those cases and deny the moral or legal validity of any claim to absolutism of the general prohibition on torture. Here is my first point of departure from either perspective.

In this article I defend an absolute prohibition on torture while at the same time arguing that the ticking-bomb case should not be brushed aside as merely hypothetical or as either morally or legally irrelevant. I suggest that the way to deal with what may be called the "extreme" or "catastrophic" case is neither by reading it out of the equation nor by using it as the centerpiece for establishing general policies. Rather, the proposal made herein focuses on the possibility that truly exceptional cases may give rise to official disobedience: public officials may step outside the legal framework, that is, act extralegally, and be ready to accept the legal ramifications of their actions. However, there is also the possibility that the extralegal actions undertaken by those officials will be legally (if not morally) excused ex post. I argue that the prospect of extralegal action supports and strengthens the possibility of formulating (and maintaining) an absolute prohibition on torture.

My focus is on what I call *preventive interrogational torture.* Henry Shue identified interrogational torture as torture whose aim is gaining information.[6] By adding "preventive" I seek to limit the discussion to that use of torture whose aim is to gain information that would assist the authorities in foiling exceptionally grave future terrorist attacks. Hence, the aim is entirely forward-looking. Preventive interrogational torture is not concerned with, for example, obtaining confessions or other evidence that may be used to bring the subject of interrogation to criminal trial. Nor is it concerned with punishing individuals for past actions.

A second clarification concerns the scope of the term "torture." Much of the legal discussion about torture revolves around the decision as to what precisely constitutes "torture." Thus, for example, the jurisprudence developed under the European Convention on Human Rights has tended to tackle the issue through the prism of a "severity of suffering" test. According to this test, a distinction can be drawn among various categories of ill-treatment (e.g., ill-treatment that amounts to "degrading" or "inhuman" treatment or to "torture") as well as between ill-treatment and treatment that does not cross the threshold of suffering that would render such treatment impermissible.[7] The "severity of suffering" test has been invoked by governments arguing that interrogation techniques utilized by their agents, while rough and coercive, did not cause so much suffering as to constitute "ill-treatment." Thus, the threshold test of suffering has been used in an attempt to fly below the radar of the absolute prohibition on torture. I am not interested in such definitional wizardry, which avoids hard questions by attempting to convince us that there is no fundamental dilemma that ought to be addressed. Rather, the argument I develop hereafter seeks to address instances where interrogation methods that clearly fall within the ambit of "torture" are used. The case of the preventive interrogational torture is truly complex. We are not served well by attempting to pretend that it is a much simpler case of definitional juggling.

The Case for an Absolute Prohibition on Torture

Torture is absolutely prohibited under all the major international human rights and humanitarian law conventions. This unconditional ban also forms part of customary international law and, arguably, amounts to a preemptory norm of international law.[8] No country around the world admits to the use of torture by its agents or openly challenges the absolute nature of the prohibition. Indeed, most governments proudly point out to specific provisions in their respective national constitutions and penal codes that prohibit torture and attach criminal sanctions to acts amounting to torture.

The case for an absolute prohibition on interrogational torture seems to me to be a compelling one. However, I do not believe that the case for an absolute ban can be made solely within the four walls of what Michael Moore called "the absolutist view of morality."[9] While nonconsequentialist reasoning supports a *ban* on torture, it does not, in and of itself, present a compelling case for an *absolute* ban. To arrive at the conclusion that absolute prohibition on torture is justified, more is needed. I anchor that necessary addition in pragmatic reasoning.

Taken from a purely Kantian perspective, the ban on torture is considered to be an unconditional duty under all circumstances. For this statement to hold true, we must conclude that the ban on torture trumps all competing values, including, for example, the right to life (e.g., we may not torture even when this is necessary to save the lives of innocent individuals). Moral absolutists must maintain their support for the absolute ban on torture even when the outcome of abstaining from use of torture in any given case is truly catastrophic, indeed, even if the survival of the whole world is at stake. *Fiat justitia et pereat mundus* (let justice be done though the world perish). This may be the case, for example, when the particular ticking bomb is a nuclear device whose activation may result in the killing of millions of innocent people. The question whether such a scenario is at all likely, while bearing considerable weight when assessing the pragmatic reasons for an absolute ban on torture, is of little significance when discussing the moral basis for such a ban. To be a true moral absolutist, one must support a ban on torture no matter what, that is, no matter how likely the harm and no matter how great the magnitude of that harm. In real life, however, even those who believe that saving the life of one (or more) innocent individuals may not justify or excuse torture of suspected terrorists are hard pressed to uphold that position in cases where there is a real risk that a harm of catastrophic proportions will materialize. As I demonstrate hereafter, many who support absolute, categorical rights, and (where relevant) prohibitions, realize that their position is untenable, not only practically but also morally speaking, when applied to such catastrophic cases.

Yet, whether one accepts that there can be no circumstances under which use of torture may be morally justified or excused or subscribes to the view that there are situations in which resort to torture may be defensible, supporting an absolute *legal* ban on torture makes sense. For the former, the prescription of an absolute prohibition on torture poses no difficulty and requires no further explanation. Yet even those who advocate the latter position ought to support an absolute legal ban on preventive interrogational torture. This position is supported by numerous arguments, and I will briefly note some of the more salient ones.

1. *Setting general policy, accommodating exceptional cases.* While ticking bomb scenarios are not merely hypothetical cases conjured up in an academic ivory tower, they are extremely rare in practice. When we set out to chart a general policy on the issue of torture we must ask ourselves whether our general policy ought to be shaped around the contours of these rare exceptions. Or is there an independent value in striking a strong position in favor of an absolute ban on torture? Those who believe, as I do, that the ticking bomb case is a hard one from both ethical and legal perspectives must be mindful of the risk of creating bad law (and ethics) to answer to the particular needs of the hard case.

However, we must also be careful not to go to the other extreme. Henry Shue warns that "artificial cases make bad ethics."[10] This is certainly an attractive proposition. Yet its problem lies in the fact that ticking bomb cases are not "artificial." They are real, albeit rare. Ignoring them completely, by rhetorically relegating them to the level of "artificial," is utopian or naive, at best. There is a difference between ignoring completely the truly catastrophic cases and focusing our attention elsewhere when designing general rules and policies. We can address the real conundrums presented by such cases in other ways.

2. *Symbolism, myths, and education.* A categorical prohibition on the use of torture is also desirable in order to uphold the symbolism of human dignity and the inviolability of the human body. Such a prohibition not only approximates what decent people believe but also what society we want to live in and belong to.[11] Moreover, even if one believes that an absolute ban on torture is unrealistic, as a practical matter, there is independent value in upholding the myth that torture is absolutely prohibited. Such a position may serve as an obvious notice that fundamental rights and values are not forsaken, whatever the circumstances, and that cries of national security, emergency, and catastrophe do not trump fundamental individual rights

and liberties. In fact, the more entrenched a norm is—and the prohibition on torture is among the most entrenched ones—the harder it will be for government to convince the public that violating that norm is necessary.

An absolute prohibition on torture plays a significant educational function. It attaches special (moral, political, social, and legal) condemnation to torture as abhorrent. Furthermore, in addition to complying with a nation's obligations under international law, upholding an uncompromising ban on torture sends a clear and strong message to other countries around the world about the impermissibility of such practices.[12]

3. *Strategy of resistance.* It may well be that use of preventive interrogational torture under certain extreme circumstances is inevitable. If government agents perceive such use to be the only way to procure critical information that is deemed necessary to foil an imminent massive terrorist attack that would result in thousands of casualties, they are likely to resort to such measures, whether they are legally permissible or not. However, even when we acknowledge that inevitability, it still makes good sense to say an absolute no to the use of torture. As Fred Schauer argues, "[r]esisting the inevitable is not to be desired because it will prevent the inevitable, but because it may be the best strategy for preventing what is less inevitable but more dangerous."[13] What is "less inevitable but more dangerous" is, for example, the expanded use of interrogational torture to less-than-catastrophic cases. Once we authorize state agents to use interrogational torture in one set of cases, it is unlikely that we will be able to contain such use to that limited subset of cases. Rather, such powers and authority are likely to expand far beyond their original intended use. Moreover, the insistence on an absolute ban on torture may slow down the rush to resort to torture practices even in truly exceptional cases. Such an absolutist position not only imposes moral inhibitions on government officials but also raises the specter of public exposure if a measure is later considered to have been unnecessary, and the (albeit remote) possibility of criminal proceedings and civil suits brought against the perpetrators.

4. *Rejection of balancing tests.* An absolute ban on torture rejects the legitimacy of pursuing any form of balancing in particular cases between the ban on torture and competing values. Such balancing is going to be factually difficult to conduct and subject to inherent biases that would result in more, rather than less, torture.

5. *Slippery slopes.* Slippery slope arguments are a significant part of the absolutists' arsenal. They come in the form of "if X then Y; Y is bad; there-

fore, even if X is good, we must refrain from X because of Y." X, in this case, is allowing the use of preventive interrogational torture in truly exceptional cases. The feared Ys include, for example: (1) use of interrogation torture for nonpreventive purposes (including for purposes of retribution and early punishment); (2) use of interrogational torture in less-than-truly-exceptional cases; and (3) expansion of the use of interrogational torture beyond the particular confines of antiterrorism, such as applying similar methods to "ordinary" criminals. This may be the result of the fact that use of torture creates a certain mindset among interrogators, as well as a broad-based constituency for torture.

In sum, the only realistic barrier against governmental abuse of powers in the context of interrogational torture may be the setting of an absolute prohibition on such practices. Even if there is a cost to be paid by such a prohibition preventing what may be deemed as necessary action in ticking bomb situations, such cost is small, because of the infinitesimal probability of such cases arising (and government not being able to effectively deal with them once they arise by utilizing legitimate measures short of torture) and it is negligible in comparison with the greater costs entailed in abuse of powers by the government in a broader—and arguably more realistic—set of cases.

Catastrophic Cases

Most absolutists end the discussion about the permissibility of interrogational torture at this point. However, the debate about torture persists. As Evans and Morgan note, "[j]ust beneath the surface . . . there is clearly a view, prevalent in many jurisdictions among security and police personnel, that torture, or means of physical or psychological pressure that we may term *near-torture,* may have to be resorted to in certain circumstances."[14] The terrorist attacks of September 11 and the ongoing war on terrorism rekindled a public and intellectual debate on the permissibility of torture and have demonstrated that the view identified in the foregoing excerpt is shared by many segments of the population beyond "security and police personnel."

To deny the use of preventive interrogational torture even when, for example, there is good reason to believe that a massive bomb is ticking in a mall is as coldhearted as it is to permit torture in the first place. It is coldhearted because in true catastrophic cases the failure to use preventive interrogational torture will result in the death of many innocent people. Upholding the rights of the suspected terrorist will lead to the negation of the rights, including the very fundamental right to life, of innocent victims. As Sissela Bok observes, "it is a very narrow view of responsibility which does not also take some blame for a disaster one could easily have averted, no matter how much others are also to blame."[15] To deny the use of preventive interrogational torture in such cases, as the Landau Commission in Israel suggested,[16] is also hypocritical: as experience tells us, when faced with serious threats to the life of the nation, government will take whatever measures it deems necessary to abate the crisis. As Justice Ben-Porat of the Israeli Supreme Court wrote in her opinion in *Barzilai v. Government of Israel*, "we, as judges who 'dwell among our people,' should not harbor any illusions. . . . There simply are cases in which those who are at the helm of the State, and bear responsibility for its survival and security, regard certain deviations from the law for the sake of protecting the security of the State, as an unavoidable necessity."[17]

Ignoring those real-life consequences of the ticking bomb case may result in portrayal of the legal system as unrealistic and inadequate. As a result, particular norms, and perhaps the legal system in general, may break down, as the ethos of obedience to law may be seriously shaken and challenges emerge with respect to the reasonableness of following these norms. Thus, legal rigidity in the face of severe crises is not merely hypocritical but is, in fact, detrimental to long-term notions of the rule of law. It may also lead to more, rather than less, radical interference with individual rights and liberties.[18] A conditional ban on torture imposes high social and individual costs, but so too does an absolute ban.

Supporting an uncompromising absolute prohibition on torture amounts to setting unrealistic standards; standards that no one can hope to meet when faced with a truly catastrophic case. As the drafters of the Model Penal Code explain, "[l]aw is ineffective in the deepest sense, indeed . . . . it is hypocritical, if it imposes on the actor who has the misfortune to confront a dilemmatic choice, a standard that his judges are not prepared to affirm that they should and could comply with if their turn to face the problem should arise."[19]

Even if each of us, as moral agents, would be supportive of an absolute prohibition on torture, we would still not want those who are entrusted with keeping us safe from harm to be strictly bound by similar constraints. We want our leaders and our public officials to possess the highest moral character. But I do not believe we want them to be brazen Kantians. Recall Kant's celebrated example of an unconditional duty, that is, the duty to tell the truth. According to Kant, the duty to tell the truth is not suspended even when an assassin (A) asks a person (B) whether a friend of B whom A wishes to murder is hiding in B's house. I agree with Sissela Bok that "[a] world where it is improper even to tell a lie to a murderer pursuing an innocent victim is not a world that many would find safe to inhabit."[20] Very few people would want to have as a friend someone who tells the assassin the truth rather than lie and save her friend. Similarly, few would want a leader who follows Kant's absolutist view to its extreme rather than act to save the lives of innocent civilians. As Judge Posner aptly put it, "if the stakes are high enough, torture is permissible. No one who doubts that this is the case should be in a position of responsibility."[21] Michael Walzer suggested that a moral politician is recognized by "his dirty hands."[22] Faced with a ticking bomb scenario, a moral person who is not a political leader, who does not bear the burden of actual decision-making, would refuse to act in an immoral way and embrace an absolutist perspective. She would keep her hands clean. A public official who is immoral would merely pretend that her hands were clean (for example, by resorting to interrogational torture but lying about it and denying the use of torture). A moral official would do the right thing to save innocent lives, while openly acknowledging and recognizing that such actions are (morally) wrong—that is, openly admitting that her hands are indeed dirty. The question then becomes not whether state agents will use preventive interrogational torture in the face of a moral principle to the contrary (they will) but rather what moral judgment and legal effect should be attached to such action.

Thus, the catastrophic case presents the open-minded absolutist with a real dilemma. Many have sought to resolve that dilemma by conceding that the catastrophic case calls for a special, exceptional treatment.[23] The nature of such exceptional treatment may be the subject of further debate, for example, as to whether it calls for the suspension or qualification of otherwise applicable moral norms (we may then talk about a justification) or whether such general moral norms continue to apply even to the exceptional case, which is still recognized as creating exceptional circumstances (when we may talk about excuses). Yet the important point is recognizing the need to engage in such further debate, that is, acknowledging the relevance and significance of the catastrophic case.

From a legal perspective, the argument about the catastrophic case implicitly acknowledges that legal norms presuppose the existence of a "normal" state of affairs and remain applicable as long as this state of affairs continues to exist. Accordingly, "[t]his effective normal situation is not a mere 'superficial presupposition' that a jurist can ignore; that situation belongs precisely to [the norm's] immanent validity."[24] In the catastrophic case, when this underlying normal state of affairs is fundamentally interrupted, the relevant legal norm may no longer be applicable as is and cannot fulfill its ordinary regulatory function. "For a legal order to make sense, a normal situation must exist."[25] General norms are limited in their scope of application to those circumstances in which the normal state of affairs prevails. Catastrophes undermine this factual basis.

Thus, extreme cases present us with a truly tragic choice. Any attempt to relegate the extreme case to mere irrelevance does not make the choice less tragic, nor does it make a real problem "go away." We can only hope to arrive at a meaningful solution to the legal and moral dilemmas presented to us by the catastrophic case by acknowledging, and accounting for, all the relevant values and interests.

The foregoing discussion still leaves us with the question of what constitutes a truly "catastrophic case." I will attempt to answer this question, which clearly is significant to the overall tenability of my project, on a different occasion. For now, it is sufficient to acknowledge that *some* catastrophic case is possible. The task of this chapter is to set out an argument for the *plausibility* of a solution based on pragmatic absolutism and official disobedience, rather than attempt to define more clearly the precise contours of such proposal.

Official Disobedience

As I tried to demonstrate in the previous two sections, there are two perspectives from which we ought to approach the question of the use of preventive interrogational torture, namely, the general policy perspective and the perspective of the catastrophic case. Unlike most absolutists and conditionalists, I suggest that both perspectives ought to be considered as valuable and relevant. We can only focus on one to the exclusion of the other at our peril. However, we must not use the two perspectives simultaneously. Instead, I suggest that the primary perspective ought to be the general one, which, as I indicated earlier, supports an absolute ban on torture based on a combination of moral and pragmatic considerations. Once this general policy is set in place, we should attend to the real problems that are presented by the catastrophic case. But can we really examine preventive interrogational torture from both perspectives and still get a coherent, morally and legally defensible picture? I believe we can.

I peg my belief on the twin notions of *pragmatic absolutism* and *official disobedience.* In the second section herein, I dealt with the former, namely with the claim that an absolute ban on torture is the right thing to do when we wed moral and pragmatic considerations. What I wish to add to this conclusion now is the argument that the way to reconcile that absolute ban on torture with the necessities of the catastrophic case is not through any means of legal accommodation (such as recognizing an explicit legal exception to the ban on torture that applies to catastrophic cases) but rather through a mechanism of extralegal action that I would term *official disobedience:* in circumstances amounting to a catastrophic case, the appropriate method of tackling extremely grave national dangers and threats *may* entail going outside the legal order, at times even violating otherwise accepted constitutional principles.

Going completely outside the law in appropriate cases preserves, rather than undermines, the rule of law in a way that bending the law to accommodate for catastrophes does not. When great calamities such as those invoked by the truly catastrophic case occur, governments and their agents tend to do whatever is necessary to neutralize the threat, whether legal or not. Yet to say that governments are going to use preventive interrogational torture in the catastrophic case is not the same as saying that they should be authorized to do so through a priori, ex ante legal rules. It is extremely dangerous to provide for such eventualities and such awesome powers within the framework of the existing legal system because of the large risks of contamination and manipulation of that system and the deleterious message involved in legalizing such actions (e.g., constitutional protections are really designed only for ordinary times and are easily suspended precisely when they are needed the most).

Instead, my proposal calls on public officials having to deal with the catastrophic case to consider the possibility of acting outside the legal order while openly acknowledging their actions and the extralegal nature of such actions. Those officials must assume the risks involved in acting extralegally. State agents may regard strict obedience to legal authority (such as the absolute legal ban on torture) as irrational or immoral under circumstances of a true catastrophic case. At the same time, such obedience is still to be expected and demanded by the imposer of such authority.[26] If we consider the role of the authority to be filled by society and identify the public official as the subject of authority, we can understand the possibility of having the latter act outside, even against, the legal authority in particular cases. Society retains the role of making the final determination whether the actor ought to be punished and rebuked or rewarded and commended for her actions. It is then up to society as a whole, "the people," to decide how to respond ex post to such extralegal actions. The people may decide to hold the actor to the wrongfulness of her actions. Alternatively, they may act to approve her actions retrospectively.

The people may determine that the use of torture in any given case, even when couched in terms of preventing future catastrophes, is abhorrent, unjustified, and inexcusable. In such a case, the acting official may be called to answer for her actions and make legal and political amends therefor. She may, for example, need to resign her position, face criminal charges or civil suits, or be subjected to impeachment proceedings. Alternatively, the people may approve the actions and ratify them. Such ratification can come in many forms, legal as well as social and political. Thus, for example, legal modes of ratification may include exercising prosecutorial discretion not to bring criminal charges against persons accused of using torture, jury nullification where criminal charges are brought, executive pardoning or clemency where criminal proceedings result in conviction, or governmental indemnification of state agents who are found liable for damages to persons who were tortured.

In addition, political and social ratification is also possible. Charles Black apparently once put the matter to his constitutional law class at Yale Law School in the following manner. "Once the torturer extracted the information required . . . he should at once resign to await trial, pardon, and/or a decoration, as the case might be."[27] While decoration can establish ex post ratification in appropriate circumstances, there may also be cases where the withholding of decoration sends a strong message of rejection. Michael Walzer, for example, notes the remarkable "national dissociation" by the British from the Royal Air Force Bomber Command. The director of the strategic bombing of Germany from February 1942 until the end of the war, Arthur Harris—whose nickname, not at all coincidentally, was "Bomber"—was not, unlike other commanders, rewarded with a peerage. In addition, and perhaps even more tellingly, even though bomber pilots suffered heavy casualties, they are not recorded by name in Westminster Abbey, unlike the case of all other pilots of Fighter Command who died during the war. Walzer describes Harris as having "done what his government thought necessary, but what he had done was ugly, and there seems to have been a conscious decision not to celebrate the exploits of Bomber Command or to honor its leader."[28] The requirement of ex post ratification ensures that public officials are not above the law. Even when acting to advance the public good under circumstances of great necessity, such actors remain answerable to the public for their extralegal actions.

The proposed solution emphasizes an ethic of responsibility on the part of not only public officials but also the general public. Public officials will need to acknowledge openly the nature of their actions and attempt to justify not only their actions but also their undertaking of those actions.[29] Such open acknowledgement and engagement in public justificatory exercise is a critical component in the moral and legal choice made by the acting officials. The public will then need to decide whether to ratify the relevant extralegal actions. In the process of deciding that latter question, each member of the public becomes morally and politically responsible for the decision. "[D]ecent men and women, hard-pressed in war, must sometimes do terrible things," writes Michael Walzer, "and then they *themselves* have to look for some way to reaffirm the values they have overthrown."[30] But it is not only the actors themselves who must attempt to find a way to reaffirm fundamental values they have violated in times of great exigency; members of the wider society must also undertake such a project of reaffirmation. Each member of society, in whose name terrible things have been done, must become morally responsible.[31] Such responsibility is assumed by and through the process of ratification or rejection of the particular terrible things that have been done.

The possibility of acting extralegally in catastrophic cases facilitates, in and of itself, an absolute prohibition on torture. Consider, for example, the conundrum in which judges find themselves. Under the proposal just advocated, courts need not be concerned with the prospect of taking an expansive view of constitutional rights coming back to haunt the nation when faced with catastrophic cases, which may necessitate limitations on those rights. The courts need not worry because if the situation is serious enough, there is always the possibility of government officials acting extralegally to protect the nation and its citizens. Hence, the very possibility of extralegal action reduces the pressures for incorporating built-in exceptions to protected rights in general and to limit the scope of the ban on torture, in particular, by way, for example, of definitional hocus-pocus "demonstrating" that certain coercive interrogation techniques fall short of "torture" and thus are not subject to the general prohibition.

Furthermore, to acknowledge the *possibility* of extralegal action is not the same thing as accepting willy-nilly limitless powers and authority in the hands of state agents. In a democratic society, where values such as constitutionalism, accountability, and individual rights are entrenched and are traditionally respected, we can expect that the public would be circumspect about governmental attempts to justify or excuse illegal actions even if such actions have been taken, arguably, to promote the general good. Moreover, we can and should expect public officials to feel quite uneasy about possible resort to extralegal measures even when such actions are deemed to be for the public's benefit. This feeling of uneasiness would be even more pronounced in nations where the "constitution is old, observed for a long time, known, respected, and cherished."[32] The knowledge that acting in a certain way means acting unlawfully is likely to have a restraining effect on government agents even while the threat of catastrophe persists.

The need to give reasons ex post, that is, the need to publicly justify or excuse (not merely to explain) one's actions, is a critical ingredient of my proposal. By requiring transparency and publicity, it emphasizes accountability of government agents. The proposed model of official disobedience puts the burden squarely on the shoulders of state agents who must act, sometimes extralegally, without the benefit of legal preapproval of their actions by, for example, the courts. Public officials have no one to hide behind. They must put themselves in the frontline and act at their own peril. If they believe that the stakes are so high that an extralegal action is merited, they may take such action and must then hope that they are able to convince the public to see things their way. As I explained earlier, the threshold of illegality serves, in and of itself, as a limiting factor against a rush to assume unnecessary powers. Moreover, the need to give reasons for the extralegal conduct may also limit the government's choice of measures ex ante. The commitment to giving reasons, even ex post, adds another layer of limitations on governmental action.[33] Moreover, the public acknowledgment of the nature of emergency actions taken by government may contribute to reasoned discourse and dialogue not only between the government and its domestic constituency but also between the government and other governments, as well as between the government and nongovernmental and international organizations. Thus, the need to give reasons is not confined to the domestic sphere. It also has international implications, both political and legal.

Justice Robert Jackson was right to suggest that "[t]he chief restraint upon those who command the physical forces of the country . . . must be their responsibility to the political judgments of their contemporaries and to the moral judgments of history."[34] At the end of the day, it is those political, moral, and—one may add to the list—legal judgments of the public that serve as the real restraint on public officials. A sense of self-indignation when rules are violated (which is the result of the social, political, and legal ethos of the community), coupled with uncertainty about the chances of ratification, militates against too easy a rush to use extralegal powers.

Ex Post Ratification

My proposal calls for maintaining an absolute ban on torture while, at the same time, recognizing the possibility (but not certainty) of state agents acting extralegally and seeking ex post ratification of their conduct. The element of ex post ratification is critical to my project.

By separating the issues of action (preventive interrogational torture) and public ratification, and by ordering them so that ratification follows, rather than precedes, action, the proposed solution adds a significant element of uncertainty to the decision-making calculus of state agents. This "prudent obfuscation"[35] raises both the individual and national costs of pursuing an extralegal course of action and, at the same time, reinforces the general ban on torture. With the need to obtain ex post ratification from the public, the official who decides to use torture undertakes a significant risk because of the uncertain prospects for subsequent public ratification. Perhaps the public would disagree after the fact with the acting official's assessment of the situation and the presumed need to act extralegally. Ratification would be sought ex post, that is when more information about the particular case at hand may be available to the public and possibly after the particular danger (which the use of preventive interrogational torture sought to avert) has been removed and terminated. Under such circumstances, it is possible that calm and rationality, rather than heightened emotions, would govern public discourse, emphasizing further the risk for the official in acting first and only then seeking approval. Of course, the public may also determine that the actions under consideration violated values and principles that are too important to be encroached on as a matter of general principle or in the circumstances of the particular case. The higher the moral and legal interests and values infringed on, the less certain the actor should be of the probability of securing ratification.

Uncertainty is also important inasmuch as it reduces the potential risk of underdeterrence that is involved in the possibility of ex post ratification. Such underdeterrence may occur if interrogators have good reasons to believe that ratification will be forthcoming in future cases where preventive interrogational torture is employed.[36] The risk of underdeterrence is the result of what may be called, following Meir Dan-Cohen, conditions of "low acoustic separation."[37] The acoustic separation model describes a universe in which the general public engages in conduct while public officials make decisions with respect to members of the public. Law contains two sets of normative messages directed to each group—the general public and public officials: one set constitutes decision rules (that is, laws addressed to officials) while the other set constitutes conduct rules (laws addressed to the general public). These sets of rules are acoustically separated and kept (in the pure model) apart. Low degrees of acoustic separation may result from the sophisticated legal mechanisms that are available to interrogators (for example, legal staff of the relevant security service), the possibility of thinking in advance about possible modes of conduct in future ticking bomb cases (even if without the ability to anticipate in advance all possible features of such cases), and the possible professional and personal links between the interrogators and the service in which they work and other state authorities (such as other law enforcement agencies).[38] Significantly, conditions of low acoustic separation create substantial risks of undesirable behavioral side effects on the part of officials, for example, by allowing decision rules—which recognize the possibility that agents who resort to preventive interrogational torture in catastrophic cases may be let off the hook—affect conduct in specific cases (i.e., state agents resorting to torture, despite the existence of an absolute ban thereon, knowing, or at least having good reason to believe, that they will enjoy immunity against criminal charges and civil claims).[39] However, it ought to be recognized that the

uncertainty that is such a critical element of the official disobedience proposal does have similar effects, to some extent, to what Dan-Cohen calls
"means of selective transmission."[40] However, whereas the means of selective transmission facilitate the channeling of different sets of norms to different constituencies (the general public and the authorities), the selectiv-
ity in my context works to draw a clear separating divide between conduct
and decision rules and minimize the risks of behavioral side effects. The
relevant conduct rules are crystal clear: they prohibit absolutely any use of
torture, whatever the circumstances. At the same time, the more uncertain
the substance and the operation of the decision rules are, and the greater
the personal risk involved in reading the substance or the operational status of those decision rules is, the greater the pull is on individual actors to
conform their conduct to the conduct rules that prohibit torture no matter what.

Indeed, even if we accept that there is a very good chance that ex post
ratification will be forthcoming eventually, there are still significant costs
attached to acting extralegally. Even if the public ratifies the decision to use
preventive interrogational torture in a specific case, there may be personal
implications for the officials involved in the decision to apply torture. Such
implications emanate, for example, from the fear that ratification will not
follow or from the fact that ratification may not be comprehensive and fully
corrective (seen from the perspective of the acting agent). Thus, for example, subsequent ratification may shield the actor against criminal charges
but not bar victims of torture from obtaining compensation in civil proceedings. Similarly, when ratification assumes the guise of an executive pardon or clemency it wipes the criminal penalty that was imposed on the individual actor, but it does not remove the ordeal of criminal prosecution
and the (moral) condemnation that is involved in criminal conviction.[41]

Once we broaden our view to incorporate international, in addition to
domestic, legal rules and norms, the costs of acting extralegally are further
elevated, introducing additional disincentives to engage in such conduct.
Even if the use of torture in any given case is domestically excused ex post,
it may be subject to a different judgment on the international plane. This
may have significant consequences, for the individual actor (the interrogator) as well as her government. First, torturers may be subject to criminal
and civil proceedings in jurisdictions other than their own, and may also be
subject to international criminal prosecution.[42] Second, the ban on torture
is nonderogable under the major international human rights conventions,

that is, it cannot be abrogated or derogated from whatever the surrounding circumstances may be. As such, no argument of public emergency can justify or excuse a deviation from the prohibition. State agents who engage in acts of preventive interrogational torture implicate their government in violation of the nation's international obligations and expose it to a range of possible remedies under the relevant international legal instruments.[43]

Recognizing the possibility of ex post ratification is not the same as authorizing the use of preventive interrogational torture ex ante. Unlike the latter, ex post ratification may serve, at most, as an ad hoc, individualized defense to specific state agents against civil or criminal charges in particular cases. It cannot serve as a general, institutional, conduct-guiding rule to be relied on ex ante. Subsequent ratification may only be available to individual public officials after the fact, as opposed to setting a priori guidelines for action. Ratification functions as an ex post excuse, rather than justification, of a particular conduct. Like other excuses, it serves not as an indication of policy goals or as mechanism to guide future behavior by state agents but rather as "expression of compassion for human failings in times of stress."[44] This expression of compassion is particularly significant for what it does *not* imply. An extralegal action, even if followed by subsequent ratification, is unlikely to establish legal precedent for the future. Although the sequence of extralegal action and subsequent public ratification may bring about an eventual change in the law, turning a political precedent into a legal one, such a shift cannot happen under the proposed solution without informed public participation in the process. In addition, because of its individualized nature, it would be hard to generalize ex post ratification into a forward-looking legal norm.

In fact, there is a strong argument that an extralegal action, even if followed by subsequent ratification, does not establish moral precedent for the future. Even those who argue that the moral obligation not to torture may be overridden in particular instances do not seem to argue that such an obligation is either canceled or terminated for all future cases. In other words, such an obligation survives a specific override, which may apply in concrete catastrophic case, and continues to apply to future cases. Furthermore, even in the catastrophic case when such obligation may be overridden, it is not canceled. Using torture, therefore, may be argued to result in a certain degree of moral loss even if we were to consider it legally permissible.[45] Seen from either perspective, a subsequent public ratification does not cancel nor terminate the general duty not to torture.

The individualized, rather than institutional, nature of the subsequent ratification is significant for yet another reason. Institutionalizing interrogational torture reinforces, by conferring an imprimatur of legality and legitimacy, social, hierarchical structures that authorize individuals, namely, the interrogators, to act violently. As Robert Cover warned in his aptly titled article "Violence and the Word," "[p]ersons who act within social organizations that exercise authority act violently without experiencing the normal inhibitions or the normal degree of inhibition which regulates the behavior of those who act autonomously."[46] In such circumstances it is much more likely that resort will be made to violence in interrogations. On the other hand, the need to act extralegally and hope for subsequent ratification focuses on individual behavior. It is not amenable to institutionalization. Interrogation manuals cannot spell it out in great detail. It is left up to the individual interrogator to determine whether to use violence in any given case. Acting at her own peril, the interrogator acts much more as an autonomous moral agent than as an agent for the hierarchical institution she serves.

Talking about Torture

In the previous sections I set out the main features of my approach to the conundrum posed by preventive interrogational torture. My proposed solution is based on the twin concepts of pragmatic absolutism and official disobedience. I argue that an absolute ban on torture is the right thing to do when we wed moral and pragmatic considerations. At the same time I suggest that in circumstances amounting to a catastrophic case, the appropriate method of tackling extremely grave national dangers and threats *may* entail going outside the legal order, at times even violating the otherwise entrenched absolute prohibition on torture.

Readers may charge me with trying to have my cake and eat it too, that is, supporting an absolute ban on torture precisely on the ground that it is not aimed to function as absolute in real-life. Perhaps this is right. Guido Calabresi notes that subterfuges often accompany our wrestling with tragic choices. "We look for solutions which seek to cover the difficulty and thereby permit us to assert that we are cleaving to both beliefs in conflict."[47] My proposal indeed attempts to cleave to both sets of values that may be involved in assessing torture, in general, and preventive interrogational torture, in particular. However, rather than cover the difficulty, I seek to expose it and ensure that it is dealt with in as transparent, open, and public manner as possible.[48]

But is public discourse, in and of itself, desirable in this context? My proposal is made in the context of an intellectual public debate about the permissibility of torture. Mine is one chapter in a book published by one of the leading academic presses and edited by a leading constitutional law scholar. Is it desirable to have such an open debate? Or is it better for the absoluteness of the ban on torture to be treated as axiomatic rather than engage in attempts to prove its desirability or usefulness? William Twining once noted (but rejected) that "philosophical analysis of the problem may provide ammunition which could be used or abused by those who seek to justify actions which reflective and reasonable men would condemn without qualification."[49] Henry Shue, who wrote a classic article that is reprinted in this book, similarly asked, "if practically everyone is opposed to all torture, why bring it up, start people thinking about it, and risk weakening the inhibitions against what is clearly a terrible business?"[50] Although Shue himself referred to such discussions as opening Pandora's box, such fears, obviously, did not prevent either Twining or Shue from writing valuable contributions to the debate. And we are the better for such articles.

The alternative to no debate over the use of torture (or, indeed, to discussion that merely consists of repeating the mantra that torture must be absolutely prohibited) is not the disappearance of the practice of torture. Thus, while we all abhor the medieval detailed codes and procedures on the use of torture, we also ought to recognize that the alternative has not been the elimination of the practice. By not discussing the practice of torture we do not make it go away; we drive it underground. Moreover, by refusing to acknowledge that the notion of torture is more complex than many supporters of the "torture-is-banned-and-that-is-all-there-is-to-it" approach would have us believe, we are running the risk of having the general public perceive the legal system as either utopian or hypocritical. After all, the central premise of this chapter is that most of us believe that most, if not all, government agents, when faced with a genuinely catastrophic case, are likely to resort to whatever means they can wield—including preventive interrogational torture—in order to overcome the particular grave danger that is involved. And most of us hope they will do so.

The prohibition on torture and the catastrophic case present us with truly tragic choices. Public officials (and, under my proposal, also members of the general public) are asked to choose between several fundamental social values, such as the right to be free from torture and the right to life.[51] We may as well make such choices in as informed a manner as possible, taking into account the widest panoply of relevant moral and legal considerations. It is in this context that public debate on torture is critical.

Notes

1. A classic discussion is Elaine Scarry, *The Body in Pain* (1985), 27–59.

2. The basic features of the paradigmatic ticking bomb case are well known: the police have in custody a person who they are absolutely certain has planted a massive bomb somewhere in a bustling shopping mall. The bomb may go off at any moment, and there is not enough time to evacuate the place. Should the bomb go off, thousands of people will die. The only lead that the police have to locate the bomb is the person in custody, but she will not reveal the location of the bomb. Police investigators are certain, beyond any doubt, that the only way of getting the information from her is by torturing her. They are also confident that if torture is applied the suspect will divulge correct information about the location of the bomb, thus giving the bomb squad a better chance of disarming it in time.

3. See, e.g., W. L. Twining and P. E. Twining, "Bentham on Torture," *Northern Ireland Legal Quarterly* 24 (1973): 305.

4. Charles L. Black, Jr., "Mr. Justice Black, the Supreme Court, and the Bill of Rights," *Harper's*, February 1961, 63, 67–68, reprinted in Charles Black, *The Occasions of Justice: Essays Mostly on Law* (1963), 89. It is worth noting that this "orders of magnitude" approach may also be shared by some who arrive at similar conclusions from a deontological, rather than consequentialist, perspective. See, e.g., Michael S. Moore, "Torture and the Balance of Evils," *Israel Law Review* 23 (1989): 280. See also Thomas Nagel, *Mortal Questions* (1979), 56: "while it seems to me certainly right to adhere to absolutist restrictions unless the utilitarian considerations favoring violation are overpoweringly weighty and extremely certain—nevertheless, when that special condition is met, it may become impossible to adhere to an absolutist position."

5. See, e.g., Winfried Brugger, "May Government Ever Use Torture? Two Responses from German Law," *American Journal of Comparative Law* 48 (200): 661; Leon Sheleff, "The Necessity of Defense of the Truth: On the Tortuous Deliberations about the Use of Torture," *Bar-Ilan* 17 (2002): 459, 485–488; Alan M. Dershowitz, *Why Terrorism Works* (New Haven, Conn.: Yale University Press, 2002), 131–163.

6. Henry Shue, chapter 2 herein, p. 51.

7. See, e.g., Malcolm D. Evans and Rod Morgan, *Preventing Torture* (1998), 73–79; Yutaka Arai Yokoi, "Grading Scale of Degradation: Identifying the Threshold of De-

grading Treatment or Punishment Under Article 3 ECHR," *Netherlands Quarterly of Human Rights* 21 (2003): 385.

8. See, e.g., Roland Bank, "International Efforts to Combat Torture and Inhuman Treatment: Have the New Mechanisms Improved Protection?" *European Journal of International Law* 8 (1997): 613; Restatement (Third) of the Foreign Relations Law of the United States, sec. 702, cmt. n (1990). See also *Siderman de Blake v. Republic of Argentina*, 965 F.2d 699, 717 (9th Cir. 1992); *Kadic v. Karadzic*, 70 F.3d 232,2 49 (2d Cir. 1995).

9. Moore, "Torture and the Balance of Evils," 297–298.

10. Shue, chapter 2 herein, p. 55.

11. Black, "Mr. Justice Black," 67.

12. John T. Parry and Welsh S. White, "Interrogating Suspected Terrorists: Should Torture be an Option?" *University of Pittsburgh Law Review* 63 (2002): 743, 763.

13. Frederick Schauer, *May Officials Think Religiously? William and Mary Law Review* 27 (1986): 1075, 1085.

14. Evans and Morgan, *Preventing Torture*, 54.

15. Sissela Bok, *Lying*, 2nd ed. (1999), 41–42.

16. Israeli Government Press Office, Commission of Inquiry into the Methods of Investigation of the General Security Service Regarding Hostile Terrorist Activity (1987), reprinted in *Israel Law Review* 23 (1989): 146, 183.

17. H.C. 428, 429, 431, 446, 448, 463/86, *Barzilai v. Gov't of Israel*, 40(3) P.D. 505, reprinted in *Selected Judgments of the Supreme Court of Israel* 1 (1988), 63. See also Pnina Lahav, "A Barrel Without Hoops: The Impact of Counterterrorism on Israel's Legal Culture," *Cardozo Law Review* 10 (1988): 529, 547–556; Mordechai Kremnitzer, "The Case of the Security Services Pardon," *Iyunei Mishpat* 12 (1987): 595.

18. See, e.g., Bruce Ackerman, *The Emergency Constitution, Yale Law Journal* (forthcoming), "If respect for civil liberties requires governmental paralysis, serious politicians will not hesitate before sacrificing rights to the war against terrorism. They will only gain popular applause by brushing civil libertarian objections aside as quixotic."

19. *Model Penal Code and Commentaries*, sec. 2.09, 372–375 (1985), quoted in Yale Kamisar, "Physician Assisted Suicide: The Problems Presented by the Compelling, Heartwrenching Case," *Journal of Criminal Law and Criminology* 88 (1998): 1121, 1143.

20. Bok, *Lying*, 42.

21. Richard A. Posner, "The Best Offense," *New Republic*, September 2, 2002, 28.

22. Michael Walzer, chapter 3 herein.

23. See Sanford Levinson's introduction, discussing the response of Charles Fried to the problem of "catastrophe." See also Oren Gross, "Chaos and Rules: Should Responses to Violent Crises Always Be Constitutional?" *Yale Law Journal* 112 (2003): 1119–1120.

24. Carl Schmitt, *Political Theology: Four Chapters on the Concept of Sovereignty*,

trans. George Schwab (Cambridge, Mass.: MIT Press, 1985); originally published 1922), 13.

25. Ibid.

26. Frederick Schauer, "The Questions of Authority," *Georgia Law Journal* 81 (1992): 95, 110–114.

27. Quoted in A. Michael Froomkin, "The Metaphor Is the Key: Cryptography, the Clipper Chip, and the Constitution," *University of Pennsylvania Law Review* 143 (1995): 709, 746.

28. Michael Walzer, *Just and Unjust Wars*, 3rd ed. (2000), 323–325. But see Robin Neillands, *The Bomber War* (2001), 401–404.

29. Mortimer R. Kadish and Sanford H. Kadish, *Discretion to Disobey* (1973), 5–12.

30. Walzer, *Just and Unjust Wars*, 325. Emphasis added.

31. But see Walzer, suggesting that members of the public may have a right to avoid, if they possibly can, those political or other positions in which they "might be forced to do terrible things."

32. Guy Howard Dodge, *Benjamin Constant's Philosophy of Liberalism: A Study in Politics and Religion* (1980), 101, quoting Benjamin Constant.

33. See Frederick Schauer, "Giving Reasons," *Stanford Law Review* 47 (1995): 633, 656–657. See also Joseph M. Bessette and Jeffrey Tulis, "The Constitution, Politics, and the Presidency," in *The Presidency in the Constitutional Order*, ed. Joseph M. Bessette and Jeffrey Tulis (1981), arguing that the need for public justificaiton may influence the choice of political acts.

34. *Korematsu v. United States*, 323 U.S. 214, 248 (1944), J. Jackson dissenting.

35. Dan M. Kahan, "Ignorance of Law Is an Excuse—but Only for the Virtuous," *Michigan Law Review* 96 (1997): 127, 139–141, discussing "prudent obfuscation" as a means to respond to the penal law's persistent incompleteness. Kahan discusses the use of vague terms in criminal laws, giving courts "the flexibility to adapt the law to innovative forms of crime ex post" (139).

36. Parry and White, "Interrogating Suspected Terrorists," 764–765.

37. Meir Dan-Cohen, "Decision Rules and Conduct Rules: On Acoustic Separation in Criminal Law," *Harvard Law Review* 97 (1984): 625, reprinted in Meir Dan-Cohen, *Harmful Thoughts* (2002), 37. For further discussion of the concept of acoustic separation in the context of interrogational torture, see Miriam Gur-Arye, chapter 10 herein. See also Dudi Zecharia, "On Torture Chambers and Acoustic Walls," *Politika* 10 (2003): 61.

38. Dan-Cohen, "Decision Rules," 640.

39. Ibid., 631–632. I should note that my proposal calls for a certain role reversal between public officials and the general public. Under my proposal, conduct rules related to the ban on torture will especially target public officials, whereas decision rules would mostly (but not exclusively) target the general public.

40. Ibid., 634–636.

41. See, e.g., Leon Sheleff, "On Criminal Homicide and Legal Self-Defense," *Plilim* 6 (1997): 89, 111–112. Similarly see Kamisar, "Physician Assisted Suicide," 1143–1144; reliance on mitigation of sentence fails to mitigate the "ordeal of a criminal prosecution or the stigma of a conviction."

42. See, e.g., Convention against Torture and Other Cruel, Inhuman, or Degrading Treatment or Punishment, adopted and opened for signature December 10, 1984, 1465 U.N.T.S. 112, articles 4–8; Rome Statute of the International Criminal Court, July 17, 1998, U.N. Doc. A/CONF.183/9 (1998), article 7(1)(f), defining torture as a crime against humanity.

43. See American Convention on Human Rights, opened for signature November 22, 1969, arts. 5(2) and 27(2), 1144 U.N.T.S. 123 (entered into force July 18, 1978); International Covenant on Civil and Political Rights, adopted December 19, 1966, arts. 4 and 7, 999 U.N.T.S. 171 (entered into force March 23, 1976); and European Convention for the Protection of Human Rights and Fundamental Freedoms, November 4, 1950, arts. 3 and 15, 213 U.N.T.S. 221. See also Winston P. Nagan and Lucie Atkins, "The International Law of Torture: From Universal Proscription to Effective Application and Enforcement," *Harvard Human Rights Journal* 14 (2001): 87.

44. George P. Fletcher, "Fairness and Utility in Tort Theory," *Harvard Law Review* 85 (1972): 537, 553.

45. See Daniel Statman, "The Absoluteness of the Prohibition against Torture," *Mishpat Unimshal* 4 (1997): 161, 190–192.

46. Robert Cover, "Violence and the Word," 95 *Yale Law Journal* 95 (1986): 1601, reprinted in *Narrative, Violence, and the Law,* ed. Martha Minow (1992), 203, 221.

47. Guido Calabresi, *Ideals, Beliefs, Attitudes, and the Law* (1985): 88.

48. Guido Calabresi, *A Common Law for the Age of Statutes* (1982), 178–181.

49. William Twining, *Torture and Philosophy, Aristotelian Society* 52 (1978): 143.

50. Shue, chapter 2 herein, p. 45.

51. Guido Calabresi and Philip Bobbitt, *Tragic Choices* (1978), 17, "it is the values accepted by a society as fundamental that mark some choice as tragic."

Reflections on the
Post–September 11 Debate
about Legalizing Torture

Alan Dershowitz

Tortured Reasoning

14

Although this is a book about the substantive issues surrounding the use of physical torture as a means to obtain information deemed necessary to prevent terrorism, I have decided to write my essay about the tortured reasoning and arguments that tend to typify much of the debate about this emotionally laden issue. I have already expressed my views with regard to controlling and limiting the use of torture by means of a warrant or some other mechanism of accountability, and these views are easily accessible to anyone who wishes to read and criticize them.[1] Here, in a nutshell, is my position.

Nonlethal torture is currently being used by the United States in an effort to secure information deemed necessary to prevent acts of terrorism. It is being done below the radar screen, without political accountability, and indeed with plausible deniability. All forms of torture are widespread among nations that have signed treaties prohibiting all torture. The current situation is unacceptable: it tolerates torture without accountability and encourages hypocritical posturing. I would like to see improvement in the current situation by reducing or eliminating torture, while increasing visibility and accountability. I am opposed to torture as a normative matter, but I know it is taking place today and believe that it would certainly be employed if we ever experienced an imminent threat of mass casualty biological, chemical, or nuclear terrorism. If I am correct, then it is important to ask the following question: if torture is being or will be practiced, is it worse to close our eyes to it and tolerate its use by low-level law enforcement officials without accountability, or instead to bring it to the surface by requiring that a warrant of some kind be required as a precondition to the infliction of any type of torture under any circumstances?

That is the important policy question about which I have tried to begin a debate. It is about how a democracy should make difficult choice-of-evil decisions in situations for which there is no good resolution.

This essay focuses on the way academics, judges, pundits, activists, reviewers, and even ordinary folk have chosen to distort, simplify, and caricature my proposal for a torture warrant. In this respect, the essay is somewhat autobiographical, but in a larger sense it is about the way provocative ideas are sometimes distorted in the interest of promoting agendas.

First, a word about how I, a civil libertarian who has devoted much of his life to defending human rights against governmental overreaching, came to advocate this controversial proposal. It began well before September 11, 2001, and it was offered as a way of reducing or eliminating the use of torture in a nation plagued with terrorism.

In the late 1980s I traveled to Israel to conduct research and teach a class at Hebrew University on civil liberties during times of crisis. In the course of my research I learned that the Israeli Security Services (the GSS or Shin Bet) were employing what they euphemistically called "moderate physical pressure" on suspected terrorists to obtain information deemed necessary to prevent future terrorist attacks. The method employed by the security services fell somewhere closer to what many would regard as very rough interrogation (as practiced by the British in Northern Ireland and by the U.S. following September 11, 2001) than to outright torture (as practiced by the French in Algeria and by Egypt, the Philippines, and Jordan). In most cases the suspect would be placed in a dark room with a smelly sack over his head. Loud, unpleasant music or other noise would blare from speakers. The suspect would be seated in an extremely uncomfortable position and then shaken vigorously. Statements that were found to be made under this kind of nonlethal pressure could not—at least in theory—be introduced in any court of law, both because they were involuntarily secured and be-cause they were deemed potentially untrustworthy, at least without corroboration.[2] But they were used as leads in the prevention of terrorist acts. Sometimes the leads proved false; other times they proved true. There is little doubt that some acts of terrorism—which might have killed many civilians—were prevented. There is also little doubt that the cost of saving these lives—measured in terms of basic human rights—was extraordinarily high.

In my classes and public lectures in Israel, I strongly condemned these methods as a violation of core civil liberties and human rights. The response that people gave, across the political spectrum from civil libertarians to law-and-order advocates, was essentially the same: but what about the "ticking bomb" case?

The ticking bomb case refers to variations on a scenario that has been discussed by many philosophers, including Michael Walzer, Jean-Paul Sartre, and Jeremy Bentham. The current variation on the classic "ticking bomb case" involves a captured terrorist who refuses to divulge information about the imminent use of weapons of mass destruction, such as a nuclear, chemical or biological device, that are capable of killing and injuring thousands of civilians.

In Israel, the use of torture to prevent terrorism was not and is not hypothetical; it was and continues to be very real and recurring. I soon discovered that virtually no one in Israel was willing to take the "purist" position against any form of torture or rough interrogation in the ticking bomb case: namely, that the ticking bomb must be permitted to explode and kill dozens, perhaps hundreds, of civilians, even if this disaster could be prevented by subjecting the captured terrorist to nonlethal torture and forcing him to disclose its location. I realized that the extraordinarily rare situation of the hypothetical ticking bomb terrorist was serving as a moral, intellectual, and legal justification for the pervasive *system* of coercive interrogation, which, though not the paradigm of torture, certainly bordered on it. It was then that I decided to challenge this system by directly confronting the ticking bomb case. I presented the following challenge to my Israeli audience: If the reason you permit nonlethal torture is based on the ticking bomb case, why not limit it exclusively to that compelling but rare situation? Moreover, if you believe that nonlethal torture is justifiable in the ticking bomb case, why not require advanced judicial approval—a "torture warrant"? That was the origin of the controversial proposal that has received much attention, largely critical, from the media. Its goal was, and remains, to reduce the use of torture to the smallest amount and degree possible, while creating public accountability for its rare use. I saw it not as a compromise with civil liberties but rather as an effort to maximize civil liberties in the face of a realistic likelihood that torture would, in fact, take place below the radar screen of accountability.

The Israeli government and judiciary rejected my proposal. The response, especially of Israeli judges, was horror at the prospect that they—the robed embodiment of the rule of law—might have to dirty their hands by approving so barbaric a practice in advance and in specific cases.

The Landau Commission, established by the Israeli government in 1987 to explore these issues, also rejected my proposal. Instead it suggested that there are "three ways for solving this grave dilemma between the vital need to preserve the very existence of the state and its citizens, and to maintain its character as a law-abiding State." These are (1) to allow the security service to continue to fight its war against terrorism in "'a twilight zone' which is outside the realm of law"; (2) "the . . . way . . . of the hypocrites: they declare that they abide by the rule of law, but turn a blind eye to what goes on beneath the surface"; and (3) "the truthful road of the rule of law," namely, that the "law itself must ensure a proper framework for the activity of the GSS [the Israeli security agency responsible for counterterrorism] regarding Hostile Terrorist Activity."

It is not surprising that when the choices are put that way, the conclusion necessarily follows that "there is no alternative but to opt for the third way." The real question was whether a legal system could honestly incorporate the extraordinary actions of the GSS without becoming so elastic as to also invite other kinds of abuses.

The Commission's answer to this question was problematic. In seeking to rationalize the interrogation methods deemed necessary by the GSS, the Commission attached "great importance" to the legal defense of "necessity." The defense of necessity is essentially a "state of nature" plea. If one finds oneself in an impossible position requiring one to choose between violating the law and preventing a greater harm, such as the taking of innocent life—and one has no time to seek recourse from the proper authorities—society authorizes one to act as if there were no law. In other words, since society has broken its part of the social contract with you, namely, to protect you, it follows that you are not obligated to keep your part of the social contract, namely, to obey the law. Thus, it has been said that "necessity knows no law."

It is ironic, therefore, that in an effort to incorporate the interrogation methods of the GSS into "the law itself," the Commission selected the most lawless of legal doctrines—that of necessity—as the prime candidate for coverage.

The Israeli law of necessity is particularly elastic and open-ended. It provides:

A person may be exempted from criminal responsibility for any act or omission if he can show that it was done or made in order to avoid consequences which could not otherwise be avoided and which would have inflicted grievous harm or injury on his person, honour or property or on the person or honour of others whom he was bound to protect or on property placed in his charge:

Provided that he did no more than was reasonably necessary for that purpose and that the harm caused by him was not disproportionate to the harm avoided.

The commission acknowledged that this "full exemption from criminal responsibility" reflects the "clash of opposing values: on the one hand, values protected by means of the prohibitions of criminal law, and on the other hand, the duty, grounded in ethical precepts, to protect one's life or bodily integrity or that of others." In other instances of conflict, such as self-defense, the law established rules of action and inaction, refusing to leave the decision solely to the subjective perceptions and priorities of the person claiming the defense, but under the rubric of "necessity," the law "foregoes the attempt to solve the problem only by [means of formal law] . . . and appeals to the sense of legality innate in the conscience of every human being." The problem, of course, is that "every human being" has a different conscience and sense of legality in situations involving the tradeoff between law violations and the protection of other values. To make matters worse, "the course test [of necessity] is what the doer of the deed reasonably believed, and not what the situation actually was."[3]

What if Palestinian rock throwers raised the defense of necessity in defense of their "honor or property"? Would the courts be forced to choose— on an entirely political basis—between conflicting claims? Or what if a suspected terrorist decides to resist the "physical pressures" of his interrogators by physical countermeasures designed to protect his honor or person—that is, what if he fights back? Could he defend himself against assault charges by invoking "necessity"?

The point of the necessity defense is to provide a kind of "interstitial legislation" to fill "lacunae" left by legislative and judicial incompleteness. It is not a substitute legislative or judicial process for weighing policy options by state agencies faced with long-term systemic problems.

To demonstrate the inappropriateness and subjectivity of the application of the necessity defense to the problems faced by the GSS, it is interesting to ask why the Commission so quickly and forcefully rejected its application to the systematic lying engaged in by agents who denied under oath that they had employed rough interrogation methods. This is what the commission says: "Here the investigator cannot rely on the defense of necessity . . . since perjury is a grave criminal offence and manifestly illegal, above which flies the black flag saying 'forbidden.'"

So held! *Ipse dixit!* But why? The GSS interrogators believed that lying was *as necessary* to their work as applying physical pressure. Both are grave criminal offenses and both are manifestly illegal. The difference surely cannot be that the immediate victims of the illegal physical pressure are suspected Arab terrorists, whereas the immediate victims of the perjury are the judges!

In fact, there are circumstances when a person who lies—or even commits perjury—should and would have the benefit of the necessity defense. For example: a person whose family is secretly being held hostage by escaped criminals is asked by the police for the whereabouts of the criminals; the criminals have threatened to kill his family unless he misdirects the police. He lies. Under these circumstances, his lie would fall within the defense of necessity. The same would be true if the person were called into court and gave the information under oath, while his family was being held under threat of imminent death by the criminals.

But systematic perjury committed over a long period of time should not be excused by necessity, because the systematic perjury is not an emergency response to a nonrecurring state-of-nature situation requiring the legislative and judiciary to delegate—in effect—their policy-making authority to the citizen, for an ad hoc weighing of choices. This is as true of the systematic long-term policy of physical pressure as it is of the systematic long-term policy of lying.

I am not necessarily suggesting by my criteria that the Commission's ultimate conclusion was wrong. I lack the information necessary to reach any definitive assessment of whether the GSS should have been allowed to employ physical pressure in the interrogation of some suspected terrorists under some circumstances. My criticism is limited solely to the dangers inherent in using—misusing, in my view—the open-ended "necessity" defense to justify, retroactively, the conduct of the GSS.[4]

The great virtue of the Landau Commission report is that it raised to the surface an important conundrum that few democracies ever openly confront. The vice of the report is that it purported to resolve that conundrum by reference to a legal doctrine that is essentially lawless and undemocratic.

In 1999 the Supreme Court of Israel confronted the issues raised in the Landau Commission report. The case, in essence, posed the following question. If an arrested terrorist knew the location of a ticking time bomb that was about to explode in a busy intersection but refused to disclose its location, would it be proper to torture the terrorist in order to prevent the bombing and save dozens of lives? The court answered no. As the president of the Supreme Court, Aharon Barak, put it: "Although a democracy must often fight with one hand tied behind its back, it nevertheless has the upper hand." It specifically outlawed many of the nonlethal techniques—"torture lite"—currently being employed by American authorities in their rough interrogations of captured terrorist suspects.

The Supreme Court of Israel left the security services a tiny window of opportunity in extreme cases. Borrowing from the Landau Commission, it cited the traditional common-law defense of necessity, and it left open the possibility that a member of the security service who honestly believed that rough interrogation was the only means available to save lives in imminent danger could raise this defense. This leaves each individual member of the security services in the position of having to guess how a court would ultimately resolve his case. That is unfair to such investigators. It would have been far better, in my view, had the court required any investigator who believed that torture was necessary in order to save lives to apply to a judge, when feasible. The judge would then be in a position either to authorize or refuse to authorize a "torture warrant." Such a procedure would require judges to dirty their hands by authorizing torture warrants or bear the responsibility for failing to do so. Individual interrogators should not have to place their liberty at risk by guessing how a court might ultimately decide a close case. They should be able to get an advance ruling based on the evidence available at the time.

In response to the decision of the Supreme Court of Israel, it was suggested that the Knesset—Israel's parliament—could create a procedure for advance judicial scrutiny, akin to the warrant requirement in the Fourth Amendment to the United States Constitution. It is a traditional role for judges to play, since it is the job of the judiciary to balance the needs for security against the imperatives of liberty. Interrogators from the security service are not trained to strike such a delicate balance. Their mission is single-minded: to prevent terrorism. Similarly, the mission of civil liberties lawyers who oppose torture is single-minded: to vindicate the individual rights of suspected terrorists. It is the role of the court to strike the appropriate balance. The Supreme Court of Israel took a giant step in the direction of striking that balance. But it—or the legislature—should take the further step of requiring the judiciary to assume responsibility in individual cases. The essence of a democracy is placing responsibility for difficult choices in a visible and neutral institution like the judiciary.

Issues of this sort are likely to arise throughout the world, including in the United States, in the aftermath of the World Trade Center disaster. Had law enforcement officials arrested terrorists boarding one of the airplanes and learned that other planes, then airborne, were headed toward unknown occupied buildings, there would have been an understandable incentive to torture those terrorists in order to learn the identity of the buildings and evacuate them. It is easy to imagine similar future scenarios.

Following the terrible events of September 11 and the reported use of rough interrogation techniques—"torture lite"—by American military and civilian officials, I tried to start a debate about the concept of a torture warrant in this country. In proposing some kind of advanced approval for the use of limited force in extreme situations, I deliberately declined to take a position on the normative issue of whether I would personally approve of the use of nonlethal torture against a captured terrorist who refuses to divulge information deemed essential to prevent an avoidable act of mass terrorism, though I did set out the argument in favor of (and against) it. I sought a debate about a different, though related, issue: if torture would, *in fact* be employed by a democratic nation under the circumstances, would the rule of law and principles of accountability require that any use of torture be subject to some kind of judicial (or perhaps executive) oversight (or control)? On this normative issue, I have expressed my views loudly and clearly. My answer, unlike that of the Supreme Court of Israel, is yes. To elaborate, I have argued that unless a democratic nation is prepared to have a proposed action governed by the rule of law, it should not undertake, or authorize, that action. As a corollary, if it needs to take the proposed action, then it must subject it to the rule of law. Suggesting that an after-the-fact "necessity defense" might be available in extreme cases is not an adequate substitute for explicit advance approval.

The possible case of a ticking bomb terrorist or terrorist with weapons of mass destruction has provided a justification for a persuasive and unregulated use of torture (or other forms of rough interrogation) by American officials, just as it had in Israel. Few are prepared to give up use of that option in really extreme cases. Instead of expressly limiting its use to such a case—and regulating it by procedural controls–many argue that is better to leave it to the "discretion" of law enforcement officials. A sort of "don't ask, don't tell" policy has emerged, enabling our president and attorney general to close their eyes to its use while being able to deny it categorically—the kind of willful blindness condemned by the courts in other contexts. With no limitations, standards, principles, or accountability, the use of such techniques will continue to expand.

These are the issues I addressed in my book *Why Terrorism Works*. These are the issues about which I have tried to begin a reasonable debate in the United States, as I had previously done in Israel. But unlike in Israel, where the debate did take place, in our country its terms were often distorted into a traditional discussion of the pros and cons of torture. Perhaps the most extreme example of this distortion took place at a conference held at John Jay College in New York, to which I was invited to deliver a keynote address about my proposal. The conference began with an emotional speech—replete with candles—delivered by a victim of torture who described how innocent people are tortured to death by brutal regimes around the world. The intended message of this introduction was that torture of the kind experienced by the speaker is bad—as if that were a controversial proposition. It was calculated to make it difficult, if not impossible, to conduct a rational discussion about ways of limiting and regulating the use of nonlethal torture in the context of terrorism prevention. Anyone who expressed any skepticism about simply reiterating a total ban on all torture was seen as the enemy of civilized human rights, even though the total "ban" now in effect has been a license for hypocrisy and pervasive torture with deniability.

Instead of engaging me in a nuanced debate about accountability and choice of evils, critics of my proposal have accused me of "circumventing constitutional prohibitions on torture,"[5] giving "thumbs up to torture," "proposing torture for captured terrorist leaders,"[6] according U.S. agencies "the right to torture those suspected of withholding information in a terrorist case,"[7] and "advocating . . . shoving a sterilized needle under the fingernails of those subjects being interrogated."[8] "Famed Lawyer Backs Use of Torture" read one headline, while another article reported that I urged governments to "put aside the moral issues."[9] One reviewer has even called me "Torquemada Dershowitz," a reference to the notorious torturer of the Inquisition. (No one, however, reminded readers that it was the liberal Jeremy

Bentham who made the most powerful utilitarian case for limited torture of convicted criminals to gather information necessary to prevent serious future crime.) Judge Richard Posner of the U.S. Court of Appeals for the Seventh Circuit alleged that I "recommend . . . that suspected terrorists be tortured for information *by having needles stuck under their finger-nails*"[10] (emphasis added)—a suggestion that he characterizes as "tinged with sadism."[11]

Anyone who reads my writings on torture—and especially the detailed chapter in my book *Why Terrorism Works*—will quickly see that each of the descriptions of my proposals is misleading.

Let me once again present my actual views on torture, so that no one can any longer feign confusion about where I stand, though I'm certain the "confusion" will persist among some who are determined to argue that I am a disciple of Torquemada.

I am against torture as a *normative* matter, and I would like to see its use minimized. I believe that at least moderate forms of nonlethal torture are *in fact* being used by the United States and some of its allies today. I think that if we ever confronted an actual case of imminent mass terrorism that could be prevented by the infliction of torture, we would use torture (even lethal torture) and the public would favor its use. Whenever I speak about this subject, I ask my audience for a show of hands on the empirical question "How many of you think that nonlethal torture *would* be used if we were ever confronted with a ticking bomb terrorist case?" Almost no one dissents from the view that torture *would in fact* be used, though there is widespread disagreement about whether it *should* be used. That is also my empirical conclusion. It is either true or false, and time will probably tell. I then present my *conditional normative* position, which is the central point of my chapter on torture.

I pose the issue as follows. If torture is, in fact, being used and/or would, in fact, be used in an actual ticking bomb terrorist case, would it be *normatively* better or worse to have such torture regulated by some kind of warrant, with accountability, recordkeeping, standards and limitations?[12] *This* is an important debate, and *a different one* from the old, abstract Benthamite debate over whether torture can ever be justified. It is not so much about the substantive issue of torture as it is about accountability, visibility, and candor in a democracy that is confronting a choice of evils. For example, William Schulz, the executive director of Amnesty International USA, asks whether I would favor "brutality warrants," "testilying warrants,"[13] and "prisoner rape warrants."[14] Although I strongly oppose brutality, testilying, and prisoner rape, I answered Schulz with "a heuristic yes, if requiring a warrant would subject these horribly brutal activities to judicial control and accountability." In explaining my preference for a warrant, I wrote the following.

> The purpose of requiring judicial supervision, as the framers of our Fourth Amendment understood better than Schulz does, is to assure accountability and neutrality. There is another purpose as well: it forces a democratic country to confront the choice of evils in an open way. My question back to Schulz is do you prefer the current situation in which brutality, testilying and prisoner rape are rampant, but we close our eyes to these evils?
>
> There is, of course, a downside: legitimating a horrible practice that we all want to see ended or minimized. Thus we have a triangular conflict unique to democratic societies: If these horrible practices continue to operate below the radar screen of accountability, there is no legitimation, but there is continuing and ever expanding *sub rosa* employment of the practice. If we try to control the practice by demanding some kind of accountability, then we add a degree of legitimation to it while perhaps reducing its frequency and severity. If we do nothing, and a preventable act of nuclear terrorism occurs, then the public will demand that we constrain liberty even more. There is no easy answer.
>
> I praise Amnesty for taking the high road—that is its job, because it is not responsible for making hard judgments about choices of evil. Responsible government officials are in a somewhat different position. Professors have yet a different responsibility: to provoke debate about issues before they occur and to challenge absolutes.

That is my position. I cannot say it any more clearly.

The strongest argument against my preference for candor and accountability is the claim that it is better for torture—or any other evil practice deemed necessary during emergencies—to be left to the low-visibility discretion of low-level functionaries than to be legitimated by high-level, accountable decision-makers. Posner makes this argument:

> Dershowitz believes that the occasions for the use of torture should be regularized—by requiring a judicial warrant for the needle treat-

ment, for example. But he overlooks an argument for leaving such things to executive discretion. If rules are promulgated permitting torture in defined circumstances, some officials are bound to want to explore the outer bounds of the rules. Having been regularized, the practice will become regular. Better to leave in place the formal and customary prohibitions, but with the understanding that they will not be enforced in extreme circumstances.

The classic formulation of this argument was offered by Justice Robert Jackson in his dissenting opinion in one of the Japanese detention camp cases:

> Much is said of the danger to liberty from the Army program for deporting and detaining these citizens of Japanese extraction. But a judicial construction of the due process clause that will sustain this order is a far subtler blow to liberty than the promulgation of the order itself. A military order, however unconstitutional, is not apt to last longer than the military emergency. Even during that period a succeeding commander may revoke it all. But once a judicial opinion rationalizes such an order to show that it conforms to the Constitution, or rather rationalizes the Constitution to show that the Constitution sanctions such an order, the Court for all time has validated the principle of racial discrimination in criminal procedure and of transplanting American citizens. The principle then lies about like a loaded weapon ready for the hand of any authority that can bring forward a plausible claim of an urgent need. Every repetition imbeds that principle more deeply in our law and thinking and expands it to new purposes. All who observe the work of courts are familiar with what Judge Cardozo described as "the tendency of a principle to expand itself to the limit of its logic." A military commander may overstep the bounds of constitutionality, and it is an incident. But if we review and approve, that passing incident becomes the doctrine of the Constitution. There it has a generative power of its own, and all that it creates will be in its own image.

Experience has not necessarily proved Jackson's fear or Posner's prediction to be well founded. The very fact that the Supreme Court expressly validated the detentions contributed to its condemnation by the verdict of history. Today the Supreme Court's decision in *Korematsu* stands alongside decisions such as *Dred Scott, Plessy v. Ferguson,* and *Buck v. Bell* in the High Court's Hall of Infamy. Though never formally overruled, and even occasionally cited, *Korematsu* serves as a negative precedent—a mistaken ruling not ever to be repeated in future cases. Had the Supreme Court merely allowed the executive decision to stand without judicial review, a far more dangerous precedent might have been established: namely, that executive decisions during times of emergency will escape review by the Supreme Court. That far broader and more dangerous precedent would then lie about "like a loaded weapon" ready to be used by a dictator without fear of judicial review. That comes close to the current situation, in which the administration denies it is acting unlawfully, while aggressively resisting any judicial review of its actions with regard to terrorism.

The *New York Times,* on March 9, 2003, reported on the "pattern" being followed by American interrogators. It includes forcing detainees to stand "naked," with "their hands chained to the ceiling and their feet shackled." Their heads are covered with "black hoods"; they are forced "to stand or kneel in uncomfortable positions in extreme cold or heat," which can quickly vary from "100 to 10 degrees." The detainee is deprived of sleep, "fed very little," exposed to disorienting sounds and lights, and, according to some sources, "manhandled" and "beaten." In one case involving a high-ranking al-Qaeda operative, "pain killers were withheld from Mr. [Abu] Zubaydah, who was shot several times during his capture."[15]

A Western intelligence official described these tactics as "not quite torture, but about as close as you can get." At least two deaths and seventeen suicide attempts have been attributed to these interrogation tactics.[16]

Intelligence officials "have also acknowledged that some suspects have been turned over [by the United States] to security services in countries known to engage in torture."[17] These countries include Egypt, Jordan, the Philippines, Saudi Arabia, and Morocco. Turning captives over to countries for the purpose of having them tortured is in plain violation of the 1984 International Convention against Torture, to which we, and the countries to which we are sending the captives, are signatories.[18]

The *Wall Street Journal* reported that "a U.S. intelligence official" told them that detainees with important information could be treated roughly:

> Among the techniques: making captives wear black hoods, forcing them to stand in painful "stress positions" for a long time and subjecting them to interrogation sessions lasting as long as 20 hours.

U.S. officials overseeing interrogations of captured al-Qaeda forces at Bagram and Guantanamo Bay Naval Base in Cuba can even authorize "a little bit of smacky-face," a U.S. intelligence official says. "Some al-Qaeda just need some extra encouragement," the official says.

"There's a reason why [Mr. Mohammed] isn't going to be near a place where he has Miranda rights or the equivalent of them," the senior federal law-enforcer says. "He won't be someplace like Spain or Germany or France. We're not using this to prosecute him. This is for intelligence. God only knows what they're going to do with him. You go to some other country that'll let us pistol whip this guy." . . .

U.S. authorities have an additional inducement to make Mr. Mohammed talk, even if he shares the suicidal commitment of the Sept. 11 hijackers: The Americans have access to two of his elementary-school-age children, the top law enforcement official says. The children were captured in a September raid that netted one of Mr. Mohammed's top comrades, Ramzi Binalshibh.[19]

There is no doubt that these tactics would be prohibited by the Israeli Supreme Court's decision described earlier, but the U.S. Court of Appeals for the District of Columbia recently ruled that American courts have no power even to review the conditions imposed on detainees in Guantanamo or other interrogation centers outside the United States.[20] That issue is now before the U.S. Supreme Court, despite efforts by the administration to preclude review.

This, then, is the virtue of explicitness. The Supreme Court of Israel was able to confront the issue of torture precisely because it had been openly addressed by the Landau Commission in 1987. This open discussion led to Israel being condemned—including by countries that were doing worse but without acknowledging it. It also led to a judicial decision outlawing the practice. As I demonstrated in *Why Terrorism Works,* it is generally more possible to end a questionable practice when it is done openly rather than covertly.[21]

My own belief is that a warrant requirement, if properly enforced, would probably reduce the frequency, severity, and duration of torture. I cannot see how it could possibly increase it, since a warrant requirement simply imposes an additional level of prior review. As I discussed in *Why Terrorism Works,* here are two examples to demonstrate why I think there would be less torture with a warrant requirement than without one. Recall the case of the alleged national security wiretap being placed on the phones of Martin Luther King by the Kennedy administration in the early 1960s. This was in the days when the attorney general could authorize a national security wiretap without a warrant. Today no judge would issue a warrant in a case as flimsy as that one. When Zaccarias Moussaui was detained after trying to learn how to fly an airplane, without wanting to know much about landing it, the government did not even seek a national security wiretap because its lawyers believed that a judge would not have granted one. If Moussaui's computer could have been searched without a warrant, it almost certainly would have been.

It should be recalled that in the context of searches, the framers of our Fourth Amendment opted for a judicial check on the discretion of the police, by requiring a search warrant in most cases. The Court has explained the reason for the warrant requirement as follows. "The informed and deliberate determinations of magistrates . . . are to be preferred over the hurried actions of officers."[22] Justice Jackson elaborated:

> The point of the Fourth Amendment, which often is not grasped by zealous officers, is not that it denies law enforcement the support of the usual inferences, which reasonable men draw from evidence. Its protection consists in requiring that those inferences be drawn by a neutral and detached magistrate instead of being judged by the officer engaged in the often-competitive enterprise of ferreting out crime. Any assumption that evidence sufficient to support a magistrate's disinterested determination to issue a search warrant will justify the officers in making a search without a warrant would reduce the Amendment to nullify and leave the peoples' homes secure only in the discretion of police officers.[23]

Although torture is very different from a search, the policies underlying the warrant requirement are relevant to whether there is likely to be more torture or less if the decision were left entirely to field officers, or if a judicial officer had to approve a request for a torture warrant. As Mark Twain once observed, "To a man with a hammer, everything looks like a nail." If the man with the hammer must get judicial approval before he can use it, he will probably use it less often and more carefully.

The major downside of any warrant procedure would be its legitimization of a horrible practice, but in my view it is better to legitimate and control a *specific* practice that will occur than to legitimate a *general* practice of tolerating extralegal actions so long as they operate under the table of scrutiny and beneath the radar screen of accountability. Judge Posner's "pragmatic" approach would be an invitation to widespread (and officially—if surreptitiously—approved) lawlessness in "extreme circumstances." Moreover, the very concept of "extreme circumstances" is subjective and infinitely expandable.

We know that Jordan, which denies that it ever uses torture, has, in fact, tortured the innocent relatives of suspect terrorists. We also know that when we captured Mohammed, we also took into custody his two elementary-school-age children—and let him know that we had them.

There is a difference in principle, as Bentham noted more than two hundred years ago, between torturing the guilty to save the lives of the innocent and torturing innocent people. A system that requires an articulated justification for the use of nonlethal torture and approval by a judge is more likely to honor that principle than a system that relegates these decisions to low-visibility law enforcement agents whose only job is to protect the public from terrorism.

As I pointed out in *Why Terrorism Works*, several important values are pitted against each other in this conflict. The first is the safety and security of a nation's citizens. Under the ticking bomb scenario, this value may argue for the use of torture, if that were the only way to prevent the ticking bomb from exploding and killing large numbers of civilians. The second value is the preservation of civil liberties and human rights. This value requires that we not accept torture as a legitimate part of our legal system. In my debates with two prominent civil libertarians (Floyd Abrams and Harvey Silverglate) both acknowledged that they would want nonlethal torture to be used if it could prevent thousands of deaths, but they did not want torture to be officially recognized by our legal system. As Floyd Abrams put it: "In a democracy sometimes it is necessary to do things off the books and below the radar screen." The former presidential candidate Alan Keyes took the position that although torture might be *necessary* in a given situation, it could never be *right*. He suggested that a president *should* authorize the torturing of a ticking bomb terrorist but that this act should not be legitimated by the courts or incorporated into our legal system. He argued that wrongful and indeed unlawful acts might sometimes be necessary to preserve the nation but that no aura of legitimacy should be placed on these actions by judicial imprimatur. Professor Elshtain makes a similar point. Though she strongly favors the use of nonlethal torture in certain extreme cases, she does not want "a law to cover such cases." Indeed, she characterizes my proposal for a torture warrant as "a stunningly bad idea." She prefers instead to have each individual "grapple with a terrible moral dilemma" rather than to have an open debate and then codify its results.[24] This understandable approach is in conflict with the third important value: namely, open accountability and visibility in a democracy. "Off-the-book actions below the radar screen" are antithetical to the theory and practice of democracy. Citizens cannot approve or disapprove of governmental actions of which they are unaware. We have learned the lesson of history that off-the-book actions can produce terrible consequences. President Nixon's creation of a group of "plumbers" led to Watergate, and President Reagan's authorization of an "off-the-books" foreign policy in Central American led to the Iran-Contra scandal. And these are only the ones we know about!

Perhaps the most extreme example of this hypocritical approach to torture comes—not surprisingly—from the French experience in Algeria. The French army used torture extensively in seeking to prevent terrorism during France's brutal war between 1955 and 1957. An officer who supervised this torture, General Paul Aussaresses, wrote an account of what he had done and seen, including the torture of dozens of Algerians. "The best way to make a terrorist talk when he refused to say what he knew was to torture him," he boasted. Although the book was published decades after the war was over, the general was prosecuted—but not for what he had *done* to the Algerians. Instead, he was prosecuted for *revealing* what he had done and seeking to justify it.[25]

In a democracy governed by a rule of law, we should never want our soldiers or president to take any action that we deem wrong or illegal. A good test of whether an action should or should not be done is whether we are prepared to have it disclosed—perhaps not immediately, but certainly after some time has passed. No legal system operating under the rule of law should ever tolerate an "off-the-books" approach to necessity. Even the defense of necessity must be justified lawfully. The road to tyranny has always been paved with claims of necessity made by those responsible for the security of a nation. Our system of checks and balances requires that all presidential actions, like all legislative or military actions, be consistent with governing law. If it is necessary to torture in the ticking bomb case, then our governing laws must accommodate this practice. If we refuse to change our law to accommodate any particular action, then our government should not take that action.[26] Requiring that a controversial, even immoral, action be made openly and with accountability is one way of minimizing resort to unjustifiable means.

I am especially pleased that Professor Elaine Scarry's essay is included in this collection, because it demonstrates how a very smart person, who has read my essay and my other writing on this issue,[27] persists on confusing my *empirical* descriptions and predictions (that torture *is* being practiced and *will be* practiced by democracies in extreme situations) with my *normative* preference (that torture *should* not be employed and that its use *should* be reduced or eliminated). Here is how Profesor Scarry erroneously characterizes my view: "He believes that in such a situation [the ticking bomb scenario] *it would be permissible* to torture if one first obtained a judicial or executive warrant." She contrasts my purported normative views with "our commitment to an unwavering prohibition on torture." But my point is precisely that we have no such commitment. In fact, our commitment instead is to "the way of the hypocrites: they declare that they abide by the rule of law, but turn a blind eye to what goes on beneath the surface." If we indeed had an unwavering commitment to prohibiting torture, I never would have begun this debate. It is because I believe that we are moving toward the worst of all possible worlds—a smug, self-satisfied willingness to condemn torture openly, while at the same time encouraging its secret use in extreme cases—that I decided to try to force this issue into the public consciousness.

What would Professor Scarry have us do instead? She would want torture to be used if it could save multiple lives, but she would leave the initial decision to the ex ante decision of "the torturers" and then leaves the post facto decision about whether the torturer did the right thing to "a jury of peers." This is extraordinarily naive, as anyone with any experience in criminal justice will quickly understand. No prosecutor would prosecute and no jury would convict if it *turned out* that the torturer was right, even if the basis on which he acted was weak or bigoted. But some juries might well convict if the torturer turned out to be wrong, even if he or she had a very strong basis on which to act. Our legal (and moral) systems should make accountability turn on a defendant's mens rea (state of mind) at the time he or she acted, not on fortuities beyond his or her control.

An analogy may prove helpful. The former head of counterterrorism, Richard A. Clark, reports that on the morning of September 11, 2001, while several planes that were believed to have been hijacked remained in the air, an excruciatingly difficult decision had to be made: whether "we need to authorize the Air Force to shoot down any aircraft—including a hijacked passenger flight—that looks like it is threatening to attack and cause large-scale death on the ground." Had a passenger jet been shot down, it is certainly possible that a terrible mistake could have been made. Perhaps that plane was not, in fact, being hijacked; or maybe the passengers were in the process of gaining control; or possibly the plane was being hijacked as leverage in negotiations and not to be crashed into a building. It would always be tragic to choose to kill innocent passengers, but it might be necessary in order to prevent even more deaths. Who should make a decision—a tragic choice—of this type and magnitude?

Surely the answer must be: the highest-ranking public official capable of doing so—someone with accountability and responsibility. No one would want to leave it to a low-ranking, anonymous Air Force pilot, without guidance or criteria (unless, of course, there was no time to pass it up to higher authorities). And certainly no one would want the fate of that pilot to be determined by "a jury of peers" after the fact. Tragic choices should be made at the top whenever feasible. And the decision whether to threaten or inflict nonlethal torture in order to prevent a mass terrorist attack is a tragic choice of evils, as is the decision to shoot down a passenger jet and kill hundreds of innocent people.

Professor Scarry also seems willing to rely on the willingness of the torturer to break the law and violate morality in an extreme case: "It is unlikely that any savior of the city would actually be inhibited by the lack of pre-existing moral and legal assurances of immunity." But that is precisely the problem: we don't want individual "saviors" to be taking ad hoc, secret, unaccountable decisions whether to inflict torture. An ex ante process would offer some protection against the evils of the current ad hoc system of deniability and unaccountability—admittedly at a cost. The real question, and one Professor Scarry avoids, is whether the cost is worth the benefits. That is the debate I have tried to begin.

Professor Scarry correctly raises the question of whether "a judge or executive branch officer, acting under the pressure of a ticking bomb, will be able to discriminate between acceptable risks." But the alternative that she apparently prefers is to leave such difficult discriminating choices to each low-ranking "savior" who believes there may be a need to torture—and to a jury of peers to decide, on an ad hoc basis, whether he struck the appropriate balance.[28]

At bottom, my argument is not in favor of torture of any sort. It is against all forms of torture without accountability. Let us continue to reaffirm not only our opposition to torture but our opposition to the kind of hypocrisy that loudly denounces torture while discreetly closing our eyes to its increasing use.

The recent disclosure of significant abuses by military intelligence and military police officers in the Abu Ghraib prison outside of Baghdad demonstrates what happens when high-ranking officials have a "don't ask, don't tell policy" toward the use of extraordinary pressures in interrogation. While our leaders in Washington and our commanders in the field adamantly denied the use of any form of torture—light or otherwise—a subtle message was being conveyed down the chain of command that intelligence and police officials on the ground could do what they had to do to obtain important information. If this had not been perceived by the soldiers as the message from above, there is no way the photographs they took would have been so openly distributed.

When the message is sent in this way—by a wink and nod—no lines are drawn, no guidelines issued, and no accountability accepted. The result was massive abuses by those on the ground, coupled with deniability by those at the top.

How much better it would have been if we required that any resort to extraordinary means—means other than routine interrogation—be authorized in advance by someone in authority and with accountability. If a warrant requirement of some kind had been in place, the low-ranking officers on the ground could not plausibly claim that they had been subtly (or secretly) authorized to do what they did, since the only acceptable form of authorization would be in writing. Nor could the high-ranking officials hide behind plausible deniability, since they would have been required to give the explicit authorization. Moreover, since authorization would have to go through the chain of command, limitations would have been imposed on allowable methods. These would not have included the kind of gratuitous humiliation apparently inflicted on these prisoners.

There are of course no guarantees that individual officers would not engage in abuses on their own, even with a warrant requirement. But the current excuse being offered—we had to do what we did to get information—would no longer be available, since there would be an authorized method of securing information in extraordinary cases by the use of extraordinary means. Finally, the requirement of securing advanced written approval would reduce the incidence of abuses, since it would be a rare case in which a high-ranking official, knowing that the record will eventually be made public, would authorize extraordinary methods—and never methods of the kind shown in the Abu Ghraib photographs.

Notes

1. Dershowitz, Alan M. *Why Terrorism Works: Understanding the Threat, Responding to the Challenge* (New Haven, Conn.: Yale University Press, 2002).

2. Interrogators routinely lied about the use of rough interrogation methods in particular cases, and thus the fruits of such interrogations were sometimes improperly introduced in criminal trials.

3. Even if the mere *public* disclosure of the problem would be dangerous to the security of the state—always a matter of degree, especially in an open democracy like Israel, where the problem will inevitably surface, as it did here—there are *secret* options (at least temporarily secret) that are far more democratic than the ones employed here. Among these are special cabinet committees or judicial panels authorized to approve special measures under extraordinary circumstances.

Perhaps I am especially skeptical of the claims of "necessity" as an American. If that defense were available in the United States, it would have been employed by Colonel Oliver North to justify his lying to Congress, and by President Richard Nixon to justify the break-in at the Democratic National Committee and its subsequent coverup. Indeed, in the United States, the defense of necessity has been used—abused—by all manner of illegal protesters, ranging from Abbie Hoffman to Amy Carter to antiabortion protesters.

4. At the very most, its unlawful conduct might have been "excused" rather than "justified." Though this distinction may sound somewhat technical, the entire enterprise of finding a conceptual hook on which to hang the Commission's policy judgments is an exercise in technicality. Indeed, the very rule of law relies on technical compliance with established norms. If such technical efforts are to be useful, they should, at least, be technically correct. And finding the conduct of the GSS to be justified, which means desirable, rather than excusable, which means merely understandable, is wrong. Perhaps the commission adopted this tactic to send a prospective message: until legislation is enacted, the GSS should *continue* to engage in the necessary and justifiable activities in which they engaged prior to the report. If this is the message the commission intended to send, it should have done so more candidly. If not, it should have avoided reliance on a legal defense that invites misunderstanding over whether the continued use of "physical pressure" is necessary and thus justified.

5. Brendon O'Leary, *Times Higher Education*, October 4, 2002.

6. *Washington Times*, March 21, 2002.

7. *Globe and Mail,* September 2002.

8. Jane Genova, October 9, 2002.

9. *National Post* (Canada), December 9, 2003, A6; *Gazette,* December 9, 2003, A7.

10. *New Republic,* October 14, 2002.

11. *New Republic,* September 2, 2002. Posner also faulted me for not considering the option of truth serum. In *Why Terrorism Works,* I do consider that option: I say "Let's start with truth serum," and then I proceed to ask "What if truth serum" doesn't work? (248) It is in answer to that question that I propose the torture warrant.

12. Although my specific proposal is for a judicial warrant, my general point relates to visibility and accountability. Accordingly, an executive warrant or an explicit executive approval would also serve these democratic values. A judicial warrant has the added virtue of a decision-maker who—at least in theory—is supposed to balance liberty and security concerns (see the Fourth Amendment). A legislative warrant for specific cases would be both cumbersome and violative of the spirit of the bill of attainder clause, though a general legislative enactment requiring judicial or executive approval would be desirable.

13. "Testilying" is a term coined by New York City police to describe systematic perjury regarding the circumstances that led to a search, seizure, or interrogation.

14. William F. Schulz, "The Torturer's Apprentice: Civil Liberties in a Turbulent Age," *Nation,* May 13, 2002.

15. Raymond Bonner, "Questioning Terror Suspects in a Dark and Surreal World," *New York Times,* March 9, 2003.

16. When Israel has employed similar (though somewhat less extreme) tactics, they were universally characterized as torture, without even noting that they were nonlethal and did not involve the infliction of sustained pain. This is what the U.N. committee against Torture concluded in 1997:

> The Committee Against Torture today completed its eighteenth session— a two-week series of meetings marked, among other things, by a spirited debate with Israel over Government-approved use during interrogations of what it termed "moderate physical pressure" in efforts to elicit information that could foil pending terrorist attacks. This morning the Committee said in official conclusion that such interrogation methods apparently included restraining in very painful conditions; holding under special conditions; sounding of loud music for prolonged periods; sleep deprivation for long periods; threats, including death threats; violent shaking; and use of cold air to chill—and that in the Committee's view, such methods constitute torture as defined by Article 1 of the Convention against Torture, especially when were used in combination, which it said appeared to be the standard case.
>
> It called, among other things, for Israel to "cease immediately" the use of those and any other interrogation procedures that violated the Con-

vention, and emphasized that no circumstances—even "the terrible dilemma of terrorism" that it acknowledged was faced by Israel—could justify torture. . . .

Members of a Government delegation appearing before the Committee contend that such methods had helped to prevent some 90 planned terrorist attacks over the last two years and had saved many civilian lives, in one recent case enabling members of the country's General Security Service to locate a bomb. The delegation repeatedly denied that the procedures amounted to torture.

Whether the procedures previously used by Israel and currently used by the United States did or did not constitute torture, the Supreme Court of Israel has now outlawed them.

17. *New York Times,* March 9, 2003, A1.

18. An Egyptian government spokesman "blamed rogue officers" for any abuse in his country and said "there was no systematic policy of torture." He went on to argue: "any terrorist will claim torture—that's the easiest thing. Claims of torture are universal. Human rights organizations make their living on these claims." The spokesman went on to brag that Egypt had "set the model" for antiterrorism initiatives and the United States is seemingly "imitat[ing] the Egyptian model." When Israel too has claimed that allegations of torture made by detainees who have provided information may be self-serving and exaggerated, Egyptian and other authorities have insisted that the detainees must be believed.

19. Jess Bravin and Gary Fields, "How Do Interrogators Make Terrorists Talk?" *Wall Street Journal,* March 3, 2003.

20. *Al Odah v. United States,* 321 F.3d 1134 (2003).

21. *Why Terrorism Works,* 155–160.

22. *U.S. v. Lefkowitz,* 285 U.S. 452, 464 (1932).

23. *Johnson v. U.S.,* 333 U.S. 10, 13–14 (1948).

24. For many, capital punishment is a moral evil that should not be, but is, employed by society. For some it is worse than nonlethal torture. The strongest argument made for it often uses extreme examples: the mass-murdering recidivist who kills while in prison and has the capacity to escape. If killing that individual were somehow deemed necessary, would Elshtein prefer that it be done by an individual state actor, after grappling with his conscience, or as a result of a codification, after democratic processes have been followed?

25. Suzanne Daley, "France Is Seeking a Fine in Trial of Algerian War General," *New York Times,* November, 2001.

26. Indeed, there is already one case in our jurisprudence in which this has already occurred and the courts have considered it. In the 1984 case of *Leon v. Wainwright,* Jean Leon and an accomplice kidnapped a taxi cab driver and held him for ransom.

Leon was arrested while trying to collect the ransom but refused to disclose where he was holding the victim. "When he refused to tell them the location, he was set upon by several of the officers . . . they threatened and physically abused him by twisting his arm and choking him until he revealed where [the victim] was being held." Although the appellate court disclaimed any wish to "sanction the use of force and coercion, by police officers," the judges went out of their way to say that this was not the act of "brutal law enforcement agents trying to obtain a confession." "This was instead a group of concerned officers acting in a reasonable manner to obtain information they needed in order to protect another individual from bodily harm or death." Although the court did not find it necessary to invoke the "necessity defense," since no charges were brought against the policemen who tortured the kidnapper, it described the torture as having been "motivated by the immediate *necessity* to find the victim and save his life." *Leon v. Wainwright*, 734 F.2d 770 11th Circuit 1984; emphasis added. If an appellate court would so regard the use of police brutality—torture—in a case involving one kidnap victim, it is not difficult to extrapolate to a situation in which hundreds or thousands of lives might hang in the balance.

27. Professor Scarry characterizes the chapter on torture as "the centerpiece of his book, *Why Terrorism Works*." It is, in fact, a brief illustrative detour (32 pages out of 271) in a book about the broad policy issues surrounding terrorism.

28. The remainder of Professor Scarry's criticisms are fully answered in the body of my essay, and I leave it to the reader to decide who is making the "errors in reasoning."

Elaine Scarry*

Five Errors in the Reasoning
of Alan Dershowitz

At the center of Alan Dershowitz's recent account of torture is the argument that a hypothetical case can be imagined in which saving a city from a nuclear, chemical, or biological bomb might depend on torturing the terrorist who placed it there or knew where it was hidden. His chapter "Should the Ticking Bomb Terrorist Be Tortured?" is the centerpiece of his book *Why Terrorism Works,* and his essay herein is again structured around the dramatic instance of the ticking bomb, which occurs at the beginning, middle, and end of his argument. He believes that in such a situation it would be permissible to torture if one first obtained a judicial or executive warrant; the prohibition against torture, dissolved by means of the warrant, would continue in place for any act of torture that had not been warranted.

The first error in Alan Dershowitz's argument is that he wrongly addresses us as a population whose members are morally impaired. (It is of course the case that if we disagree with him we are perceived to be deficient:

---

*A reader wishing to learn my own view of torture should see the opening chapter of *The Body in Pain.*

An accurate understanding of torture cannot—in my view—be arrived at through the ticking bomb argument, which (quite apart from what any one advocate may intend) opportunistically provides a flexible legal shield whose outcome is a systematic defense of torture.

Why, then, should the ticking bomb argument be answered? In the years following 9/11, the ticking bomb argument has come to seem omnipresent and urgent, not only because of Alan Dershowitz's startling articulations of it but because our own leaders have repeatedly cited imminent nuclear, chemical, or biological threats as reasons for modifying constitutional and international rules on an array of matters (many of which Alan Dershowitz himself would fiercely oppose).

Answers must therefore be given to the ticking bomb argument, even though the arguments (both for and against it) provide a false location for achieving a genuine understanding of torture.

the charge of "hypocrisy" to any who believe the prohibition against torture should remain firmly in place recurs at intervals throughout his two essays; but the problem I wish to identify is more grave and applies to us whether we agree or disagree with him; and I believe it distorts his reasoning about the key questions.) Let us see precisely how this is so.

Introducing an "imaginable" occasion for torture that has no correspondence with the thousands of cases that actually occur has the effect of seeming to change torture to a sanctionable act. As Henry Shu urges in his essay herein, the unwavering prohibition against torture must be kept in place; and should the unlikely "imaginable" instance actually ever occur, the torturer would have to rely on convincing a jury of peers that the context for the act was exceptional.

But exposing the defect of the ticking bomb argument requires that we go further. Anyone, we are told, who had the choice between on the one hand torturing and saving-the-city and on the other hand not torturing and not saving-the-city would be likely to choose the first. That may be. But so, too, anyone confronted with the choice between on the one hand saving-the-city and being herself imprisoned, or on the other hand not saving-the-city and not being imprisoned, would almost certainly also choose the first. That is, torturing should be perceived with the same acute aversion with which one's own legal culpability and one's own death are perceived; and while it is possible that a jury would exonerate someone in this situation, it does not follow that any such guarantee should be provided before the fact. Nor should someone enter into the act expecting exoneration after the fact. That one might *have to do* something someday that is wrong does not mean the act has ceased to be "wrong" and "punishable." It is unlikely that any savior of the city would actually be inhibited by the lack of preexisting moral and legal assurances of immunity.

It is a peculiar characteristic of such hypothetical arguments on behalf of torture that the arguer can always "imagine" someone large-spirited enough to overcome (on behalf of a city's population) his aversion to torture, but not so large-spirited that he or she can also accept his or her own legal culpability and punishment.

The first major error in Alan Dershowitz's argument, then, is that he severely midjudges the compatriots to whom, and about whom, he is speaking. He rules out, at the outset, the possibility that if one of us had the chance to save the Earth from the scourge of a nuclear weapon, the person would forfeit his or her liberty or even life to carry out that act. The entire argument is premised on the idea that the population lacks the simple attribute of courage. The act of inflicting torture requires no courage (the aversiveness is wholly borne by someone else), whereas the forfeit of one's future liberty requires that some portion of the severe adversity be endured by the actor himself.

Dershowitz tells us—both in his book and in the present essay–that he repeatedly asks his students and lecture audiences to raise their hands if they believe someone who could stop a nuclear bomb by torturing would do so; he reports that invariably many hands rise in the air. What if he followed that simple experiment with another: "Raise your hand if you believe that someone who saw she had it within her power to save hundreds of thousands of lives would forfeit her own liberty or give her own life?" Will not as many hands go up when this question is posed as when the imaginary opportunity to torture is posed? In fact, many more people (such as soldiers) have shown themselves willing to give their lives to save other human beings than have ever shown themselves willing to perform an act of torture, so it is unclear why any legal impunity needs to offered to cover the unlikely ticking bomb situation.

The way a person's legal culpability for torture enables him to test the situation in front of him can be seen by noticing not just the final action that is taken but the stations along the way. If I believe I am in the presence of someone who knows where an armed nuclear bomb is ticking away, I must ask myself *how certain* I am that this person actually knows that information. Now the testing ratio comes into play. If I say "I am confident enough that he holds this knowledge that I am willing to torture him," then I ought also to be able to say "I am confident enough that he holds this knowledge that I am willing to forfeit my liberty and possibly my life in order to procure that knowledge." If I instead find myself saying "Come to think of it, I'm not quite sure enough that I can give up my liberty to it," it is the signal to revise my assessment of confidence that torturing him would produce any knowledge worth having. Performing this test is more accurate (and certainly more rapid) than finding a judge who can issue a warrant, unless we design the warrant situation as one in which any judge who generates the warrant also agrees to go to jail.

In addition to the two defects of the argument on behalf of issuing warrants to permit torture in the ticking bomb situation—first, that it assumes a cowardly population incapable of acting without prior guarantees of immunity, and second, that it eliminates the procedure for testing one's level of confidence—there is a third problem. The ticking bomb scenario is often described as highly improbable. What makes it improbable is not the existence of a ticking bomb (it is entirely possible that a terrorist or a deranged state leader will one day try to use a nuclear bomb, or a chemical or biological weapon capable of killing hundreds of thousands). What instead makes the ticking bomb scenario improbable is the notion that in a world where knowledge is ordinarily so imperfect, we are suddenly granted the omniscience to know that the person in front of us holds this crucial information about the bomb's whereabouts. (Why not just grant us the omniscience to know where the bomb is?)

In the two and a half years since September 11, 2001, five thousand foreign nationals suspected of being terrorists have been detained without access to counsel, only three of whom have ever eventually been charged with terrorism-related acts; two of those three have been acquitted.[1] When we imagine the ticking bomb situation, does our imaginary omniscience enable us to get the information by torturing one person? Or will the numbers more closely resemble the situation of the detainees: we will be certain, and incorrect, 4,999 times that we stand in the presence of someone with the crucial data, and only get it right with the five thousandth prisoner? Will the ticking bomb still be ticking?

Almost all aspects of our post–September 11 world bring us face to face with our lack of omniscience. We have failed, in two and a half years, to find the anthrax murderer, despite the fact that the precisely identified strain of anthrax limits the pool of eligible candidates to a tiny handful of people; this is not like finding a needle in a haystack, it's like finding a needle in a bright red pincushion that contains one needle and nineteen straight pins. We have gone to war against a country that was "known" to have weapons of mass destruction, only to find it had none. We knew our troops would be welcomed as liberators, at least by the Shi'ites, who are now killing our soldiers as the Sunnis hang our civilians from bridges. And yet, despite our overwhelming miscalculation, mismeasurement, and inability to solve mysteries both before and after they happen—or to put it in the fairest light, despite the excruciating difficulty of ever being right—we are asked to entertain the possibility of lifting the unconditional prohibition against torture, and to do so by imagining that one of us will recognize the ticking bomb accomplice the moment we see him.

Oddly, and conversely, torturing a person in order to get information about a ticking bomb is sometimes introduced in situations where the information is already available through means that require inflicting no cruelty. Although Alan Dershowitz usually formulates the ticking bomb license-to-torture as a case in which hundreds of thousands of people stand to die from a nuclear, chemical, or biological weapon, he at one point asks us to imagine that we are back on September 11; and that by capturing and torturing the hijacker on one of the planes we can learn the target of another plane and enable the people in that targeted building to evacuate. But a great deal of information about the plane that eventually hit the Pentagon was known from FAA air controllers, radar images, and a passenger cell phone call placed directly to the Justice Department. For fifty-five minutes before the plane hit the Pentagon, it was clear that American Airlines Flight 77 was highly likely to be one of the hijacked planes, since it was off course, was not answering air controllers, and had turned off its secondary radar; for twenty minutes before it hit the Pentagon, it was certain (because passenger Barbara Olson phoned her husband, Theodore Olson, in the Justice Department) that the plane was under the control of hijackers; for twelve minutes before it hit the Pentagon, an air controller saw it on primary radar headed for Washington; for nine minutes before it hit the Pentagon, a C-130 watched it flying fast and low.[2] We need to wonder why we were not able to use this available information to get people out of the Pentagon and other Washington buildings, rather than supposing that it would have been helpful to torture someone to learn its target.

To summarize, then, the ticking bomb scenario, with warrant as a license to torture, presents us with three major problems: (1) it assumes a population that is (against robust evidence) cowardly and self-regarding—able and willing to torture but unable and unwilling to themselves suffer harm; (2) it assumes a population that is (against robust evidence) omniscient; and (3) by providing legal immunity, it eliminates the felt-aversiveness to cruelty that acts as a way to test one's level of conviction that thousands of lives are at risk and that one is uniquely positioned to act as their savior.

Alan Dershowitz has asked us to put aside our commitment to an unwavering prohibition on torture, to enter into an open debate with him, and to step into that debate by passing through the threshold of the ticking bomb case, a case whose framing assumptions are erroneous. But it may be useful to proceed forward and examine some of his other arguments, for it is apparent that here, too, he presents us with errors both in the substance and the style of the reasoning; and perhaps if the errors are articulated, he will be persuaded to return to his own original position, which (he several times tells us) was until recently a blanket condemnation of torture.

The proposal we are asked to contemplate is one in which a judge or an executive branch officer will issue a warrant licensing the holder of the warrant to torture, and the claim is that the existence of the warrants will, by introducing judicial scrutiny and by providing a documentary record, reduce the number of incidents of torture that take place and increase the accountability of those carrying out such acts.

This is a puzzling claim. We are asked to assume that a judge or executive branch officer, acting under the pressure of a ticking bomb, will be able to discriminate between acceptable and unacceptable cases. Are acceptable cases those that involve weapons of mass destruction (and therefore tens of thousands of deaths) and unacceptable cases those that involve smaller numbers of injuries? Or is some factor other than number of persons the key, as at many moments appears to be the case in Dershowitz's own examples? Dershowitz might fairly complain that we only lack an answer to that question because so far the debate has not really gotten underway, and therefore the practical details of the arrangement have not been worked out.

But there does already exist a solid basis for our skepticism that a warrants system will produce coherent discrimination. The court set up to issue warrants under the Foreign Intelligence Surveillance Act (FISA) has declined only one requested warrant in twenty-five years: the estimated number of warrant requests is twenty-five thousand.[3] If a torture warrant court were based on this model,[4] the incidence of torture would not be likely to decline, nor would the level of accountability increase.

But let us assume that the torture warrant court would, unlike the FISA court, operate with a high level of resistance and would grant only a small number of warrant requests (those providing strong evidence that extreme injury is about to take place very soon, and also providing strong evidence that one specified prisoner holds the key that will enable us to prevent the injury). In other words, let us assume that a coherent principle of discrimination is at work, and now let us see if we can decipher how this will decrease the incidence of torture and increase the level of accountability. Nothing about the results appears to let us reach this conclusion.

Under this new system, the prohibition against torture will dissolve in those cases where the torturer obtains a warrant but will continue in place for any act that has not first been warranted. Of these two groups of persons, the permitted and the prohibited, is it the first group, the second group, or the two groups together that enable us to achieve a level of accountability that surpasses the level available under our longstanding blanket prohibition of torture? Clearly, it cannot be the second group. All acts of torture that are carried out without a warrant (either because the torturers refuse to consult the court, or because they surreptitiously carry out their acts of torture even after their application for warrants have been turned down) will be undocumented—or, more accurately, they will have only the level of documentation that we have today under the blanket prohibition (a point that will be returned to). Is it, instead, the first group that will be accountable? We will, by virtue of the warrant, have a record of the person's actions, the reasons for those actions, the outcome (assuming the warrant holder does not stray from what he or she requested and what the judge granted) and can now request to see concrete evidence of the ticking bomb that was dismantled. But since the torturer has, by means of the warrant, already been released from the usual constraints against torture, in what does his or her accountability consist? Didn't the judicial review, by taking account of his or her proposed actions, release him or her from further accountability? It may be that we can review his or her actions: would this mean we should understand the warrant as a temporary grant of permission that is, upon review, subject to retrospective revocation, at which point the torturer's exemption from punishment would dissolve? Long experience with search warrants suggests the opposite: search warrants, far from facilitating review, historically have tended to close the door on review. In *The Bill of Rights: Creation and Reconstruction*, Akhil Amar describes the way the search warrant has often acted as a shield against the charge of trespass.[5]

The torture warrant system, then, appears to leave us with an unknowable number of illegal instances that cannot be reviewed (that is, cannot be reviewed in any way that is not already available to us under our current blanket prohibition) and a knowable number of legal instances that because they have been warranted are unlikely to be reviewed—even in the way that is currently available to us under the blanket prohibition system. Under the proposed system, our ability to review acts of torture has gotten no better, and actually appears to have gotten worse, than under our present blanket prohibition.

Alan Dershowitz, then, credits the warrant system with a power of documentation and accountability it does not appear to have. Conversely, he undercredits the forms of documentation and accountability that already exist under the present across-the-boards prohibition. He seems to believe that if someone wants the ban on torture to be absolute yet acknowledges that torture occurs, the person must be a hypocrite who pretends to denounce brutality while letting it take place "under the radar." The most baffling moment in his essay comes when he accuses William Schulz, the executive director of Amnesty International USA, of having an insufficient understanding of the purpose of accountability. Because William Schulz opposes warrants for torture, as well as warrants for brutality, testilying, and prisoner rape, Alan Dershowitz asks Schulz: "Do you prefer the current situation in which brutality, testilying and prisoner rape are rampant, but we close our eyes to those evils?"

Does Alan Dershowitz not know, or has he somehow forgotten, that Amnesty International's major work in the world is relentlessly to document instances of torture that have taken place, to make a public record, and through that record, to bring public pressure to bear on stopping the acts of torture even as they are taking place? Torture is itself a ticking bomb (it inflicts grave and widespread physical injury); Amnesty works to stop it, not only before it goes off but often in the very midst of its explosion. The suggestion that Amnesty, because it opposes warrants, prefers that "we close our eyes" is astonishing, given that no group has so steadily required us to keep our eyes on torture. This does not mean that the record is close to complete. Amnesty International continually reminds us that its own records are incomplete, that it can document instances of torture only in countries where Amnesty members are permitted to speak with prisoners. Many other research bodies—newspapers, human rights groups, congressional or U.N investigative groups—also contribute to the widespread commitment, and ability, to document torture.[6]

We encounter, then—in addition to the three major problems earlier summarized in the ticking bomb frame—a fourth and fifth major problem in the proposal for warranting torture. The fourth is that Alan Dershowitz credits the warranting system with a power to provide documentation and accountability that it does not appear to have. The fifth is that his proposal greatly undercredits the forms of documentation and accountability already available to us. These allow us continually to strive for some measure of accountability, while keeping national and international prohibitions on torture fully in place.

Although I have focused here on the framing assumptions and substance of his argument, problems also occur in the form and style of that argument. He often exposes the flaw of a particular idea (e.g., the necessity defense), form of sequencing (e.g. slippery slope), or phrase (e.g., "torture lite")—seeming in each case to repudiate it in unequivocal terms—only to bring that idea, form of sequencing, or phrase back into the service of his own proposal, usually without identifying it by its earlier name or label. The phrase "nonlethal torture," though it literally designates a horrifying set of practices, is in the context of his essay used as though it meant "moderation," without announcing that cruel linguistic trick in the way "torture lite" openly does. He critiques the "necessity" defense, accurately identifying it as "the most lawless of legal doctrines" and warning us that it is so elastic it can accommodate any person and any position; yet his warrant system gives center stage to the necessity defense, bestows on it a material form, and turns it into a formal procedure. Through this method of repudiating, then using, phrases, forms of sequencing, and ideas, he protects his arguments by giving them deniability. Were we to fault him for relying on the "necessity defense," he would look startled, indignant, and quote back to us the four pages in which he has discredited that defense. Thus we arrive at the climactic moment in his essay where he quotes those who fault him for countenancing the legitimation of torture—quotes them with astonishment, as though he cannot comprehend where on earth such descriptions (straightforward summaries of his view) could possibly have come from.

No one should take Alan Dershowitz lightly (even when face to face with his light, bright spirit). He means business. He intends to open a debate. He intends that debate, in turn, to reopen the law, to alter it, to replace the blanket prohibition on torture with partial legitimacy. He assumes—rightly—that he and those to whom he addresses himself have the power to change law and legal practice. He dedicates his book on the ticking bomb to the "nearly ten thousand students" he has taught over thirty-eight years at Harvard Law School (many of whom now hold legal positions around the country and the world). "You are our future," he tells them. "Preserve it from our enemies."

Let us hope that his former students and all other readers will see the errors in his reasoning and conclude that the best way to preserve the future from "our enemies" is to reaffirm each day the blanket prohibition on torture, and to work with newspapers, human rights groups, and investigative bodies to document and hold those who torture accountable for their acts.

Notes

1. David Cole, lecture, Harvard Law School, September 24, 2003.

2. The inability to act on available information is described in more detail in Elaine Scarry, *Who Defended the Country?* ed. Joshua Cohen and Joel Rogers (Boston: Beacon Press, 2003).

3. David Cole, *Enemy Aliens: Double Standards and Constitutional Freedoms in the War on Terrorism* (New York: New Press, 2003), 68; Dan Eggen and Susan Schmidt, "Secret Court Rebuffs Ashcroft," *Washington Post*, August 23, 2002, 1.

4. Alan Dershowitz does sometime appear to be assuming the warrant court will be, like the FISA court, secret. He at one point speaks of a "special cabinet committee or judicial panel authorized to approve special measures under extraordinary circumstances" (n. 3).

5. Akhil Reed Amar, *The Bill of Rights* (New Haven, Conn.: Yale University Press, 1998), 71–73. Amar writes: "In the end, the Fourth Amendment framers accepted some warrants as necessary but imposed strict limits on these dangerous devices. Warrantless searches did not pose the same threat because those searches would be subject to full and open after-the-fact review in civil trespass cases featuring civil juries" (73).

6. For an example of the documentation of acts of torture (and those who have trained torturers) gathered by multiple research groups, see Timothy Kepner, "Torture 101: The Case against the United States for Atrocities Committed by School of the Americas Alumni," *Dickinson Journal of International Law* (2001). Kepner assesses the potential liability of the School of Americas in a domestic court, using the Alien Tort Act and the Torture Victim Protection Act of 1991; he takes into consideration complications that arise from the Federal Tort Claims Act, the Combatant Activity Exception, the Foreign Country Exception, and the Political Questions Doctrine.

Richard A. Posner

Torture, Terrorism, and Interrogation

The well-grounded fears of international terrorism that were aroused by the attacks on the United States of September 11, 2001, have led to a reconsideration of extreme measures for the protection of the nation,[1] and among them is the use of torture to obtain information from suspected terrorists. At least three questions should be addressed: What methods of interrogation should the word "torture" connote? What criterion should be used to determine how coercive an interrogation should be permitted, whether or not it should be deemed torture? And what should be the legal regime for the application of the criterion to particular interrogations? Those are the three questions I address in this brief essay.

As a valuable essay by Sanford Levinson explains, the word "torture" has been broadly defined in certain United Nations conventions and other more-or-less official documents,[2] and more narrowly defined in others,[3] but all these are what philosophers call "persuasive definitions"—definitions that do not describe how a word is used but how the definer would like it to be used. The word "torture" lacks a stable definition. Almost all official interrogation is coercive, yet not all coercive interrogation would be called "torture" by any competent user of the English language, so that what is involved in using the word is picking out the point along a continuum at which the observer's queasiness turns to revulsion. Not only will different observers fix different points, but the means of coercing information are so various that the continuum itself is not clearly demarcated. Is it worse to question a person under bright lights or to threaten to beat him up? To question him in relays or to pretend that he is being held in a secret facility in a distant country?

What I think is clearly true as a matter of linguistic usage, at least in the culture of the United States and the countries we consider our peers, is that the infliction of actual physical pain to extract information is torture. I am inclined to go further and suggest that any deeply offensive touching, even if it does not inflict actual pain—I have in mind such things as shaking a person or pouring cold water on his or her head—would be regarded as torture by most Americans who have opinions on such matters, though I am not certain of this. When, however, there is no touching, though there may be sleep deprivation, close confinement in chilly or dirty cells, bright lights (the old "third degree"), shouting, threats, truth serums, and lies, I think it becomes an option whether to call the interrogation torture or merely coercive. (Blindfolding, though it involves touching, seems to me on the borderline; likewise manacling, at least if the person being questioned is violent.) Some though not all forms of coercive interrogation that do not involve any physical contact at all are nonetheless forbidden, in normal circumstances anyway (obviously a critical qualification, to which I'll return), as violating the self-incrimination clause of the Fifth Amendment, but we do not have to call them "torture," since torture is not the only thing that the self-incrimination clause forbids.

I am suggestiong that as we move up the pressure curve we encounter a kink, an inflection point, when the coercion changes from the psychological to the physical. After that point is reached, the affixing of the term "torture" to describe the interrogation is, I am inclined to believe, mandatory, even if the physical contact is not painful, provided it is deeply offensive; before the point is reached, however, the use of the term is optional, unless the psychological methods employed are mild, in which event the label of "torture" would clearly be inappropriate.

I do not consider the drawing of a sharp line between the psychological and the physical to be arbitrary. A major project of modernity is to make people squeamish in order to discourage recourse to violence, especially political violence, the most dangerous kind—is, in other words, to turn the beast of prey that is natural man into a tame domestic animal, as Nietzsche put it.[4] The inviolability of the body is a symbol of that project, and the best practical argument for barring the use of violence to defend property rights, for prohibiting flogging as a form of punishment, and for abolishing capital punishment or at least making it painless—and for affixing the "torture" label certainly to the infliction of pain, and probably to any offensive touching, when aimed at extracting information.

We should respect the line that separates psychological from physical coercion, and permit it to be crossed only *in extremis;* but we need not feel the same reluctance to impose a degree of psychological pressure that might challenge the conventional limitations, for example, the requirement of giving a person in custody the *Miranda* warnings before questioning him, and desisting from questioning if he requests a lawyer. Such limitations do not come out of any constitutional text; the language of the Fifth Amendment is that "no person . . . shall be compelled in any criminal case to be a witness against himself." A "witness" is someone who testifies, not someone who makes a statement out of court, under pressure or otherwise. The current law of self-incrimination has been made by the Supreme Court out of constitutional whole cloth, and it can be unmade if occasion requires.

Suppose a terrorist is known to be at large with a suitcase full of aerosolizers filled with smallpox virus; his confederate is caught and refuses to answer any questions, instead demanding a lawyer. Does the Constitution entitle him to remain silent? If not, what pressures on him to reveal the whereabouts of his companion does the Constitution permit? These are the wrong questions if the relevant constitutional provisions are as malleable as I think they are. The right questions are, *should* the Constitution entitle the person to remain silent and, if not, what degree of pressure to get him to talk *should* the Constitution be interpreted to permit? The right answer to the first question is no, and to the second, "as much pressure as it takes." That is, what is required is a balance between the costs and the benefits of particular methods of interrogation. The costs and benefits need not be entirely, or for that matter in any respect, monetized or even monetizable or otherwise quantifiable. Certainly the costs include the horror that the term "torture" evokes, but the costs can be outweighed by the benefits if torture is the only means by which to save the lives of thousands, perhaps tens or hundreds of thousands, of people. In so extreme a case, it seems to me, torture must be allowed.

And perhaps in less extreme cases. Suppose your child has been kidnapped. The kidnapper is caught, reveals that the child is locked in an underground vault, explains that the supply of oxygen in the vault is limited, and refuses to indicate the whereabouts of the vault. I think the use of torture to extract the information would be proper in such a case, provided there was no alternative method of extracting it. But the less certain is the need for or the expected efficacy of torture, the more lives have to be at risk to justify it under the balancing, or cost-benefit, or sliding-scale approach

I am defending. If there is only a small probability that a terrorist is at large with a nuclear bomb or plague germs, the fact that, should the risk materialize, thousands or millions of people will die becomes a compelling argument for torture, in comparison to a case in which there is the same probability that a dealer in illegal drugs is at large.

I anticipate three objections from civil libertarians. The first is that torture, like slavery, is always wrong. Maybe so, but there is such a thing as a lesser wrong committed to avoid a greater one. There is such a thing as fighting fire with fire, and it is an apt metaphor for the use of torture and other extreme measures when nothing else will avert catastrophe. And while "the end justifies the means" is a dangerous slogan, it is dangerous because it ignores the possibility that the end does not justify the means because the end, while a good one, is not as valuable as the means are costly. That is a danger that a balancing test avoids.

The second objection is that torture is an ineffectual method of interrogation. This is not so much an objection, however, as a plea in avoidance, since if it is true that torture is always ineffectual, it will always flunk a cost-benefit test. Torture may well be a clumsy and inefficient method of interrogation, as well as a method that should be reserved for the gravest of emergencies because of its costliness in the broadest sense of "cost," as well as its frequent inefficacy, but it is hard to believe that it is always and everywhere ineffectual; if it were, we would not have to spend so much time debating it. It is true that extracting accurate information is not the only motive for torture; others include extracting false confessions, intimidating the population or particular subgroups, and sadism. Given these motives, which can incidentally help us understand the abhorrence, and the terrible historical record, of the practice (think of the Inquisition, and of Stalin's show trials), it is possible in principle that torture, though resorted to frequently, is a completely inefficacious method of obtaining true information. But this is very unlikely; the practice is too common.

The second objection is that recourse to torture so degrades a society that it should be forsworn even if the death of many innocents is an assured consequence.[5] That is a proposition falsified by history. In very recent times, France (in Algeria), the United Kingdom (in its struggle with the Irish Republican Army), and Israel (in combating the intifada) have all used torture to extract information, yet none is a country that has "sunk . . . into barbarism."[6] Torture is uncivilized, but civilized nations are able to employ uncivilized means, at least in situations of or closely resembling war, without becoming uncivilized in the process. I suspect that this is particularly true when the torture is being administered by military personnel in a foreign country. *Inter armes silent leges.*

Assuming that the current war against international terrorism will involve episodes in which resort to highly coercive methods of interrogation—methods that may or may not demand the label of torture but that will be more coercive than current constitutional understandings permit—we must consider what if any means should be used to bring the methods within the law. The issue is sharply posed by the chapter on torture in Alan Dershowitz's recent book on terrorism.[7] I agree with much of what he says in that chapter. He says what only the most doctrinaire civil libertarians (not that there aren't plenty of them) deny, that if the stakes are high enough torture is permissible. No one who doubts that should be in a position of responsibility. The position articulated by Ariel Dorfman in his foreword to this book—"I can only pray that humanity will have the courage to say no, no to torture, no to torture under any circumstance whatsoever, no to torture, no matter who the enemy, what the accusation, what sort of fear we harbor, no to torture no matter what kind of threat is posed to our safety, no to torture anytime, anywhere, no to torturing anyone, no to torture"[8]—is not only overwrought in tone but irresponsible in content. It is also notably abstract; I would be curious whether Dorfman would maintain his position in the context of concrete cases, such as the kidnapping case I described earlier. Dershowitz cites a federal court opinion that approved a police officer's choking an actual kidnapping suspect until he revealed where the kidnap victim was. Dershowitz also gives the telling example of the Phillipine authorities who in 1995 "tortured a terrorist into disclosing information that may have foiled plots to assassinate the pope and to crash eleven commercial airliners carrying approximately four thousand passengers into the Pacific Ocean."[9] He points out that since terrorists are more dangerous than ordinary criminals, the dogma that it is better for ten guilty people to go free than for one innocent person to be convicted may not hold when the guilty ten are international terrorists who, moreover, are seeking and may succeed in obtaining weapons of mass destruction. And he asks a good question: "What moral principle could justify the death penalty for past individual murders and at the same time condemn nonlethal torture to prevent future mass murders?"[10]

But I am distressed that Dershowitz should think it appropriate to indicate that his preferred form of "nonlethal torture" is inserting a sterilized needle under the suspect's fingernails.[11] One might have expected that before recommending the infliction of physical pain Dershowitz would have explored the adequacy of, for example, a combination of truth serum, bright lights, and sleep deprivation. Maybe he has explored these alternatives and found them wanting, but there is no indication of that in the book. Moreover, it is unlikely that a single method of extracting information from the unwilling would be optimal in all cases. Some people may be less susceptible to physical pain than to other forms of inducement or coercion.

Dershowitz believes that the occasions for the use of torture should be regularized by requiring a judicial warrant for the needle treatment. Which brings me to the third question I said I would discuss. I think, to begin with, that he exaggerates the significance of the warrant as a check on executive discretion. A warrant is issued in an ex parte proceeding, and usually the officer seeking the warrant has a choice of judges or magistrates from whom to seek it. So there isn't much actual screening, in most cases. And it is probably inevitable that in national security cases the judicial officers authorized to issue such warrants will be chosen in part for their sensitivity to security concerns. Moreover, the warrants and the affidavits supporting them, as well as the judges' reasons for granting the warrants, would be likely to remain secret. The requirement of a warrant would no doubt make the officers seeking them a little more careful, but perhaps not much more truthful or candid. Dershowitz's argument for a judicial screen is particularly surprising given his well-known distrust of judges' competence and probity. I should think he would worry that requiring a warrant in cases of coercive interrogation would operate merely to whitewash questionable practices by persuading the naive that there was firm judicial control over such interrogations.

There is a more interesting argument for leaving the decision whether to employ highly coercive means of interrogation that violate conventional constitutional norms to executive discretion, rather than dragging in courts and the rest of the apparatus of formal law. If legal rules are promulgated permitting torture in defined circumstances, officials are bound to want to explore the outer bounds of the rules; and the practice, once it were thus regularized, would be likely to become regular. Better, I think, to leave in place the customary legal prohibitions, but with the understanding that of course they will not be enforced in extreme circumstances. Abraham Lincoln suspended habeas corpus during the early months of the Civil War.

The Constitution almost certainly does not authorize the president to suspend habeas corpus.[12] Lincoln did it anyway and was probably right to do so—the Union was in desperate straits, and its survival was more important than complying with every provision of the Constitution, since, had the rebellion succeeded, the Constitution would have gone by the boards. It does not follow that the Constitution should be amended to authorize the president to suspend habeas corpus; for he might be inclined to test the scope of that authority. The fact that Lincoln was acting illegally must have given him pause, and must also have reduced the danger of what civil libertarians profess to fear (though there is no support for the fear in U.S. history), which is a ratchet effect by which restrictions of civil liberties in times of national emergency would persist when the emergency ended and become a platform for further restrictions the next time there was an emergency.

Likewise it is unnecessary and probably, from the civil liberties standpoint, counterproductive to enact a statute authorizing torture—a statute that, as Dershowitz argues, might well be deemed constitutional, provided that no effort was made to introduce a confession obtained by torture in judicial proceedings against the person tortured. After all, if there is no use of a confession in a judicial proceeding, there is not even an attenuated sense in which an out-of-court declaration makes the declarant a "witness" against himself or herself within the meaning of the Fifth Amendment's self-incrimination clause, though it could still be argued that highly coercive interrogation is a deprivation of a form of liberty (liberty as physical and perhaps psychological integrity), and that if the deprivation is extreme enough to "shock the [judicial] conscience," then there is a denial of due process of law within the meaning of the Fifth and Fourteenth Amendments.

Regularizing the use of extreme measures against terrorists would, moreover, amplify a valid concern of civil libertarians that I have not yet mentioned—that once one starts down the balancing path, the protection of civil liberties quickly erodes. One starts with the extreme case, the terrorist with plague germs or a nuclear bomb in his traveling case, or the kidnapper who alone can save his victim. Well, if torture is legally justifiable if the lives of thousands are threatened, what about when the lives of hundreds are threatened, or tens? And the kidnap victim is only one. By such a chain of reflections we might be moved to endorse a rule that torture is justified if, all things considered, the benefits, which will often be tangible (lives, or a life, saved), exceed the costs, which will often be nebulous. It is better I think to stick with our perhaps overly strict rules, trusting executive officials to break them when the stakes are high enough to enable the officials to obtain political absolution for their illegal conduct.

Notes

1. Richard A. Posner, *Law, Pragmatism, and Democracy,* chap. 8 (2003).

2. Sanford Levinson, "'Precommitment' and 'Postcommitment': The Ban on Torture in the Wake of September 11," *Texas Law Review* 81 (2003): 2013. See also the useful discussion in John T. Parry, chapter 8 herein.

3. This is especially emphasized in Parry's chapter herein.

4. See especially the second essay in *On the Genealogy of Morals.*

5. The argument is made by Henry Shue in his "Response [to Sanford Levinson, "The Debate on Torture: War against Virtual States," *Dissent* (summer 2003): 79], *Dissent* (summer 2003): 90, 91.

6. Ibid., 91.

7. Alan M. Dershowitz, *Why Terrorism Works: Understanding the Threat, Responding to the Challenge* (New Haven, Conn.: Yale University Press, 2003). The discussion that follows is based in part on my review of Dershowitz's book. See Richard A. Posner, "The Best Offense," *New Republic,* September 2, 2002, 28. Let me take this opportunity to try to correct a mistaken impression created by an unfortunate choice of words at the beginning of the review, where I said: "Although a professor at the Harvard Law School, [Dershowitz] is not a scholar. His principal activities, when he is not actually in class teaching, are defending notorious criminal defendants, such as O. J. Simpson, Claus von Bülow, Michael Tyson, and Jonathan Pollard, appearing on television talk shows, and writing books (often best sellers) and articles of a journalistic character on current events, such as the Clinton-Lewinsky scandal and the 2000 presidential election deadlock." This may have sounded as if I were denying that he had ever written scholarly articles or asserting that he is incapable of scholarship or that he is an incompetent scholar. What I meant was that the focus of his work is no longer scholarship but rather advocacy and polemics, and that the work should be evaluated accordingly. *Why Terrorism Works* is not a scholarly book, but it is a valuable contribution to the debate over the use of extreme measures against international terrorism, and my review of it was favorable, though not uncritically so.

8. Foreword, p. 17.

9. Dershowitz, *Why Terrorism Works,* 137.

10. Ibid., 148.

11. Ibid., 144, 148.

12. Posner, *Law, Pragmatism, and Democracy,* 273.

Richard H. Weisberg

Loose Professionalism, or Why Lawyers Take the Lead on Torture

GEN'L. JACK D. RIPPER: "Were you ever a prisoner of war,
  Mandrake?"
GROUP CAPTAIN LIONEL MANDRAKE: "Yes . . . the
  Japanese."
RIPPER: "Did they torture you?"
MANDRAKE: "Yes, yes, Jack. They did."
RIPPER: "Did you talk?"
MANDRAKE: "No—but I don't think they really wanted me
  to talk. They were just having a bit of fun, that's all."
—Stanley Kubrick, *Dr. Strangelove*

Others in this symposium have amply demonstrated that the practice of torture through the years—apart from the physical and psychic pain visited on the victims—has been fraught with risks to those who inflict it as well. The torturer through history can be characterized as naive (in his hope that confession or disclosure will be accurate) or as cynical (in his indifference to the inaccuracy that usually follows from the practice), or as self-absorbed (in his need for the torture victim to utter formulas that support the torturer's worldview) or as sadomasochistic (in his literal brutality, often tempered by the phrase "this hurts me more than it hurts you"). None of these descriptions reflects well on the torturer or the society condoning the practice. Against these risks, periodically, apologists for the practice invoke special emergency conditions (whether spiritual or geopolitical), as though the world had never before seen such conditions. Where the premodern torturer perceived some unique threat to the soul, the modern torturer sees it to the nation-state, and his or her postmodern apologist manages to forget history in an unwise and ironic rush to cloak the torturer's brutality in the language of utilitarianism.

I want to discuss the professional consequences—specifically to the world of lawyers and law professors—of this rush to rationalization. Using especially the historical example of Vichy, I will associate with that unfortunately analogous "emergency challenge" to (French) legal professionalism the current tendency among some otherwise right-thinking (American) lawyers to justify what had previously been considered an unthinkable practice. Then and there it was racism; now and here it is torture. I will call the phenomenon of legal discourse that slips dangerously toward the known-to-be-wrong as "loose professionalism." I find it especially in the spearheading contribution to this symposium of Sanford Levinson—which cites allied remarks of Alan Dershowitz and Richard Posner on the subject—as well as in other essays included here.

Two points at least bear clarification early: first, I am not suggesting that the legal community can or should completely avoid discussions of torture; no—I am suggesting on the all-too-infrequent historical model of early protest against aberrational practices that lawyers so inclined should speak out directly and forcefully *against* the practice. (Hence Professor Levinson misunderstood me at an earlier stage in this debate when he suggested that people with my perspective on torture did not want to have "this conversation in public" but instead opted "to avert our eyes to what is actually going on." There *should* be such a "conversation" about torture, including, as its preferably most powerful intervention an emphatic *no* to the practice!) Second, I am not suggesting that those who, instead, begin to rationalize torture necessarily favor the practice; what I am saying is that the lessons of history are clear in demonstrating that such rationalizations not only help the practice to thrive but often provide (as in Vichy-created racism) the main reasons for its baleful success.

In mid-October 1940, with Nazi occupiers in Paris and a new French regime down in Vichy legislating aggressively against Jews, Professor Jacques Maury leveled a frontal protest against racism. A specialist in public law from the University of Toulouse, Maury could not believe that statute writers from his own country had jumped the gun on German demands and exceeded even the Nuremberg model of "racial" definition and persecution. As I reported in a book-length study of the French legal profession under Vichy,[1] many lawyers at the time privately found Vichy's premature violation of France's egalitarian traditions to be grotesque. They, like Maury, believed at the beginning that the French system simply would not deign to recognize or enforce racist practices. Maybe the occupiers would eventually impose anti-Semitism on the indigenous population, but the Nazis surely had not yet made that difficult political decision by October 1940, when Vichy on its own promulgated the first of what would become almost two hundred home-grown laws against the Jews. So Professor Maury published openly what most of his colleagues believed: it was unacceptable for a government acting in the name of France to violate "our long-held rule safeguarding equality in their rights as well as their responsibilities to all French people."

A "conversation" had begun about racism. If government ministers under Marshal Petain wished to define and punish people on the basis of their "racial" or "religious" heritage, the rest of the legal community's willingness to do so remained quite unclear. Jacques Maury voiced his unwillingness, and he did so loudly and clearly. His professional assumption was that the strange un-French law would die aborning. No one yet had introduced into the conversation a discourse of rationalization, obfuscation, or utilitarianism. Instead, among the first prominent words from a lawyer was Maury's unambiguous rejection of the practice. Maury—no "Ivan Karamazov [saying, as Levinson has understood Dostoevski's character] "let justice be done though the heavens fall!,"—on the contrary was speaking a pragmatic *professional* language of French legal tradition.

Risking considerably more than an American lawyer might today protesting the practice of torture, Jacques Maury published his professional opinion of the new law's validity in the Parisian equivalent of the *Yale Law Journal;* it was a frontal attack on racism. He did not assume, as the rationalizers of torture seem to do today, that since the practice exists we are required to micromanage it by bringing our exquisitely refined lawyer-like skills to justify at least some part of it.

Tragically, Maury's protest went no further than the two articles he published in the fall of 1940. If Maury had been punished for his indictment of the new practice, either by the Nazis or the Vichy regime itself, there might have been reason for his colleagues to reject his mode of frontal protest. But he was not punished for his words at all. Three years later, his academic career thriving, we find him instead still writing about these laws, which had been developed along the lines of an accepting discourse instead of the conversation of protest he had vainly opened as the Occupation was just beginning. Documents show that, in the absence of any help at the beginning from his confreres at the bar or in academia, Maury himself dropped the discourse of principled protest and instead (like those others) worked within the laws and made them live.

By 1942 and 1943—with the deportations from France proceeding apace and according to Vichy legal definitions—Jacques Maury's strict professionalism had been transmogrified. Like the rest of his colleagues at the bench and bar (and in academia), Maury instead wrote and talked about the ambiguities surrounding the status of the Jew in Vichy. Like everyone else, he had become a loose professional. Direct protest against the very idea of such laws had disappeared.

What happened between the publication of his protest in late October and the loose professionalism of the high-deportation period? The transmogrification had, as it turns out, little to do either with external German pressure or with indigenous anti-Semitism itself. It did not happen, as it turns out, that Maury's legal colleagues accepted this bizarre change in their laws and traditions because they were afraid of the Nazis. Fewer still wished to pander to the Germans so that France could politically fit into Hitler's "new Europe." Ample documentation proves that French lawyers quickly perceived that the Nazis were willingly permitting French laws and judicial structures to proceed virtually unchanged; that Maury himself went unpunished—that the Vichy laws deliberately distanced themselves from (and often exceeded) Nazi racial models—further indicated that the Germans had prudently decided to let Vichy go its own way, even abiding broad-scale debate by the French as to the direction and philosophy behind such laws.

Anti-Semitism existed, of course, among lawyers as among the wider population. At the bar, there was a special resentment of the recent influx of "foreign Jews." But there was an even deeper resentment that Vichy legislation worked to disbar and sometimes imprison respected Jewish colleagues whose families had been in the country since Napoleon or before and whose brothers and fathers had died fighting for France during the twentieth century. There was no love of this legislation.

Analogous to the rationalizers of torture today, most Vichy-era lawyers would say wistfully: "Nobody in France likes official discrimination on the basis of race and religion. *But . . ."* Everything that really counted in the discourse that followed Maury's late-1940 strict professionalism began with that word *but.*

Confronted with a clear choice between opposing the practice and working within it, the French legal community took up the new laws as they would a rich and potentially fine new wine. Like today's micromanagers of torture, they found the "middle ground," the loopholes, the ambiguities, and in so doing they made the new and unusual vintage into a highly palatable professional brew. As many veterans of Vichy whom I interviewed twenty or so years ago told me, had French lawyers (like those in Italy) or the population as a whole (like that in Denmark) rejected the racist laws, history would have told a different and probably far more benign wartime story than the one France has to live with today.

Whatever their personal feelings and their finer professional instincts— to be detected in archival records of private musings by French lawyers across the spectrum (even in the Vichy ruling circle itself)—the entire relevant legal community spent four years collectively reversing their country's 150-year-long egalitarian traditions. And they did this not only under no significant German pressure but sometimes in the face of the occupier's annoyance that the Vichy approach went too far, implicated too many groups, and involved a case-by-case legalistic scrutiny that was foreign to Nazi jurisprudence and precedent.

Although the practice of torture violates all of our traditions, lawyers of impeccable credentials are starting to "pull a Vichy" on their community.[2] Lacking the will to mount a Maury-style protest, they seek to cabin torture within a spectrum of acceptable and unacceptable procedures and definitions. In this sense they exceed the unfortunate example of Vichy in three ways: first, if they instead chose to enter the debate at the level of direct protest, they would encounter none of the personal and professional risks run by Maury in the fall of 1940. Maury's finer instincts moved him at first to protest despite many conceivable risks to his own well-being; today's apologists, who are under no external threat, traduce such instincts. Second, unlike the Vichy lawyers, who knew that racial laws were an actual unavoidable fact, apologists for torture today cannot be absolutely sure that an American variation on the practice actually exists in any widespread way. Thus what looks—sadly enough—like an apologetics for torture actually also stands as a potential goad to decision-makers to adopt or expand a practice that may currently be no more than a blip on the radar screen.[3] In Vichy, the legal community's eventual looseness managed to *enhance,* grotesquely, the racial laws' chances of succeeding; today, loose professionalism may in fact *create the practice.* Third, today's loose professionals have World War II and its lessons fully behind them; Maury and his colleagues—like the Church in Europe, which also spoke a discourse of apology or accommodation when even Hitler might have stopped his most extreme practices if there had been unambiguous protest early—*wrote* that unfortunate history. Today's professional communities need to *learn* it.

The complex discourse of loose professionalism is on the move, but the Vichy example should give us pause. We should not confuse conversational complexity (even among lawyers) either with intelligence, appropriateness, or even sophistication. These virtues, and perhaps especially the last of the three, implicitly justify the arguments made on behalf of *some* forms of torture. No one, after all, wants to seem wide-eyed when facing—for example—the "ticking bomb" hypothetical. So even if one admits the severe costs of breaking the taboo against torture, surely it would be unwise to forgo the benefits of saving thousands of lives by torturing the one who knows where the bomb is.

But—as David Cole and I, among others, have pointed out—the hypothetical itself lacks the virtues of intelligence, appropriateness, and especially sophistication. Here, as in *The Brothers Karamazov—pace* Sandy Levinson—it is the complex rationalizers who wind up being more naive than those who speak strictly, directly, and simply against injustice. "You can't know whether a person knows where the bomb is," explains Cole in a recent piece in the *Nation;* "or even if they're telling the truth. Because of this, you end up sanctioning torture in general."

Let us continue to be alert to what governments may be doing. And, if there is evidence that our government practices torture, let us avoid loose professionalism by entering the debate with a firm protest against the practice. Let us not lead, in the name of some skewed idea of *Realpolitik,* with our collective, liberal chins.

Notes

1. *Vichy Law and the Holocaust in France* (NYU Press, 1996).
2. Ironically, some of these actually try to embellish their arguments by citing unspecified examples of the use of torture by the French Resistance during this same

Vichy period. While there are some isolated reported cases of harsh methods used by the embattled Maquis, history has dealt appropriately and in documented detail with the Nazis' actual torture of members of the Resistance, most notably perhaps Jean Moulin. References to the French Resistance to justify torture are historically suspect and professionally perverse.

3. May and June 2004 brought to public attention several memoranda and other internal documents of the Bush Administration that offer compendious rationalizations by Administration lawyers tending to soften the taboo against torture. They raise serious questions not only about the merits of their legal analyses, but also about what is the "professional responsibility" of lawyers who believe themselves under pressure to justify what is in fact moral evil.

CONTRIBUTORS

Alan Dershowitz is the Felix Frankfurter Professor of Law at the Harvard Law School. Among his many books is *Why Terrorism Works: Understanding the Threat, Responding to the Challenge* (Yale University Press 2002).

Ariel Dorfman holds the Walter Hines Page chair at Duke University. His latest books are *Blake's Therapy,* a novel, and *Other Septembers, Many Americas,* a collection of essays (both from Seven Stories Press), as well as *Desert Memories: Journeys through the Chilean North* (National Geographic).

Jean Bethke Elshtain is the Laura Spelman Rockefeller Professor of Social and Political Ethics at the University of Chicago.

Oren Gross is Associate Professor and Vance K. Opperman Research Scholar, University of Minnesota Law School. Some of the issues discussed in his article herein are developed further in his article "Is Torture Warrant Warranted? Pragmatic Absolutism and Official Disobedience," *Minnesota Law Review* 88 (2004).

Miriam Gur-Arye is Judge Basil Wunsh Professor of Criminal Law at Hebrew University of Jerusalem.

Oona A. Hathaway is Associate Professor of Law at Yale Law School. She has written a series of articles and is working on a book on the influence of international law on state behavior.

John Langbein is Sterling Professor of Law and Legal History at Yale University.

Sanford Levinson holds the W. St. John Garwood and W. St. John Garwood, Jr., Regents' Chair in Law at the University of Texas Law School and is Professor of Government at the University of Texas, Austin.

Fionnuala Ní Aoláin is Professor of Law at the Transitional Justice Institute at the University of Ulster (Northern Ireland) and Visiting Professor of Law at Minnesota Law School. Professor Ní Aoláin is also a member of the Irish Human Rights Commission and was appointed by the secretary-general of the United Nations to serve as an expert to its Commission on the Status of Women with regard to its 2002–2006 thematic work on the equal participation of women in conflict prevention, management and conflict resolution, and postconflict peace-building. She was also one of three nominees by the Irish government to a judicial position on the European Court of Human Rights in 2004.

Mark Osiel is Professor of Law at the University of Iowa and the author of three books on legal responses to mass atrocity, including, most recently, *Mass Atrocity, Ordinary Evil, and Hannah Arendt: Criminal Consciousness in Argentina's Dirty War.*

John T. Parry is Associate Professor of Law at the University of Pittsburgh School of Law.

Richard Posner is a judge on the U.S. Court of Appeals for the Seventh Circuit and Senior Lecturer at the University of Chicago Law School.

Elaine Scarry is the Walter M. Cabot Professor of Aesthetics and the General Theory of Value at Harvard University. She is the author, among other works, of *The Body in Pain* (1985).

Henry Shue is a Senior Research Fellow in Politics at Merton College, Oxford, and Visiting Professor of Politics and International Relations at the University of Oxford. Best known for his book *Basic Rights* (2nd ed., 1996), he is currently writing primarily about moral issues concerning the resort to war and the conduct of war.

Jerome H. Skolnick is Affiliated Professor at and Codirector of the Center for Research in Crime and Justice at the New York University School of Law and the Claire Clements Dean's Professor (Jurisprudence and Social Policy) Emeritus, at the University of California at Berkeley School of Law.

Michael Walzer is Professor at the School of Social Science at the Institute for Advanced Study, Princeton, New Jersey.

Richard Weisberg is the Floersheimer Professor of Constitutional Law at Cardozo Law School of Yeshiva University and director of its Holocaust/Human Rights Center. His most recent book is *Vichy Law and the Holocaust in France.*

INDEX

Defense, U.S. Department of, 29
Defenseless, assault upon, 49–54
Denmark et al. v. Greece (1976), 215, 222
Deontology, 78–79, 81, 82, 229
Depression decade, 107
Dershowitz, Alan, 27, 31, 34–35, 37, 83, 178, 257–283, 285–290, 295–298, 300
Dickerson case, 115
Dirty hands, dilemma of, 24, 61–74, 238
   reflection on, 77–88
Dirty Hands (Sartre), 61, 73, 74
Dirty War, in Argentina, 23, 36–38, 77, 129, 131–140
Discourses, The (Machiavelli), 69
Donnelly v. United Kingdom (1973), 221
Dorfman, Angelica, 9–11
Dorfman, Ariel, 3–18, 4, 27, 30, 295
Dostoevski, Feodor, 15–17, 301
Drugs, 145, 154, 296
Due process-voluntariness standard, 113, 115, 122, 151
Dunking test, for witches, 54

Economist, 30, 38
Egypt, 26, 154, 200, 203, 204, 258, 269, 279
Eichmann, Adolf, 129, 131–132, 134, 135
Eighth Amendment to the United States Constitution, 150, 151, 156
Electric shocks, 79, 147, 148, 215
Elizabeth I, Queen of England, 100
El Mostrador, 12
Elshtain, Jean Bethke, 25, 77–89, 272–273, 279
English Reformation, 100
Enker, Arnold, 179
Enlightenment, 97–98
Enríquez, Edgardo, Senior, 6
Escalation of torture, 153–156
Estadio Nacional, Santiago, 14
Ethnic cleansing, 7
European Commission of Human Rights, 148, 222, 227
European Committee on the Prevention of Torture, 219
European Convention for the Prevention of Torture and Inhuman or Degrading Treatment or Punishment, 213, 218

European Convention on Human Rights (ECHR), 213–225, 232
   problem of violations involving Article 3, 220–223
   standards for defining torture, 214–218
   terrorist suspects and, 224
   uniqueness of approach of, 218–220
European Court of Human Rights, 25, 110, 148, 213–220, 222–225
European law of torture, 94–99, 101
   abolition, 97–99
   safeguards, 95–97
   two-eyewitness rule, 94–95, 97–99
European Union, 219, 223
Evans, Rod, 236
Extradition of suspects, 26–27, 38, 154, 199–200, 269
Eye contact with suspect, 174, 175

Fair fight, notion of, 51
Falanga, 215
Fifth Amendment to the United States Constitution, 120, 121, 150, 151, 292, 293, 297
Food, deprivation of, 110, 147, 148, 176, 216, 269
Foreign Intelligence Surveillance Act (FISA), 286
Foucault, Michel, 109, 110
Fourteenth Amendment to the United States Constitution, 120, 121, 150, 151, 297
Fourth Amendment to the United States Constitution, 263, 267, 271
Fourth Lateran Council of 1215, 94
France
   Algerian independence struggle and, 34, 111, 258, 273, 294
   Vichy period and, 300–305
Frankfurter, Felix, 114
Frederick the Great, 97
French Resistance, 304–305
Fried, Charles, 31–32, 34
Frog crouch, 168, 173, 186

Gabrielli Rojas, Hernán, 13, 14
Gallardo, Sabas, 133
Gays and lesbians in military, 31